# OUTREACH AND RENEWAL

CISTERCIAN STUDIES SERIES: NUMBER TWO HUNDRED THIRTY-SIX

# OUTREACH AND RENEWAL

## A First-Millennium Legacy for the Third-Millennium Church

James McSherry

α

Cistercian Publications
www.cistercianpublications.org

LITURGICAL PRESS
Collegeville, Minnesota
www.litpress.org

A Cistercian Publications title published by Liturgical Press

**Cistercian Publications**
Editorial Offices
Abbey of Gethsemani
3642 Monks Road
Trappist, Kentucky 40051
www.cistercianpublications.org

1      2      3      4      5      6      7      8      9

**Library of Congress Cataloging-in-Publication Data**

McSherry, James.
    Outreach and renewal : a first-millennium legacy for the third-millennium church / James McSherry.
        p. cm. — (Cistercian studies series ; no. 236)
    Includes bibliographical references (p.     ).
    ISBN 978-0-87907-236-0 (pbk.) — ISBN 978-0-87907-798-3 (e-book)
    1. Church history—Primitive and early church, ca. 30–600.
    2. Church history—Middle Ages, 600–1500.    3. Fathers of the church.    I. Title.    II. Series.
    BR162.3.M427    2011
    270.1—dc22                                    2010050204

# CONTENTS

# Abbreviations

*The following abbreviations are used throughout the footnotes:*

ACW   Ancient Christian Writers. Westminster, MD: Newman Press; New York: Paulist Press, 1946–.

ANF   The Ante-Nicene Fathers of the Christian Church. Grand Rapids, MI: Eerdmans, 1996.

CF   Cistercian Fathers Series. Kalamazoo, MI: Cistercian Publications, 1970–.

CUAP   Catholic University of America Press.

ECL   *Early Christian Lives: Life of Antony by Athanasius, Life of Paul of Thebes by Jerome, Life of Hilarion by Jerome, Life of Malchus by Jerome, Life of Martin of Tours by Sulpicius Severus, Life of Benedict by Gregory the Great.* Translated by Carolinne White. London: Penguin Books, 1998.

ECW   *Early Christian Writings: The Apostolic Fathers: The First Epistle of Clement to the Corinthians. The Epistles of Ignatius; The Epistle of Polycarp of Smyrna; The Martyrdom of Polycarp; Didache.* Translated by Maxwell Staniforth. Early Christian Writings. New York: Dorset Press, 1993.

FCh   Fathers of the Church. Washington, DC: Catholic University of America Press, 1948–.

JB   Jerusalem Bible.

NPNF   A Select Library of the Nicene and Post-Nicene Fathers of the Christian Church. Edited by Philip Schaff et al. Grand Rapids, MI: Eerdmans, 1996–98; Peabody, MA: Hendrickson, 1999.

WF   *The Western Fathers: Being the Lives of SS. Martin of Tours by Sulpicius Severus, Ambrose by Paulinus, Augustine of Hippo by Possidius, Honoratus of Arles and Germanus of Auxerre.* Translated by F. R. Hoare. New York: Sheed and Ward, 1954.

# PREFACE

Several years ago I read Daniel Conneely's *Letters of Saint Patrick*, in which the missionary's work is viewed in the context of the patristic era. The experience led me to revisit a group of spiritual guides whose names and inspiring exploits were common currency until the sixties of the last century but who have fallen from public view in recent times. The fathers of the Church were products of the late classical and early medieval world of a rapidly disintegrating empire. They served a body which was so beleaguered that one of their number, Gregory the Great, feared shipwreck from the storms through which he guided it.

The fathers' emulation of the ascetics and association with monasticism inspired their passionate commitment to sharing the Gospel message, defending it against attack, renewing the Church in its decline, and salving the fears and material needs of peoples enduring war, famine, and poverty. While both fathers and ascetics may have been larger than life in their willingness to endure sacrifice and criticism in support of the faith of fellow Christians, they never failed to retain their humanity. Their rich legacy supplies the theme of this study.

I am indebted to the scholars whose lucid assessments of the lives and works of the fathers were consulted during the research process. Their writings led me, in turn, to the translations of the sources on which much of *Outreach and Renewal* is based. I refer here not merely to monumental series like Fathers of the Church or Ante-Nicene and Post Nicene Fathers, but to the many individual renderings of patristic works acknowledged in the bibliography.

I wish to thank Father Mark Scott, executive editor of Cistercian Publications, for the patience and insight with which he steered the enterprise in the direction of publication. His advice and encouragement, delivered with sensitivity and humor, ensured that *Outreach and Renewal* advanced much more smoothly and steadily than I could have anticipated. Sincere thanks also to Stephanie Nix, Colleen Stiller, and Lauren L. Murphy of Liturgical Press, valued guides through the demanding final stages of preparation for publication. Finally, not least to my wife Kathleen I express my gratitude for her understanding, tolerance, support, and invariably pertinent observations on the work in hand.

# INTRODUCTION

Acts of the Apostles opens with the birth of the Church at Pentecost, when the disciples, "filled with the Holy Spirit," answered Christ's call to "proclaim the good news to the whole creation."[1] Referring to the numerous people of differing origins and degrees who heard the apostolic message of salvation at that time, Saint Luke speaks of those who responded with faith remaining true to the "teaching and fellowship, to the breaking of bread and the prayers." Luke goes on to trace the progress of the faith from Palestine to Syria, through Asia Minor, to Greece and Rome. Just thirty years after Christ's initial call to the apostles, Saint Paul was contemplating a journey to Spain.[2]

The successors of the apostles continued to praise the beneficent God who had created human beings in his own image and restored them to favor when they fell from grace. They urged the faithful to respond with love, worship, and acceptance of God's will. Many of these spiritual guides were later acclaimed as fathers of the Church.[3] Most of the fathers were bishops and ascetics; some were martyred in the early persecutions. In the apostolic tradition, they proclaimed the Good News of redemption, and reminded Christians that, as members of a community which is both human and divine, individual believers and the entire body of faithful are in perennial need of renewal.

Aware that human frailty had been a feature of even the apostolic era, the fathers of the fourth century were equipped to counter the decline in

---

[1] Acts 2:1–4; Mark 16:15.

[2] Acts 2:42–47; Rom 15:23–24.

[3] Irenaeus, *Against Heresies*, 4.26.2, revised. Cleveland Coxe, Alexander Roberts, and James Donaldson, The Ante-Nicene Fathers of the Christian Church, vol. 1 (Grand Rapids, MI: Eerdmans, 1996) 497.

faith and religious practice which accompanied the advent of religious freedom. Seeking to support believers and inspire them to persevere in their baptismal commitment, they invoked God's grace and gave a priestly witness which recalled the example of the martyrs. They also emulated the ascetics who, from the early fourth century, began to leave the imperial cities for the deserts of Egypt, where they served God and neighbor through prayer and self-sacrifice. Recognizing that these individuals were worthy of emulation, fathers like Basil, Jerome, Gregory of Nazianzen, and Ambrose adopted the same simplicity of life and dedication to God's service. They encouraged bishops and priests to live communally and frugally, sharing their resources in the spirit of the early Church.

The vigor of the ascetic movement was such that, by the fifth and sixth centuries, Gaul and Ireland in the far west had become noted centers of monasticism. A number of influential biographies celebrated admired ascetics like Antony the desert father and Martin of Tours. Antony's story was written in the mid-fourth century. Martin's was published in 398. The same year saw the appearance of Augustine's *Confessions*, in which the writer traces his personal journey from arrant pride to humility, from unbelief to a faith worthy of the desert ascetics. Just over fifty years later, Patrick, an obscure bishop whose life of mission resembled Martin's, wrote his brief and moving *Confession*. A millennium and a half later, Christians still gain inspiration from these spiritual testimonies.

The role of the fathers was defined by Augustine when, in the early fifth century, he described his predecessors as "brilliant advocates" placed by God at different times and in different places for the good of the Christian body and the inspiration of believers.[4] On their difficult and often dangerous mission they were fortified by a strong sense of spiritual comradeship, captured by Gregory of Nazianzen in his oration on the death of Basil. In the famed bishop, whom he had known since boyhood, he found the "faithful friend" of Ecclesiasticus, "a sturdy shelter" and "a treasure" whose excellence was immeasurable. And since Basil was also "a child of light, a man of God," he was "truly a gift from God."[5]

---

[4] Augustine, *Against Julian*, 2.10.33, trans. Matthew A. Schumaker, The Fathers of the Church, 35 (Washington, DC: Catholic University of America Press, 1981) 97.

[5] Gregory of Nazianzen, Oration 11.1, trans. Martha Vinson, FCh 107:30; Sir 6:14–15.

The patristic era began with Clement of Rome, who was martyred around AD 100. Its approaching end was signaled by the death of Gregory the Great in 604. In the course of those centuries, fathers of east and west met the spiritual, moral, and material needs of fellow Christians. Clement's generation endured persecution by the Roman state. By Gregory's time, persecution was long past. However, with the empire moving toward extinction, entire societies were suffering the horrors of invasion and internecine warfare, which further undermined belief and practice.

From first to last, the fathers preached the Gospel with a confidence that was alive to the realities of Christian living. In a surviving letter, Clement sought to resolve disagreements and divisions among Christians. Five centuries later, in a time of extreme social disruption, Gregory saw the Church as a ship threatened on every side by dangerous billows, with some of its timbers damaged by the buffeting.[6] From the beginning, the faith was threatened by dangers from within and without. Direct attack through misrepresentation and persecution was answered by apologists and martyrs. Divisions, heresies, or schisms involving individuals or groups in the believing community were combated by the fathers and resolved by Church councils.

The work of the fathers and ascetics did not end with the death of Saint Gregory, for devoted followers continued to propagate patristic teaching through the first millennium and beyond. Within a century of the pope's passing, the English monk Bede was relaying the Good News in works that retained their popularity for centuries. Lauding Gregory as his inspiration and the source of his country's conversion, he hailed the contribution of Irish ascetics to the spiritual regeneration of the north of England. It was an achievement facilitated by Ireland's comparative freedom from the ravages of barbarian invasion.

Irish commitment to monasticism had begun with the missions of Palladius and Patrick, which were initiated thirty years after the death of Martin of Tours. It was a period dominated by some of the most influential patristic teachers. Ireland's early adherence to the monastic ideal was rewarded early in the second millennium, when, at the nadir of its own decline, its church was supported by Anselm and Bernard, ascetics who were among the most celebrated followers of the fathers.

---

[6] Gregory the Great, Letters 1.43, trans. James Barmby, *The Nicene and Post-Nicene Fathers of the Christian Church*, vol. 12 (Grand Rapids, MI: Eerdmans, 1997) 87–88.

In the seventh century, English monks led a mission to the pagan lands of western continental Europe, a venture which culminated in the work of Boniface, apostle to the German people. Boniface's mission proved to be a stepping-stone to Charlemagne's famed social and religious renaissance, whose leading scholastic lights were products of the cathedral schools and monasteries of Europe. Drawing on the teachings of the fathers, they promoted education of the clergy, study of the Scriptures, and renewal of the liturgy. Though it incorporated a darker aspect, this renewal was of great assistance to future generations of Christians through its transcription and preservation of the Scriptures, the works of the fathers, and, not least, the *Rule of Saint Benedict*.

During the final centuries of the first millennium, as fragmentation of the Carolingian Empire brought further religious decline, ascetic followers of the fathers led another revival. Cluny was founded in the early tenth century. In the eleventh, Pope Gregory VII, a former monk, emulated his sixth-century namesake by inviting monastic communities to join him in a major work of spiritual renewal.

It was in the context of Gregory's reform that Christians benefited from the works and example of two ascetics whose influence has persisted into the present century. Anselm developed Augustine's synthesis of philosophy and theology, reason and faith in writings that are still fresh and accessible. Bernard's continuing contribution to monasticism is universally acknowledged. His letters illuminate the great issues of the twelfth century, while the biblical commentaries, passion for asceticism, and fearless defense of the faith have seen him hailed as "last of the fathers." Anselm should share that honor, for the witness and writings of both men helped to ensure an effective presentation of the apostolic teaching through the second millennium and beyond.

# 1

# THE FATHERS AND THE APOSTLES

The fidelity to Scripture and apostolic tradition that marked the patristic era was exemplified by the apostolic fathers of the first and second centuries, whose proximity to the age of the apostles has always fascinated Christians. Many were martyred, and their writings accorded an esteem approaching that of Scripture. With Christ's sojourn on earth so tantalizingly close in time, their immediate successors were conscious of a passing generation who had "known those who had known the Lord." Irenaeus, bishop of Lyons, who died in the year 200, wrote of these associations. In a poignant letter to his friend Florinus, now fallen into heresy, he reminds him that, as a boy in Smyrna, a Greek town in Asia Minor, he himself had seen Florinus in the company of their bishop, Polycarp the martyr. Irenaeus vividly recalls how Polycarp spoke of his relations with John and with others who had seen Jesus. Treasuring those words about "the Lord, his miracles and his teaching," he is overwhelmed by the realization that they came from one "who had gathered them from those who had seen the Word of Life."[1]

The authority of Clement of Rome, first of the fathers to leave writings which have survived, was enhanced by his reference to Peter and Paul as the "noble examples of our own generation." In AD 94, on behalf of the Church at Rome, Clement wrote to the Christians of Corinth about their bitter dispute over the selection of church leaders. He deplores the rivalry and jealousy which have overtaken a people previously

---

[1] Eusebius, *Ecclesiastical History*, 5.20.2–8, trans. Kirsopp Lake, Loeb Classical Library, vol. 1 (London: Wm. Heinemann, 1926) 497–98; Irenaeus, *Against Heresies*, 3.3.4; ANF 1:416.

so sober, selfless, and humble.[2] Lamenting that the eye of faith has grown dim and that, driven by selfishness, each is following his own desires, Clement reminds his readers of the great figures of the recent past, including Peter and Paul, who had been victims of the envy of others. Urging members of the divided community to seek unity through humility and love, he advises them to draw close to Christ, "who belongs to the lowly of heart." This will enable them to turn their backs on pride and the sins associated with it. By restoring their wrongfully deposed leaders, they will be following the wishes of the apostles, who learned from Christ himself that there would be "dissensions over the title of bishop." Jesus had ruled that, on the deaths of those appointed, "other accredited persons should succeed them in their ministry." Clement's conclusion is unequivocal. Since those ousted in Corinth had been validly appointed, "with the full consent of the Church," they should be reinstated.[3]

With his assured presentation of Church teaching and invocation of the apostolic age, Clement set the pattern for future patristic writers, who remained alert to Christ's prayer that his followers, while living in the world, would not live in accordance with its spirit. Clement and his successors recognized that, even in apostolic times, Christians had struggled to be faithful. Paul, in his day, had detailed the snares threatening the Corinthians. Naming deep disagreements, immorality, even idolatry, he begged wayward believers to be united in their belief and practice.[4] If they are "to live lives that are self-controlled, upright, and godly," they should avoid being "conformed to this world" around them.[5] Writing in the mid-second century, Hermas surveyed the weaknesses afflicting the Christian body, which included neglect of the worship due to God among those who "reach out for this world and glory in their riches." When persecution comes, he says, such people put their wealth before their faith.[6]

As they encouraged Christians to seek renewal through faith, self-sacrifice, and simplicity of life, the earliest fathers endorsed Paul's as-

---

[2] Clement, *First Letter*, 5, trans. Maxwell Staniforth, *Early Christian Writings: The Apostolic Fathers* (New York: Dorset Press, 1993) 25.

[3] Clement, Ep 1.3, 16, 44; ECW 25, 31, 46.

[4] John 17:15; 1 Cor 1:10–11; 1 Cor 5; 1 Cor 8.

[5] Titus 2:12; Rom 12:2.

[6] Hermas, *The Shepherd*, First Vision 1, trans. M.-F. Marique, FCh, vol. 1 (New York: CUAP, 1981) 249.

surance that, though buffeted, bowed, and even knocked to the ground, believers would survive through the power of faith:

> So we do not lose heart. Even though our outer nature is wasting away, our inner nature is being renewed day by day. For this slight momentary affliction is preparing us for an eternal weight of glory beyond all measure.[7]

There is practical guidance from the fathers for those who are troubled. Clement speaks of the good to be gained from proper observance of the liturgy: "There ought to be strict order and method in our performance of such acts as the Master has prescribed for certain times and seasons."[8] For Ignatius the martyr, participation in the Eucharist, the central act of Christian prayer and worship and "the medicine of immortality," is the cure for all evil and adversity.[9] Counseling the Philippians against slander, love of money, injustice, and other breaches of God's law, Polycarp preaches temperance, compassion, and forbearance. The weapons in the fight against evil are "watching unto prayer and continuing steadfast in fasting, beseeching steadfastly the all-seeing God to lead us not into temptation."[10]

From the Church's earliest days, spiritual mentors encouraged perseverance in Christian living by giving exemplary support to believers. Asking the Philippians to follow the rule of life which they have received from him, Paul advises them to look to those who are already doing so: "Observe those who live according to the example you have in us." He refers to his own acceptance of "the loss of all things" for Christ's sake: "Indeed, in Christ Jesus I became your father through the gospel. I appeal to you, then, be imitators of me."[11] The fathers adopted the same pattern of ministry. Polycarp professes that, in his moral teaching, he himself is following "our blessed and glorious Paul."[12] Clement urges the Corinthians to draw close to the saints, "for those who cling to them shall become saints."[13] From the *Didache*, written before AD 150, believers

---

[7] 2 Cor 4:16–17.
[8] Clement, Ep 1.40; ECW 44.
[9] Ignatius, *Letter to the Ephesians*, 20; ECW 82.
[10] Polycarp, *Letter to the Philippians*, 7; ECW 147.
[11] Phil 3:17, 8; 1 Cor 4:15–16; see 1 Cor 11:1.
[12] Polycarp, *Letter to the Philippians*, 3; ECW 145.
[13] Clement, Ep 1.46; ECW 47.

learn that, by "seeking the company of holy men" each day, they will be better able to resist the various forms of immorality surrounding them.[14]

Early Christians endured trials which were sustainable only through God's grace, for the persecution predicted by Christ was a continuing reality for two centuries after the birth of the Church. As successive imperial administrators invoked repressive laws, there were inevitable lapses from faith, but corresponding acts of heroic witness. John alone among the apostles escaped martyrdom. Peter and Paul were executed in Rome. Widely invoked was Stephen, put to death at Jerusalem around AD 35.[15] Father and martyr Ignatius of Antioch was, like Clement, a link with those who had "known the Lord." On the long journey from his see of Antioch to Rome, where he was to die in the arena, he wrote letters to seven Christian communities. Less concerned for his own plight than for the well-being of his fellow believers, he reminded them that Jesus died to win salvation for all.

It is little wonder that the early fathers saw in the Christian way of life a demanding journey, a race in which an eternal prize was to be won, even a battle to overcome evil. All were images which reflected the thread of self-denial, renunciation, and asceticism found in the Gospels. The metaphor of the good fight came naturally to Paul, who warned his converts to stand their ground, "and fasten the belt of truth around your waist, and put on the breastplate of righteousness. As shoes for your feet put on whatever will make you ready to proclaim the gospel of peace."[16]

Finding a fellow spirit in Polycarp, bishop of Smyrna, Ignatius cautioned him against error and spoke of the necessity for constant prayer. Encouraging the young prelate to "stand your ground with firmness, like an anvil under the hammer," he reminded him that, as bishop, he must be willing to endure trials of all kinds.[17] Taking Ignatius's words to heart, Polycarp later asked the Philippians to imitate the Lord Jesus Christ and "stand firm in these ways, taking the Lord for your example. Be fixed and unshaken in your faith."[18] In 155, forty-five years after meeting Ignatius, Polycarp died in another persecution. He was described by his biographer as "not only a famous teacher, but a martyr without peer,

---

[14] *Didache*, 4; FCh 1:229.
[15] Acts 7:60.
[16] Eph 6:14–15.
[17] Ignatius, *Letter to Polycarp*, 3; ECW 128.
[18] Polycarp, *Letter to the Ephesians*, 10; ECW 148.

and one whose martyrdom all aspire to imitate, so fully does it accord with the Gospel of Christ."[19]

In those early centuries the Christian faith was subjected to campaigns of misrepresentation by pagan writers, who accused believers of superstitious practices and excesses. The attacks were answered by apologists like Justin, who had been a follower of Plato before his conversion. Already believing in the existence of a single supreme being who was infinitely good, he found the ultimate truth in the faith of Christians who remained "fearless of death and of all other things that are counted fearful."[20] In his *Apology*, addressed to the emperor Antoninus Pius, Justin employed the concepts of Greek philosophy, presenting Jesus as the Logos, or Word of God, who had become incarnate to save mankind through his death and resurrection. His efforts to convince the pagans of Rome that Christian belief was "the true philosophy" led to his martyrdom in the year 165.

Despite the dangers and disappointments of the times, the Church continued to thrive throughout the Roman world. Half a century after Justin's death, the African Christian apologist Tertullian, addressing those "rulers of empire" who hated Christians so much, ably resolved the paradox of the faith's continued advance despite Rome's hostility. Insisting that imperial cruelty would not prevail, he exclaimed, "The more you mow us down, the more we grow; the blood of Christians is seed."[21]

As belief in the one true God continued to spread within a largely pagan milieu where worship of natural objects was commonplace, the fathers found signs of God's presence everywhere. Clement observes that the earth, the oceans, the seasons, and the heavens obey the divine laws. In the seasonal renewal of nature, even in the passing days, he sees a figure of the resurrection and claims that, by doing good in the world, Christians are imitating God, who "as the architect and Lord of the universe takes a delight in working." Clement used this sense of God's hand in the harmony of the universe to persuade the Corinthians that, by rejecting disharmony, shunning division, and defeating envy, they would enjoy "the life that knows no death, the shining splendor

[19] *Martyrdom of Polycarp*, 19; ECW 162.
[20] Justin, *Apology*, 2.12, rev. A. Cleveland Coxe, ANF, vol. 1 (Grand Rapids, MI: Eerdmans, 1996) 192.
[21] Tertullian, *Apology*, 1.50, trans. Emily Joseph Daly, FCh, vol. 10 (Washington, DC: CUAP, 1977) 125.

of righteousness, the truth that is frank and full and the faith that is perfect assurance."[22]

With their faith in a generous and merciful God firmly grounded in the apostolic teachings, the early fathers concurred with the assurance of Saint Paul that nothing in this life "will be able to separate us from the love of God in Christ Jesus our Lord." It was a comfort for Christians subject to intolerable pressures to be told by a Church father like Clement that, in the person of his Son, God chose to come on earth "a babe in arms or a root in waterless soil, with not a trace of shapeliness or splendor about him." In quoting Isaiah, Clement was also invoking the memorable words of Paul:

> His state was divine,
> yet he did not cling to his equality with God,
> but emptied himself
> to assume the condition of a slave,
> and became as men are.[23]

In the light of the Church's treatment by the state, it is ironic that the initial advance of the Gospel message in the Roman world was facilitated by the unprecedented stability brought by the pagan Augustus, who became emperor just twenty-seven years before the birth of Christ and died in the fourteenth year of the Christian era. Since he was named in Scripture, many Christians, conscious of God's providential design for creation, saw in the emperor's reign a means of "preparing the nations for his teaching," with the "Augustan peace" the divinely chosen moment for the Savior's birth.[24] In the pagan poet Virgil's celebration of Aeneas's greatest virtue, pietas, there were those who found a prophetic insight into the new relationship about to be forged between God and his creatures. Some Christians even detected, in the poet's *Eclogues*, allusions to the coming of the Savior:

> Now the last age of Cumae's prophecy has come;
> The great succession of centuries is born afresh.

---

[22] Clement, Ep 1.19–20, 35–36; ECW 33–34, 41–42.

[23] Rom 8:38–39; Clement, Ep 1.16; ECW 31; see Isa 53:2–3; Phil 2:6–7.

[24] See Luke 2:1; Origen, *Against Celsus*, 2.30, trans. Frederick Crombie, *Writings of Origen*, vol. 2 (Edinburgh: T & T Clark, 1872) 35–36.

Now too returns the virgin; Saturn's rule returns;
A new begetting now descends from heaven's height.

In the year 394, Jerome, most acerbic of the fathers, summarily dismissed such exaggerated attempts to identify prophetic elements in the works of pagan poets. In one of his letters he drily observes that the credulous might see in the words of the *Aeneid*, "Hail only Son, my might and majesty," a veiled reference by God the Father to the Son and find in the verse "such words he spoke and there transfixed remained" an allusion to the Savior's words on the cross. These gullible people forget that it is perfectly possible to read the following verses without "calling the Christless Maro a Christian":[25]

Now comes the virgin back and Saturn's reign,
Now from high heaven comes a Child newborn.

All such speculation, declares Jerome, is puerile, since it "resembles the sleight-of-hand of a mountebank." It is idle to try to teach what you do not know, he bitingly observes, and, "if I may speak with some warmth, it is worse still to be ignorant of your ignorance."[26]

Though believing that human history unfolded within the context of God's providence, Augustine, like Jerome, rejected such fanciful speculations about the pagan poets. Against Virgil's elevation, in the *Aeneid*, of the heroic earthly dispensation established by Augustus, the author of the *City of God* asserts his intention to defend that glorious city against those who prefer their own gods. The Roman poet's celebration of the power of Augustus, as son of a god, to "show mercy to the conquered and beat down the proud" is dismissed as a claim for usurpation by a creature of the exclusively divine ability to "resist the proud, but give grace to the humble."[27]

---

[25] Virgil, *The Eclogues*, 4.4–7, trans. Guy Lee (London: Penguin Books, 1988) 57–67; Maro: Publius Virgilius Maro; Virgil, *Aeneid*, 1.664, trans. Robert Fitzgerald (London: Harvill Press, 1983) 27.

[26] Jerome, Ep 53.7, trans. W. H. Fremantle, NPNF, vol. 6 (Grand Rapids, MI: Eerdmans, 1996) 99.

[27] Augustine, *City of God*, 1. Preface, trans. Henry Bettenson (London: Penguin Books, 2003) 5; see Prov 3:34; Jas 4:6; 1 Pet 5:5; Virgil, *Aeneid*, 6.843–74, trans. J. W. Mackail (London: MacMillan, 1908) 144.

# 2

# THE TWO CITIES
## CALLED TO SERVE

Some of the most celebrated fathers of the Church ministered in the turbulent times which prevailed from the mid-fourth century to the end of the fifth. In the east, the long-lived Athanasius, bishop of Alexandria, who died in 373, was a redoubtable opponent of the Arian heresy and an early advocate of asceticism. Basil of Caesarea, his brother Gregory of Nyssa, and their friend Gregory of Nazianzen were able spiritual teachers and committed ascetics. John Chrysostom's devotion to the Gospel brought him exile and death in a remote part of the empire. Basil and his brethren had their counterparts in the west. In 386 Jerome left Rome to establish a monastery in Bethlehem. Augustine was baptized by Ambrose, bishop of Milan, at Easter 387. Returning to Africa in the following year, he formed an ascetic community. A decade after Augustine's death in 430, another prominent Church father, Leo, was elected to the see of Rome.

These learned and cultured individuals rejected the benefits of educational achievement, family inheritance, or high office for the life of service favored by Christ and the apostles. Their immediate exemplars were humble ascetics like Antony, the desert hermit, or lowly bishops like Martin and Patrick, who were unburdened by educational or social eminence. While other prelates within the empire confined their ministry to urbanized centers, Martin frequently journeyed from Tours to evangelize the pagan peoples of Gaul's remote countryside. Patrick brought the faith to a non-Roman people living on the western edge of Europe. Leaving his native place to "live among barbarians, a stranger and exile for the love of God," he served in remote places "beyond which no one dwells."[1] He and Martin endured the scorn of more accomplished churchmen.

The context in which the fathers of those times exercised their ministry was forged by Constantine's accession in the early fourth century, when the Roman Empire began to turn a friendly face to the Church. Believers who had experienced Diocletian's recent persecution were now able to practice their faith without fear. They could even aspire to public office. Magnificent basilicas rose in the cities. Bishops became respected and influential figures in society. Many among the nobility turned to the faith. Church numbers steadily grew, especially in urbanized areas. Christianity enjoyed a further seal of approval when, in 391, the emperor Theodosius issued an edict recognizing it as the official religion.

Though this liberation was viewed by many believers as the ultimate act of providence, its benefits were not unalloyed, for the inevitable influx of converts brought a diminution in religious faith and religious practice. Surrounded by the decadence of an empire in decline, Christians were tempted by the spirit of a beckoning secular world. Pagan influences lingered not only in the countryside but in the cities, where many influential families maintained their faith in ancient cults. Some believers fell under the spell of the Gnostics, who taught that access to truth is the preserve of a privileged few and that material creation is intrinsically evil.

An added danger threatened all citizens of the Roman world. From the mid-third century the empire was severely tested by surrounding peoples. By the first decade of the fifth century, as Roman soldiers were being withdrawn from Britain to help hold back the Goths, the province was harried and plundered by Irish and Pictish raiders. In one such incident Patrick was seized and taken into captivity, "with so many thousands of people."[2] Farther east, the Goths, pressed hard by Huns from Asia, had surged into Italy. Contained for a time, they entered Rome on 24 August 410. For ten days their leader Alaric and his forces plundered the city. The disaster evoked widespread recognition of a terrifying truth. A great power which, for centuries, had ensured order and civility in Europe, Africa, and the Near East was no longer able to protect its people.

[1] Patrick, *Letter to Coroticus*, 1, trans. Ludwig Bieler, *The Works of Saint Patrick*, Library of Ancient Christian Writers, No. 17 (Westminster, MD: Newman, 1953) 41.

[2] Patrick, *Confession*, 1, Bieler, 21.

In Bethlehem, Jerome was so overcome by the misfortunes of the victims that "day and night I could think of nothing but the welfare of the community." With his monastery caring for refugees, he was unable to continue his work: "Long did I remain silent, knowing that it was a time to weep."[3] Even two years later he could not contemplate the calamity without emotion: "My voice sticks in my throat and, as I dictate, sobs choke my voice. The city which had taken the whole world was itself taken." The event was not unexpected. In the year before the catastrophe, Jerome had reflected on the number of imperial cities overrun by barbarians and asked, "If Rome can perish, where shall we look for strength?"[4] His conclusion, expressed three years after the sack of the city, has grim implications for the fate of all empires: "When the bright light of all the world was put out . . . the whole world perished in one city . . . who could believe that Rome, built up by the conquest of the whole world, had collapsed, that the mother of nations had become also their tomb."[5]

Moved by the pitiful state of survivors disembarking at his own town of Hippo in North Africa, Augustine helped to relieve their sufferings. However, he did not share the prevailing apocalyptic view of Rome's fall. In the *City of God*, written to rebut claims by pagans among the Roman aristocracy that the beginnings of Rome's decline coincided with the advent of Christianity, he asserts that Rome's very rise contained the seeds of its destruction, for it was built on the motivating principle of so many great kingdoms, a lust for power fueled by unremitting wars, disguised as missions for the protection of life and liberty. In the absence of justice, he asks, "What are kingdoms but gangs of criminals on a large scale?"[6] Pride had made the fall inevitable.

An accomplished student of the classics, Augustine was aware that Virgil's *Aeneid*, written to honor the emperor, had proclaimed Jupiter's promise that Rome would enjoy rule without end. Augustus had claimed virtues appropriate to God alone and, like other Roman leaders, had even been deified. Under him, the world's values had prevailed. The magnitude of the fall caused Augustine to conclude that, while earthly empires come and go, "the glorious city of God" endures, and that true

---

[3] Jerome, Ep 126.2; NPNF 6:252; Eccl 3:4.

[4] Jerome, Ep 127.12, 123.17; NPNF 6:257, 237.

[5] Jerome, *Commentary on Ezekiel*, 1. Preface, trans. W. H. Fremantle, NPNF, vol. 6 (Grand Rapids, MI: Eerdmans, 1996) 500.

[6] Augustine, *City of God*, 4.4; Bettenson, 139; see 1 Pet 5:5.

justice, which never found a place in Rome, can exist only "in that commonwealth whose founder and ruler is Christ."

Differing so much, these cities have been formed by two loves, the earthly one by love of self, reaching the point of contempt for God, the heavenly by love of God, "carried as far as contempt of self."[7] Christians represent that part of the kingdom of heaven "on pilgrimage in this world." Forming a "single pilgrim band" drawn from all nations, they continue toward their eternal destiny. In God alone will all find the true peace that is everlasting.[8] While the faithful people of God and the worldly suffer the same disasters caused by evil, there will be widely differing outcomes: "The fire which makes gold shine makes chaff smoke; the same flail breaks up the straw and clears the grain; and oil is not mistaken for lees because both are forced out by the same press."[9]

Despite contrasting the two cities so trenchantly, the realistic Augustine refused to isolate the Christian ethos from its earthly setting. Developing his theology of the Church in response to the Manichaeans and Donatists, who favored the formation of groups confined exclusively to "the pure," he insisted that the Christian community, containing the wheat and chaff, good fish and bad of Matthew's Gospel, is called to enhance society's welfare and foster its peace, which is born of a "well-ordered concord" between individuals, or within families and societies.[10] While there will be those among the godly who will not remain faithful to their commitment, the ungodly will always be able to enter God's city by repenting and confessing the faith.

While acknowledging that man's fallen nature ensures the imperfection of earthly peace and justice, Augustine affirms that Christians cannot divorce themselves from the world, because "the two cities are intertwined and mingled with each other, until the last judgment separates them."[11] Pilgrims to the heavenly city will continue to serve and glorify God while observing society's norms and obeying its laws. As bishop, Augustine contributed personally to the well-being of his community, not least by devoting substantial time daily to arbitrating civil disputes

---

[7] Augustine, *City of God*, 2.21, 14.28; Bettenson, 75, 593.

[8] Augustine, *City of God*, 1.35; 19.11; Bettenson, 45; 865–66; see Rom 8:25; Ps 94:15.

[9] Augustine, *City of God*, 1.8; Bettenson, 14.

[10] Augustine, *City of God*, 19.13–14; Bettenson, 870–74.

[11] Augustine, *City of God*, 19.17; Bettenson, 877.

between citizens. However, while welcoming the empire's current favorable attitude to the Church, he withheld unconditional approval. Christian leaders, ruling justly, should be "slow to punish, ready to pardon." Then, like other believers, they can be happy in the present, "through hope," and look forward to the final happiness which is promised.[12]

With their lives rooted in the culture of the empire, the fathers of the time were uniquely equipped to face the challenges of the secular world. Most were from far-flung provinces, but their Roman citizenship represented a potent bond. Almost all were products of Christian families whose hopes for their offspring focused on education, through which able and ambitious students could attain high status in society. Many traveled far to study in noted centers of learning. As young men, Basil of Caesarea and Gregory of Nazianzen achieved academic excellence in Alexandria, Constantinople, and Athens, while John Chrysostom studied in his native city of Ephesus. Gregory and John were celebrated theologians and orators. The able Basil became an acclaimed pastor and administrator. In the west, where Latin was the medium of education, Ambrose, whose father had been Praetorian Prefect of Gaul, enjoyed the best education of the day. He studied Greek, as did Jerome, who later applied an impressive mastery of that language to his monumental work of biblical translation and commentary.

Jerome was a gifted twelve-year-old when he left Dalmatia, modern Slovenia, for Rome. Cultivating his formidable literary and linguistic gifts, he absorbed the highest learning of the city. Sulpicius Severus and his friend Paulinus, Church fathers with roots in Gaul, were noted for their literary accomplishments. Paulinus shared with Gregory of Nazianzen the distinction of being a poet. Since the fathers of Augustine and Patrick were decurions who owned some property and enjoyed moderate status in their respective communities, their sons would have shared similar expectations.

Patrick was haunted in old age by the neglected educational opportunities of his early life. Bitterly regretting his lack of learning, he traced it to enslavement in Ireland and the thoughtlessness of youth. Augustine did not disappoint the hopes of his parents, who made sacrifices to ensure his educational success. At sixteen, he spent a year at home in Tagaste, while his father sought funds to finance his higher education

---

[12] Augustine, *City of God*, 5.24; Bettenson, 220.

in Carthage.[13] He excelled in the study of rhetoric, which was essential to social advancement, especially in the areas of law or administration: "Here is learned the use of words! Here eloquence is acquired, most necessary for winning cases and expressing thoughts."[14]

Many Church fathers of the fourth and fifth centuries initially contemplated or pursued a secular career, but were later won to exclusive service of God. Basil confesses that, as a student in Athens, he "wasted much time in vanity and spent my youth in the vain labor of acquiring a knowledge made foolish by God." In the year 356, returning home weighed down with academic honors, suddenly, "as if roused from a deep sleep" he "looked upon the wondrous light of the truth of the Gospel." Awakened to the "futility of the wisdom of rulers of this earth," he saw that the "great means of perfection was selling one's possessions, sharing with needy brethren and complete renunciation of solicitude for this life."[15] Less than a decade later, Jerome had a similar experience when, with Bonosus, he made his way from Rome to Trier, the western imperial capital, where both youths hoped to find positions in state service. Years later, Jerome reminded another friend that he "first began to seek and serve" his Creator while he and Bonosus "lodged in the same house and shared the same food by the half-barbarous banks of the Rhine."[16]

Jerome's was a commitment willingly undertaken by all the fathers. Paulinus, member of the Roman senate and disciple of the ascetic Martin, sacrificed all to become a monk. Later, he was appointed bishop of Nola in Italy. His wife Teresia also followed the dedicated way. The turning point for both was the death of their only child. Sulpicius Severus followed the same path in similar circumstances. Visiting Tours, he was urged by Martin to follow the example of Paulinus. "There," Martin exclaimed, "there is someone for you to follow, there is someone to imitate."[17] Martin rightly sensed that the successful young lawyer, whose wife had recently died, was ready to change his way of life.

---

[13] Augustine, *Confessions*, 2.3.5, trans. John K. Ryan (New York: Image Books, 1960) 67.

[14] Augustine, *Conf*, 1.16.26; Ryan, 59.

[15] Basil, *Letters*, 223.2, trans. Agnes Clare Way, FCh, vol. 28 (Washington, DC: CUAP, 1953) 127.

[16] Jerome, Ep 3.5; NPNF 6:6.

[17] Sulpicius Severus, *Life of Saint Martin of Tours*, 25, trans. F. R. Hoare, *The Western Fathers* (London: Sheed and Ward, 1954) 41–42.

Augustine's journey to enlightenment, like Jerome's, was initially colored by worldly ambition, which in 383 led him across the Mediterranean to Rome. By 384 he was master of rhetoric in Milan, then capital of the western empire. Symmachus, Prefect of Rome, had recommended him for the post, which was a stepping-stone to high office in the imperial service. But Augustine was unhappy, and, on a day when he was "preparing to make an address in praise of the emperor," he suddenly saw, even in the gaiety of a drunken beggar, happiness greater than any he could gain through realizing his ambitions. His restlessness, arising from an aspiration to pursue the "most ardent search for truth and wisdom," brought him to a heretical sect, then to Platonic philosophy, and ended in baptism by Ambrose. Just over a decade later, Augustine thanked God for his first, providential encounter with the famed bishop: "All unknowing, I was led to him by you, so that, through him, I might be led, while fully knowing it, to you."[18]

Conversion of life was not limited to the fathers of the time. A slave in Ireland at sixteen, Patrick spent six years herding animals in all seasons. In his sufferings and those of his fellow captives he came to see the will of God, who "brought over us the wrath of his anger," for he and his friends had "turned away from God and did not keep his commandments." It was a providential chastisement which led him to the truth. Transformed from a heedless Christian to one who, in a single day, would say "as many as a hundred prayers, and almost as many in the night," Patrick rejoiced that his travails had brought him in an especial way to God, who "guarded me and comforted me as a father would his son."[19]

Martin's path to God was very different. His humility and goodness are captured in the short biography written by Sulpicius Severus, who was a disciple and a friend. A former Roman soldier and native of Pannonia, modern Hungary, he was reared in Pavia by pagan parents. Against their wishes, he went to a church at the age of ten and "asked to be made a catechumen." As a soldier, he astonished comrades by his dedication to Christian ideals. Though still not baptized, he engaged in works of charity, "assisting the wretched, feeding the needy, clothing the naked, keeping nothing himself from his pay beyond what was necessary for his daily food." Finally, having decided to turn his back on military

---

[18] Augustine, *Conf*, 5.13.23; Ryan, 130.
[19] Patrick, *Conf*, 1, 2, 16; Bieler, 21, 25.

life, he risked death by telling the emperor, "I have been your soldier up to this time; let me now be God's."[20] For over a millennium after his death in 399, Martin was among the best-loved saints of Europe.

Patrick answered God's call in his youth; Augustine, at thirty-three. Ambrose heard it in his mid-thirties. An accomplished orator and legal advocate, Ambrose was appointed to the Judicial Council by Probus, Praetorian Prefect of Italy. He then became governor of the provinces of Aemilia and Liguria, with headquarters at Milan, the western imperial capital at that time. When Auxentius, Arian bishop of the city, died in 374, there was a disputed succession. As governor, Ambrose moved quickly to forestall any public disorder. He could not have foreseen the outcome. Known as a devout catechumen who was orthodox in his beliefs, he was asked by the citizens and clergy to become their spiritual leader. After initial hesitation on his part, he was baptized, ordained priest, and consecrated bishop.[21]

Through their own journeys to conversion and subsequent experience in an environment which tested religious faith and practice in so many ways, the fathers of the time learned that Christians deserved a supportive and exemplary pastoral witness. They looked to predecessors like Polycarp for inspiration. In the second century, the martyr had written to the Philippians on the need for devoted priests. They must be "men of generous sympathies, with a wide compassion for humanity," whose business is "to reclaim the wanderers, keep an eye on all who are infirm, and never neglect the widow, the orphan, or the needy. Their care at all times should be for what is honorable in the sight of God and men."[22] As martyrs, Polycarp and his peers had given the ultimate example of service. With the age of persecution now past, their successors adopted a form of witness which spoke directly to a new generation. The ascetic or monastic way signified their absolute commitment to God, a link with the apostolic tradition and an assured means of emulating the example of the martyrs.

The ultimate source of inspiration for ascetics was the Gospel counsel to the rich young man: "If you wish to be perfect, go, sell your possessions, and give the money to the poor . . . then come, follow me." On hearing these words, Peter had assured Jesus that he and his brethren had indeed

---

[20] Sulpicius Severus, *Life of Saint Martin*, 2, 4; WF 12–14.16.
[21] Paulinus, *Life of Saint Ambrose*, 6–9; WF, 152–55.
[22] Polycarp, *Letter to the Philippians*, 6; ECW 146.

"left everything, and followed him."[23] From the earliest days, the Church praised men and women who, for the good of the community, dedicated themselves exclusively "to the Lord's affairs." Dedicated women were allotted a special place at celebrations of the Eucharist. Noting that widows make "constant intercessions for everyone," Polycarp advised them "to observe discretion as they practice our Lord's faith."[24] In his letter to the Smyrnaeans, Ignatius greeted "those virgins who are called widows," while Justin Martyr paid tribute to the many men and women, Christians since childhood, who remained virgins at the age of sixty or seventy years.[25]

Since most fathers of the fourth and fifth centuries were bishops, they could not commit themselves exclusively to the monastic round of prayer, study, and manual work but pursued their ministry in the spirit of asceticism. They encouraged fellow priests to imitate them. In *Duties of the Clergy* Ambrose told clerics that their sense of mercy and justice should reflect God's. They must share the fortitude of the martyrs and follow Paul in offering their lives as examples to be followed.[26] Jerome was particularly insistent that priests should devote themselves exclusively to God and his people and avoid paying the least lip service to mammon. Employing shock tactics to expose those seduced by worldliness, he satirizes clerics who delight in ostentation, entertain men of the world, engage in rumor-mongering, fawn on influential people, or cultivate wealthy, high-born women. With a cold eye, he portrays others carefully "walking on tip-toe over wet roads" to protect their fine clothes and good leather shoes. Such barbed pen pictures are accompanied by the inevitable caustic exclamation: "These are bridegrooms rather than clergymen!"

Further biting images from Jerome's gallery of self-indulgent clergymen cast ridicule on connoisseurs of the good things of life, including those who amass private fortunes and gourmets who "know several kinds of fish by name or can tell unerringly on what coast a mussel had been picked."[27] There is exaggeration here, for Jerome was a master of mockery and invective. Yet Augustine would have concurred with his conclusions, for experience told him that, while there would always

---

[23] Matt 19:21–30; Luke 5:28.

[24] Polycarp, *Letter to the Philippians*, 4; ECW 145.

[25] Ignatius, *Letter to the Smyrnaeans*, 13; ECW 123; Justin, *Apology*, 1.15; ANF 1:167.

[26] Ambrose, *Duties of the Clergy*, 1.28, 2.17, trans. H. De Romestin, NPNF, vol. 10 (Grand Rapids, MI: Eerdmans, 1970) 10:22–23, 57.

[27] Jerome, Ep 22.28; NPNF 6:34.

be devoted priests, there would also be those who "enjoy the temporal honors and secular advantage connected with the office." He concluded that "both types will continue in the Catholic Church even to the end of time."[28] Over the years, he encountered a rich variety of priestly weakness. There were the disobedient, the restless or the conniving, or those who indulged in "strife and deceit." For some, the attractions of money or ambition were too great. When disciplined, a few ran off and joined the schismatics. Augustine identifies the source of such failures and their cure. Pride, which also leads to the desire for pleasure, praise, and honors, is overcome only by turning to God and living "wholly in his sight."[29]

As a bishop in pursuit of Gospel simplicity, Augustine lived communally with his clergy. In the spirit of Saint Paul, who wished servants of God to serve "without seeking food and clothing from anyone," he accepted gifts only if they could be used by all the brethren, who would "receive what they need from the common supply."[30] His sensitive application of this principle is evident in one of his final letters, to the virgin Sapida. She had made a robe for her brother, who died before it could be completed. Offered the garment, Augustine accepted it, praising Sapida's affection for her brother, but reminded her that she should gain greater comfort from the fact that "he for whom this was prepared" is now clothed "with incorruptibility and immortality."[31]

On one occasion, the bishop's reluctance to become personally immersed in financial affairs led to a profound embarrassment. After leaving the administration of church finances and property to capable clergy and household stewards, he discovered that Januarius, a priest of his own house, had broken the vow of poverty by secretly retaining property. When enquiries revealed that other clergy had similarly offended, Augustine dealt with the matter in two sermons. To underline the Gospel principle by which he and his community of priests lived, he had the key passage of Acts read aloud to the entire congregation: "There was not a needy person among them, for as many as owned lands or houses sold them and brought the proceeds of what was sold. . . . and

---

[28] Augustine, *Letters*, 208.2, trans. J. G. Cunningham, NPNF, vol. 1 (Peabody, MA: Hendrickson, 1999) 558.

[29] Augustine, Ep 22.7; NPNF 1:240–41.

[30] Augustine, *On the Work of Monks*, 3–4; 5.32, trans. Mary Sarah Muldowney, FCh, vol. 14 (Washington, DC: CUAP, 1981) 381–82; see Acts 20:33.

[31] Augustine, Ep 263.1–4; NPNF 1:91–93.

it was distributed to each as any had need." Assuring his listeners that he had revealed all he knew, he promised that, should a similar scandal arise, he would be equally open about it.[32]

A further disappointment came through the actions of another member of his household. When the nominee for the bishopric of Fussala withdrew on the eve of consecration, Augustine nominated Antonius, whom he thought he knew so well. Once settled in his see, the new bishop was accused of oppression and extortion. Writing to Pope Celestine in 423, Augustine admitted his error of judgment in appointing the man: "As for myself, I must confess to your holiness . . . I am so racked with anxiety and grief that I think of retiring from the responsibilities of the episcopal office, and abandoning myself to demonstrations of sorrow corresponding to the greatness of my error."[33] Augustine's response to such behavior would have been shared by all the fathers, whose attitude to the priesthood resembled that of the youthful John Chrysostom. Knowing that even the apostle Paul had approached the duties of spiritual ministry "in fear and trembling," the austere John queried the situation of those who, like himself, seek their own and "fail to go beyond the commandments of Christ."[34]

Augustine concluded that, in a spiritual guide, sincere belief, simplicity of life, and exemplary service of God and neighbor are more important than worldly wisdom or academic success. The lives and works of Martin and Patrick embodied this ideal. Though relatively unlearned, their generous response to God enabled them to bring many to belief. Patrick's summons came after his escape from slavery when, in a dream, a man named Victoricus, coming "as it were" from Ireland, gave him one of the "countless" letters he carried. The young man heard the "voice of the Irish" who lived "beside the Wood of Voclut near the western sea," crying in unison, "We beg you, youth, come and walk among us once more." Writing the *Confession* in old age, Patrick is grateful that "the Lord gave them according to their cry."[35]

Martin also heard the call through the voice of the people. At the request of Bishop Hilary of Poitiers, he had established his hermitage in Ligugé. Moved by his reputation for holiness, the people of Tours

---

[32] E. Van der Meer, *Augustine the Bishop*, trans. B. Battershaw and G. R. Lamb (London: Sheed and Ward, 1983) 200–206; Acts 4:34–35.

[33] Augustine, Ep 209.10; NPNF 1:562.

[34] John Chrysostom, *On the Priesthood*, 3.7, trans. W. R. W. Stephens, NPNF, vol. 9 (Grand Rapids, MI: Eerdmans, 1996) 48.

[35] Patrick, *Conf,* 23; Bieler, 28.

asked him to become their bishop. When he resisted the invitation, they resorted to subterfuge: "A citizen of Tours named Rusticus came and knelt at his knees and got him to come out by pretending that his wife was ill." Once on the public road, Martin was escorted by a great throng, and "it was practically as a prisoner that he reached the city." Concluding that the peoples' request had been divinely inspired, his reluctance changed to enthusiastic acceptance.[36]

Patrick and Martin were motivated by a faith as firm as that expressed by Saint Paul and echoed by Augustine: " 'The word is near you, on your lips and in your heart' (that is, the word of faith that we proclaim); because if you confess with your lips that Jesus is Lord and believe in your heart that God raised him from the dead, you will be saved."[37] The nature of the faith and commitment which they shared is captured in Sulpicius Severus's words about Martin:

> What human sorrows did he not, for the hope of eternity, endure, in pain, in hunger, in night watchings, in nakedness, in fasting, in the insults of the envious, in the persecutions of the wicked, in care for the sick, in anxiety for those in peril? Who was in sorrow and Martin did not sorrow too? Whose fall was not his shame? Who perished and he did not sigh? And all this in addition to his daily and varied warfare against the forces of human and spiritual wickedness.[38]

The source of Martin's acclaim throughout the Christian world is captured in a single luminous incident. While still in the army and not yet a Christian, he was entering Amiens during a dark winter which had been "so fearfully hard beyond the ordinary that many were dying of the intense cold." At the city gate a "coatless beggar" vainly begged passersby to have pity on him. Drawing his sword, Martin cut his military cloak in two, giving half to the man. His biographer records the outcome. In the night, Christ, wearing the beggar's cloak, appeared to the generous soldier, saying, "Martin is still only a catechumen, but he has clothed me with this garment."[39]

---

[36] Sulpicius Severus, *Life of Saint Martin*, 9; WF 22–23.
[37] Rom 10:8–9; Patrick, *Conf*, 4; Bieler, 22; Augustine, *Sermons*, 212.1; FCh 38:117.
[38] Sulpicius Severus, Ep 2; WF 54.
[39] Sulpicius Severus, *Life of Saint Martin*, 3; WF 14–15.

# 3

# THE SPIRIT OF ASCETICISM

Christ's call to carry the cross is heard by all believers, for the spirit of self-sacrifice which characterized the lives of Jesus and his disciples lies at the heart of the Church's devotional and ethical life. The disciples responded to the even more urgent call contained in the counsel of perfection which, by the early fourth century, was moving many Christians to become hermits or members of monastic groups in the Egyptian desert. In the mid-century Athanasius wrote his biography of Antony, who answered Christ's invitation to the rich young man by retreating from the city of Alexandria to a life of prayer in the desert. Antony, who was visited by many people seeking spiritual solace and advice, left his hermitage on only two occasions. During Maximin's persecution of 311 he supported Christians facing trial in Alexandria and ministered to those sentenced to work in the mines and prisons. Shortly before his death in 356, he returned to the city and publicly condemned Arianism.

Responding to the monks who had asked him to write the *Life of Antony*, Athanasius offered characteristic words of encouragement: "Brothers, you have entered on the most noble contest, striving either to equal the monks of Egypt or to outdo them in seeking after moral perfection by means of rigorous self-discipline. May God grant fulfillment of the desire expressed in your prayers."[1] Monasticism's potent attraction was ably articulated by John Cassian, who, with his friend Germanus, spent several years in the Near East, where they visited the Egyptian ascetics. In the early decades of the fifth century, John distilled

---

[1] Athanasius, *Life of Antony*, preface, trans. Carolinne White, *Early Christian Lives* (London: Penguin Books, 1998) 7.

the wisdom of the desert fathers into two books, the *Institutes* and the *Conferences*. From Abbot Paphnutius he had learned the three types of call that can transform an individual's life. The first, a direct summons from God, heard by both Abraham and Antony, so pervades the heart that a man or woman is inspired to lead a committed life. The second call comes through a human agency, such as the good example or teaching of a saintly individual. The third involves compulsion, as when a person is threatened by death or endures a great loss.[2]

The behavior of the desert ascetics could be eccentric, even extreme, but in the fourth century the young Basil fell under their influence. Traveling through Egypt, Palestine, Syria, and Mesopotamia, he was captivated by the sincerity of their witness: "I admired their continence in living and their endurance in toil. I was amazed at their persistence in prayer and their mastery of sleep . . . I called these men's lives blessed in that they did indeed show in their bodies the mortification of Christ."[3] Returning to Pontus around 360, Basil established a monastic community. Assuring his friend Gregory of Nazianzen that he would attain the ultimate truth by joining him, he painted an idyllic picture of the monastery's sylvan setting, lauding the beauties of God's creation, the "lofty, densely wooded mountain, with trees of every color and variety, the cold transparent streams, the abundant flowers, the multitudes of songbirds and fish, the land fragrances and river breezes." He claimed that it was a place which nourished every kind of fruit, "the sweetest of which is the solitude," so conducive to contemplation.[4]

Despite penning this utopian vision, Basil was a realist. As bishop of Caesarea, he later founded monasteries in busy towns, whose inhabitants benefited from the example of prayerful communities living in harmony with God and neighbor. Reminding the wealthy of their responsibility to society, he extolled monastic emphasis on worship of God, distribution of possessions, and care for the needy. When Basil died, his friend Gregory marveled at the charity and austerity of a man who had provided shelter for strangers, training for those who lacked skills, medical treatment for the poor, and housing for the homeless: "Others had their cooks and rich tables, refinements of cuisine, elegant carriages and soft

---

[2] John Cassian, *The Conferences*, 1.3–4, trans. Boniface Ramsey, ACW 57 (New York: Paulist Press, 1997) 121.

[3] Johannes Quasten, *Patrology*, vol. 3 (Westminster, MD: Newman Press, 1960) 205.

[4] Saint Basil, Ep 1–185; FCh 13:46–47.

flowing garments. Basil had the sick, the dressing of their wounds and the imitation of Christ, cleansing leprosy not by word, but in deed."[5]

A similar pattern of conversion and renunciation was experienced by others. Around the year 360 Martin became a hermit at Ligugé.[6] Typically choosing the most extreme test, Jerome arrived in the Syrian desert, where he spent almost three years as a hermit before conceding that the solitary life was not for him. Later, in Bethlehem, he founded the monastic community which he guided till his death in 420. It was from Pontiacus, a visitor to Milan, that Augustine heard of Antony, whose name and deeds had been unknown to him "till that very hour." He listened avidly as Pontiacus related the story of two young men, serving at the western imperial court in Trier, who abandoned their possessions and followed God after reading Athanasius's biography of the ascetic. At the same time, he learned that Ambrose, whom he so admired, had founded a monastery just outside the city walls and that it was "filled with good brothers."[7]

To Basil and Augustine, monastic life was the supreme example of a worshipping Christian community, whose harmonious rhythm of prayer, work, study, order, and calm represented a reflection of the peace of heaven and a means of transforming the world.[8] On being ordained priest in Hippo, Augustine established a community of monks in the cathedral garden. Possidius, his first biographer, describes how those "servants of God" bound themselves, in the spirit of the early Christians, to "hold everything in common and distribute it to each as the need arose." Later, as bishop, Augustine lived in community with his priests: "The clergy and he were all fed and clothed in the same house, at the same table and from a common purse." Possidius states that the house and adjoining monastery provided at least ten bishops, "holy and venerable, chaste and learned," for the church in his part of Africa.[9]

Ambrose too embraced the spirit of asceticism. On becoming bishop, the former governor of Aemilia and Liguria "gave away to the

---

[5] Gregory of Nazianzen, *Oration on Saint Basil*, 61–63, trans. Leo P. McCauley, FCh, vol. 22 (Washington, DC: CUAP, 1968) 80–82.

[6] Sulpicius Severus, *Life of Saint Martin*, 7; WF 20; *Creeds, Councils and Controversies*, ed. J Stevenson (Cambridge: SPCK, 1989) 20.

[7] Augustine, *Conf*, 8.6.14–15; Ryan, 191–92; see Luke 5:11.

[8] Possidius, *Life of Saint Augustine*, 2; WF 196.

[9] Possidius, *Life of Saint Augustine*, 5.1, 11.3; WF 198, 206; see Acts 2:44–45, 4:35.

Church or the poor all the gold and silver at his disposal . . . leaving nothing for himself he could call his own." His biographer is unambiguous about the motive: "It was as a soldier stripped and unhampered that he wished to follow Christ our Lord."[10] Ambrose's friend Paulinus, former governor of Campania and product of a distinguished senatorial family, founded a religious community at Nola, where he was afterward appointed bishop. Ambrose relayed the disbelief of Paulinus's peers, pagan and Christian, that "a man of such family, such background, such genius, gifted with such eloquence, should retire from his seat in the senate and that the succession of so noble a family should be broken."[11] Writing to Licentius, profligate and still pagan son of his former patron Romanianus, Augustine urged him to go to Campania and learn how Paulinus, "that eminent and holy servant of God, shook off great worldly honors without hesitation" to serve Christ.[12]

The fathers' commitment to asceticism enabled them to devote their lives exclusively to service of God and neighbor. They were at one in rejecting the allure of wealth, privilege, and the secular rewards of learning. Paulinus put it well: "Let the orators keep their literature, the philosophers their wisdom, rich men their wealth, and kings their kingdoms. Christ is our glory, property and kingdom."[13] When he wrote this to a friend who, like him, had been a provincial governor, he was surely thinking of his spiritual mentor, "blessed father Martin," in whom he found the simplicity, self-denial, and holiness prized by the fathers.[14] Martin is credited with popularizing monasticism in Gaul. He left neither books nor letters, but his life and work place him irresistibly in the company of the fathers. Pressed into the army because of his father's rank of military tribune, he had resigned while serving in Gaul. There he was baptized and met his spiritual guide, Hilary, bishop of Poitiers, Church father and champion of Christian orthodoxy.

Later, as bishop of Tours, Martin insisted on maintaining his ascetic practices, and established a monastery at Marmoutier, two miles from the city. It was a place "so secluded and remote that it had all the

[10] Paulinus, *Life of Saint Ambrose*, 38; WF 177.
[11] Ambrose, *Letters* 28, trans. Mary Melchior Beyenka, FCh, vol. 26 (Washington, DC: CUAP, 1954) 144.
[12] Augustine, Ep 26.5–6; NPNF 1:248.
[13] Paulinus of Nola, Ep 38.6; ACW 35:190.
[14] Paulinus of Nola, Ep 18.9; ACW 35:176.

solitude of the desert," protected on one side by the rock face of a high mountain and "enclosed by a gentle bend of the river Loire." The abbot-bishop was soon surrounded by disciples. Coming from every sector of society, holding all in common, they lived frugal lives, dressed in coarse clothing, and ate sparingly. They sheltered and prayed in wooden huts, or in caves hollowed out of the hillside, coming together to participate in communal worship. Sulpicius Severus wonders at the numbers of young aristocrats who joined their company: "These, though far differently brought up, had forced themselves down to this degree of humility and patient endurance, and we have seen numbers of them afterwards made bishops."[15]

Martin's example led to the foundation of monastic communities throughout Gaul. Established by Honoratus in 410, Lérins became the most widely known. The monastery of Auxerre was founded by Saint Germanus, who had resigned from the military governorship of much of northern Gaul to follow the ascetic way. He became bishop of Auxerre in 418. Eleven years later, Germanus's orthodoxy prompted Pope Celestine to send him to Britain, where the Pelagian heresy was gaining ground. Within two years, Palladius, a prominent member of the group which had accompanied Germanus on his mission, was consecrated bishop to "the Irish who believe in Christ."[16] Writing shortly before the year 700, Muirchú named Germanus as the young Patrick's teacher after the escape to Gaul.[17] That Patrick's apostolate in Ireland had a prominent ascetic dimension is evident in his assessment of his missionary success not merely in terms of the great numbers baptized but in the numerous "sons and daughters of the kings of the Irish seen to be monks and virgins of Christ." So many are they, he claims, that they are beyond his power to number.[18] These ascetic converts elicit several references in his writings.

The fathers were at one in commending the dedicated life to both men and women. On returning to Rome from the desert in 382, Jerome was gratified to find several devout women of the city following the ascetic way. "The saintly Marcella," a wealthy widow, whose life was

[15] Sulpicius Severus, *Life of Saint Martin*, 10; WF 24–25.

[16] Prosper of Aquitaine, *Chronicle*, trans. Liam De Paor, *Saint Patrick's World: The Christian Culture of Ireland's Apostolic Age* (Dublin: Four Courts Press, 1993) 79.

[17] Muirchú, *Life of Saint Patrick*, De Paor, 178.

[18] Patrick, *Conf*, 41; Bieler, 34; *Letter to Coroticus*, 12; Bieler, 44.

"worthy of the Gospel," had committed herself to asceticism after meeting Athanasius, the biographer of Antony, during his exile in Rome. She and her friend Paula turned their houses into centers of devotion.[19] Many other women joined them in lives of prayer, study, and service. Learning of Jerome's scholarship, Marcella drew on his extensive scriptural knowledge to guide her friends in study of the Bible. She even set herself the task of learning Hebrew.

Meanwhile, certain influential members of Roman society felt threatened by the numbers of young women of marriageable age who were following the new way. Supporting the ascetics with his customary pugnacity and lack of tact, Jerome incurred the intense dislike of many in the city but had a powerful protector in Pope Damasus, who valued his learning and secretarial assistance: "Damasus of blessed memory spoke of none but me."[20] When Damasus died in 384, Jerome and Paula left for Palestine, where they established two religious houses in Bethlehem. Jerome was abbot of the men's monastery. When Paula died in 404, her daughter Eustochium became superior of the women's community and continued to run the pilgrim hostel founded by her mother. Jerome left a moving account of Paula's inspiring life and death. He also recorded the passing of Marcella during the fall of Rome, recalling the happier times when she and her dedicated friends had served God so faithfully.[21]

Other resourceful women were promoting asceticism in the east. Macrina, sister of Gregory of Nyssa and Basil, helped her mother to rear the family after her father's early death. It was she who encouraged Basil to consider his future when he returned from higher education in Greece "excessively puffed up by his rhetorical abilities and disdainful of all great reputations." When another talented brother, Nautacrius, a hermit, was killed in the wilderness, she persuaded her grieving mother to abandon the comforts of a prosperous life and join with family servants in a worshipping community of women "as if all belonged to the same rank."[22]

Other women were equally intrepid. Egeria, a Spanish virgin, was an early pilgrim to the Holy Land. For the sisters in Galicia she wrote an account of her visits to the biblical sites of Asia Minor, Palestine, Sinai, and

---

[19] Jerome, Epp 54.18, 127.5; NPNF 6:108, 254–55.

[20] Jerome, Ep 45.3; NPNF 6:59.

[21] Jerome, Epp 108, 127; NPNF 6:195–212, 253–58.

[22] Gregory of Nyssa, *Life of Saint Macrina*, trans. Virginia Woods Callahan, FCh, vol. 58 (Washington, DC: CUAP, 1967) 168, 170–71.

Egypt. The hazardous journey took three years, from 381 to 384. Egeria's short book contains valuable information on individuals in the Palestinian church of the time. There are also descriptions of liturgical practices, such as celebration of the Eucharist and antiphonal singing of the psalms. Her portrayal of the ceremonies of holy week includes details of processions to the large cross erected outside the *anastasis*, the basilica commemorating the resurrection of Christ. A highlight of the book is an account of the Good Friday veneration of the cross, led by the bishop of Jerusalem.[23]

Another woman who ended far from home was Melania the elder, a prominent member of the Roman nobility and relative of Paulinus of Nola. When her husband and two sons died in 372, she abandoned great wealth to "embrace poverty and humility" in a Jerusalem convent. She was admired for her fearless defense of the desert monks against the emperor Valens, promoter of the Arian heresy. Visiting Paulinus at Nola after twenty-five years in Palestine, Melania evoked his unqualified admiration: "What a woman she is! A soldier for Christ with the virtues of Martin, though of the weaker sex." In her disregard for mere material status the bishop sees a greater nobility of spirit than that shown by her famous consular family. He recalls that, when she arrived at his church wearing her "old black rags," she was accompanied by a large group of relatives, all members of the Roman aristocracy, who "joined with the peaceful voices" of the ascetics as they sang the psalms.[24]

Melania's niece, who shared her name and her regard for the spiritual life, sold much of her property and land to the benefit of the poor and the work of the Church. When she and her husband Pinianus decided to emancipate their slaves, the family made an unsuccessful appeal to the emperor to overturn the decision. After the death of Pinianus, the younger Melania emulated her famous aunt by founding and leading a community of devout women in Jerusalem. Though many people of the time attempted to dissuade women from following the ascetic way, Ambrose remained an enthusiastic advocate. His book, *On Virginity*, was dedicated to his sister Marcellina, who received the veil from Pope Liberius in Saint Peter's and continued to live in the family home, praying, fasting, and engaging in good works.[25] Criticized by prominent families,

---

[23] *Travels of Egeria*, 36.1–36.9, trans. John Wilkinson (Oxford: Oxbow Books, 2006) 154–57.

[24] Paulinus of Nola, Ep 29.6–13; ACW 35:105–17.

[25] Ambrose, *Concerning Virgins*, 3.1.1; NPNF 10:381.

who preferred their daughters to marry and lead conventional lives, Ambrose continued to support the women's choice, though advising them against extremes of austerity.[26] Augustine favored the sisterhood and wrote a rule for nuns in the convent in Hippo, where his widowed sister had been superior until her death.[27]

Patrick too encouraged female asceticism, and one young woman, whom he describes as a "blessed Irishwoman of noble birth," resembled the patrician ladies of Rome and Milan in needing no persuasion to become "a virgin of Christ." Her bishop expresses his joy that, responding to the divine call, "she most laudably and ardently chose" to dedicate herself entirely to God. Patrick's delight at her decision is enhanced by the knowledge that, not long before, Irish families like hers had been "worshipping idols and things impure."[28] Bishops of the time valued the example of girls of high social status rejecting lives of ease for total commitment to God. Writing to Proba, a devout member of the Roman aristocracy, Augustine celebrates the consecration to virginity "of the daughter of your house," because it glorifies God and brings blessings on the family. He prays that many young women, of all social levels, will follow the girl's example.[29]

Patrick's appreciation of asceticism rivaled that of Basil, Ambrose, Jerome, and Augustine. His description of the degrees of virginity, including those of widows and married couples who practice continence, echoes patristic teaching. Sharing Ambrose's willingness to defend dedicated Christian women who experience family hostility, he lauds those willing to endure "persecutions and false reproaches from their parents." The plight of female slaves is a particular concern. Though they are most prone to suffering, "even to the extent of terror and threats," he rejoices that few are deterred from persevering in their chosen way. Their strength to endure he attributes to God: "Through grace, they continue steadfast in their following of him, even though they are forbidden."[30] By supporting them with such conviction, Patrick challenged the incomprehension of Christians still influenced by their largely pagan milieu.

---

[26] Ambrose, *On Virginity*, 6.27–28, trans. Daniel Callam (Toronto: Peregrina, 1996) 16.

[27] Augustine, Ep 211; NPNF 1:563–68.

[28] Patrick, *Conf*, 41–42; Bieler, 34.

[29] Augustine, Ep 150; NPNF 1:504.

[30] Patrick, *Conf*, 42; Bieler, 34–35.

Despite the fathers' efforts, not all Christians of the time acknowledged the spiritual benefits of a life dedicated exclusively to God. In Rome, an ex-ascetic, Jovinian, campaigned against monasticism, causing some monks and nuns to abandon their religious vocation and marry. Ambrose and his fellow bishops wrote a letter of protest to Pope Siricius. Reminding him that, in attacking monastic life, Jovinian and his kind claim to be honoring married life, Ambrose asks, "What praise is possible to marriage if virginity receives no distinction?"[31] He consciously balances his criticism by observing that, in extolling chastity, Saint Paul "does not do away with the grace of marriage, nor has he so exalted marriage as to check the desire for chastity." To Ambrose the Church is a field, rich in the diversity of fruit and flowers, in which is found the spring flowers of virginity side by side with "the gravity of widowhood" and the fruits of marriage.[32]

The fathers' acceptance of chastity, or virginity, signifying their absolute commitment to God and fellow Christians, reflected Paul's consciousness of its exemplary value in guiding his Corinthian converts, who were living in a city notorious for its licentiousness. Urging faithfulness to family life, the apostle points to his own dedicated way of life, undertaken for the glory of God. Though accepting that it is not for all, he clarifies why that way of life is fitting for him: "The unmarried man is anxious about the affairs of the Lord, how to please the Lord."[33] A past master of the telling phrase, Jerome expresses his preference for the ascetic life more colorfully, remarking that the Christian wishing to give all as God's soldier must remember that no soldier takes a wife to battle.

At one with the fathers on this final degree of self-sacrifice, Patrick was an exemplar for the monks and virgins in Ireland.[34] His father had been a deacon and his grandfather a priest, but he chose the way of total commitment, convinced that, through grace, he would continue his work with the Irish, a trust received from God, "who bade me to come here and stay with them for the rest of my life."[35] Unaffected by the lure of material success, Patrick is certain "that poverty and adversity are better suited to me than lucre and luxury." His words are reminiscent of

---

[31] Ambrose, Ep 44; FCh 26:225.

[32] Ambrose, *Concerning Widows*, 13.79; 14.83, trans. H. De Romestin, NPNF, vol. 10 (Grand Rapids, MI: Eerdmans, 1997) 405.

[33] 1 Cor 7:32; see 1 Cor 5:1–13; 1 Cor 6:1–20.

[34] Patrick, *Conf*, 55; Bieler, 38.

[35] Patrick, *Conf*, 43–44; Bieler, 35; *Letter to Coroticus*, 1; Bieler, 41.

Ambrose's about Paulinus, who, in leaving Gaul for Italy, "is now poor instead of rich and has said farewell to home, country and kindred in order to serve God with greater zeal."[36]

For Patrick, as for his fellow ascetics, there was no turning back when following Christ. Freeborn by birth, he sold his "noble rank, neither ashamed nor sorry, for the good of others." No longer can he invoke the protection of Roman law, as Paul did when about to be flogged.[37] Driven by "zeal for God," he had arrived in Ireland an exile for Christ, having given up homeland and family, and "my life to the point of death."[38] Indeed, in denouncing Coroticus, a fellow Briton and leader of a predatory band that has murdered some of his flock and abducted others, he acknowledges his absolute kinship with the Irish: "The wickedness of the wicked has prevailed over us. We have been made, as it were, strangers. Perhaps they do not believe that we have received one and the same baptism, or that we have one and the same God and Father. For them it is a disgrace that we are Irish."[39]

Having sacrificed all for God, the fathers and their ascetic brethren recognized the need for God's help if they were to be faithful to the end. In a simple story, related with typical facility, Jerome illuminates the part played by grace in the life of the dedicated person. His *Life of Malchus* illustrates the reply of Jesus to the prospective disciple who proposed that he should first go and bid farewell to his people at home: "No one who puts a hand to the plow and looks back is fit for the kingdom of God."[40] Against his abbot's wishes, Malchus, who has been a monk for many years, leaves the monastery to visit his widowed mother, sell property, and establish a monastery in his native place. On his way across the desert he is captured by Saracens and sold into slavery. His master gives him the task of tending sheep and then commands him to marry a fellow slave. Escaping, both flee across the burning wastes for three days, only to be tracked to a cave by their pursuers. Saved from certain death by a fierce lioness, Malchus is able to return, contrite, to his monastic community. In the vastness of the desert, hunted like a wild beast, "with nothing to see but the earth and

---

[36] Ambrose, Ep 28; FCh 26:144.

[37] Patrick, *Letter to Coroticus*, 10; Bieler, 43; see Acts 22:25–30.

[38] Patrick, *Letter to Coroticus* , 1–2; Bieler, 41.

[39] Patrick, *Letter to Coroticus*, 16; Bieler, 45; "Strangers" translates *extranei*: strangers, foreigners, or aliens.

[40] Luke 9:62.

the sky," he had given thanks to God as his judge "because I discovered in the desert the monk whom I had been about to lose in my own country."[41]

Neither the fathers nor their ascetic brethren yielded to the temptation of Malchus. Writing to Novatus, Augustine noted that, though the tie that bound him to Severus, a close friend from boyhood and now a fellow bishop, surpassed "even the bond of kinship," they met seldom, "neither by his wish nor by mine, but because of our giving to the claims of our mother the Church precedence above the claims of this present world, out of regard for that coming eternity in which we shall dwell together and part no more."[42] Patrick, an aged man, still harassed by enemies intent on destroying his good name, dreamed of final visits to family in Britain and brethren in Gaul. He accepted that it was a dream which would never be realized, for he was committed, in faith and sincerity, to his people. Insistent that he would continue to preach the Gospel to the "heathen Irish" till he died, he prayed that God would give him perseverance "and deign that I be a faithful witness to Him to the end of my life for my God."[43]

Shortly before his death, Augustine calmly considered the finality of his commitment and that of his fellow bishops. In May 429 the Vandals had crossed from Spain into Africa. Within a year, they controlled much of Numidia. Stories of destruction, massacre, and rape abounded. Urgent requests for guidance arrived at Hippo, with Bishop Honoratus asking whether he and his fellow prelates should move to towns which were more secure. In his reply, Augustine surveyed the various choices confronting those committed to responsibility for the spiritual welfare of others and concluded that a bishop may leave if he is specifically sought by the enemy, or in circumstances where there are other spiritual leaders to care for the flock. However, it is generally permissible to do so only if the faithful themselves are fleeing. Should they choose to stay, their pastor must do the same. The minister who runs away, when the consequence is the withdrawal from Christ's flock of that nourishment by which its spiritual life is sustained, is a "hireling who sees the wolf coming and flees because he does not care for the sheep."[44] Augustine died in Hippo on 28 August 430 while his city, crowded with refugees, was under siege by the Vandals.

---

41. Jerome, *Life of Malchus*, 5–7, ECL 123–26.
42. Augustine, Ep 84.1; NPNF 1:363.
43. Patrick, *Conf*, 58; Bieler, 39.
44. Possidius, *Life of Saint Augustine*, 30.1–14; WF 232–42.

# 4

# MARTYRS, ASCETICS, AND FATHERS

I n their endeavors to fortify the faith of fellow Christians subject to
the influence of a world which tolerated Christianity but was largely
indifferent to its message, the fathers of the fourth and fifth centuries invoked the example of the martyrs. Jerome captured the prevailing
situation in a wry observation on the paradox of a Church which, growing under persecution, had been "crowned by the martyrs," yet under
the Christian emperors had become "more powerful and wealthy but
less rich in Christian virtues."[1] Half a century later, on the feast of Saint
Laurence, Leo the Great celebrated the achievement of all martyrs: "By
the imitation of his charity and by the likeness to his suffering, they are
nearer to Our Lord Jesus Christ, who died for all." Speaking of Christ's
passion, he observed that the words "thy will be done" lay at the heart
of man's salvation, for they had "instructed all the faithful, inflamed all
confessors, crowned all martyrs."[2]

Jerome had been a devotee of the martyrs since his youth. As a
student in Rome, he joined friends of the same age and interests on
Sundays to visit the tombs "which were dug in the depths of the earth."
Ambrose was another enthusiast. Claiming Gervasius and Protasius as
soldiers of Christ and protectors of the Church, he placed their remains
in his basilica, observing that, unlike soldiers of this world, they were
soldiers of Christ, who triumphed through prayer and suffering.[3] Each

---

[1] Jerome, *Life of Malchus*, 1; ECL 121.
[2] Leo, *Sermons*, 85.1; 58.5, trans. Jane P. Freedland and Agnes J. Conway, FCh,
vol. 93 (Washington, DC: CUAP, 1995) 363, 353; Ambrose, Ep 61; FCh 26:379.
[3] Jerome, *On Illustrious Men*, trans. ed. Thomas P. Halton, FCh, vol. 100 (Washington, DC: CUAP, 1999) xxiii; Ambrose, Ep 61; FCh 26:379.

year, on June 29, feast of saints Peter and Paul, Ambrose's friend and fellow bishop, Paulinus, visited Rome, where he prayed with other pilgrims "at the sacred tombs of the apostles and martyrs." When he built a basilica at Nola, he placed the relics of martyrs at the altar. Through the generosity of Ambrose, he was able to do the same at his second church, which was not far from Nola.[4]

Augustine, who later in life was a devotee of Stephen, celebrated the martyrs' feats and the magnitude of their reward: "Where are they now, do you think, these saints? They are with God. They sit at the heavenly banquet where the Lord feasts them upon his divinity."[5] He pondered the paradox of Peter and Paul, who, humiliated in their deaths, were now honored, with many visiting their shrines. Rejoicing that an obscure fisherman was enjoying greater acclaim than the emperors, the bishop urged his people to love the things loved by the martyrs, "even though you don't need to endure what they endured."[6]

Carthage, where Augustine had studied, taught, and later, as bishop, often preached, held the grave of the martyred bishop whom he called "the blessed Cyprian."[7] It was there, just half a century after Cyprian's death, that Perpetua and her servant Felicity met the same fate during Diocletian's persecution of 303. The African people preserved their poignant story, recounted, in part, by Perpetua herself. Just twenty-two, she was "well born, liberally educated, honorably married, with an infant son at the breast," having a father, mother, and two brothers, one a catechumen like herself. Surrounded by the horrors of prison life, the darkness, the intolerable heat, the rough handling by soldiers, she and Felicity, who was also mother of an infant, died with dignity in the amphitheatre.[8]

Martin would have known of the martyrs of Lyons, who died in the persecution of 177 under the emperor Marcus Aurelius. Patrick's sojourn in Gaul would have brought him the same story. Among the victims were the slave girl Blandina, fifteen-year-old Ponticus, and their aged bishop Photinus, "very weak in body and scarcely breathing from

---

[4] Paulinus of Nola, Epp 32.17, 43.1; ACW 35:150–51, 227–28.

[5] Van der Meer, *Augustine*, 473.

[6] *Saint Augustine's Political Writings*, ed. E. M. Atkins and R. J. Dodaro (Cambridge: University Press, 2001) 53.

[7] Augustine, *Conf*, 5.8.15; Ryan, 123.

[8] Quasten, *Patrology*, vol. 1, 181; D. Attwater, *The Penguin Dictionary of the Saints* (Middlesex: Penguin Books, 1975) 273.

sickness."[9] When all was over in the amphitheatre, the martyrs' bodies were thrown to the dogs, and then burned. Their ashes were scattered in the River Rhône "so that not a single trace of their bodies might be left on earth." Irenaeus, who survived because he had been in Rome during the persecution, acknowledged their witness: "They are indeed martyrs whom Christ judged worthy to be taken up as soon as they had confessed him, putting his seal on their witness by death; but we are simple, humble confessors."[10]

Patrick, whose Irish converts were so brutally killed shortly after baptism, recalls the "twelve dangers" in which his own life was at stake and expresses gratitude for God's protection. Now, in old age, he is still willing to give "even my life without hesitation and very gladly for his name."[11] Offering himself as "a living victim to Christ my Lord," he prays that he may be permitted to share the fate of the martyrs and shed his blood "with those exiles and captives for his name, even though I should be denied a grave, or my body be woefully torn to pieces limb by limb by hounds or wild beasts, or the birds of the air devour it."[12] Patrick's aspiration was shared by Paulinus, who in the year 395 was ordained priest after distributing his property and possessions. In a letter to his friend Sulpicius, he quoted Saint Paul: "I pray, my brother, that we may be found worthy to be cursed, censured and ground down, and even to be executed in the name of Jesus Christ."[13]

Though willing to die for their beliefs, the fathers and ascetics of the fourth and fifth centuries acknowledged that the era of the martyrs was past and embraced the new martyrdom of the ascetic way. Conceding that Martin did not suffer the torture endured by the prophet Isaiah, and that, unlike the apostle Paul, he "shed no blood," Sulpicius claims that Martin achieved martyrdom through his life of self-sacrifice. He presents Martin as an exemplary churchman who awakens in the reader "a desire for true wisdom, for the heavenly warfare and for a valor inspired by God."[14]

---

[9] Quasten, *Patrology*, vol. 1, 180.

[10] Musurillo, 81–83; Eusebius, *Ecclesiastical History*, vol. 1, 5.1.1–5, 2.1–5; Loeb, 409–41, 211–17.

[11] Patrick, *Conf*, 35, 37; Bieler, 31, 32.

[12] Patrick, *Conf*, 59; Bieler, 39; see Ps 79:1–2, 12–13.

[13] Paulinus of Nola, Ep 1.8; 2.2; ACW 35:34; 2 Cor 1:1–7.

[14] Sulpicius Severus, Ep 2; *Life of Saint Martin*, 1, preface; WF 54; 11–12.

Tempered by their asceticism and fortified by absolute commitment to God, the fathers of the Church, with lowly bishops like Martin and Patrick, emulated the martyrs by resisting the excesses of powerful men. Patrick fearlessly condemned Coroticus and his soldiers as killers and abductors of his "dearest ones." Expressing incredulity that some of the perpetrators professed to share with him the same kingdom of God where they have "one God for Father," he avers that he can no longer regard the Britons among them as "fellow citizens, or fellow citizens of the holy Romans." They have basely slain innocent captives and sold others as slaves to a pagan land "where sin abounds openly, grossly, impudently."[15]

The guilty men have even sold some survivors to "the abominable, wicked and apostate Picts" and mocked the messengers sent as negotiators. The bishop's disgust is palpable: "You prefer to kill and sell them to a foreign nation that has no knowledge of God. You betray the members of Christ, as it were, into a brothel."[16] As a former slave, he has no illusions about the fate of the female survivors, who will be doled out as prizes "for the sake of a wretched temporal kingdom which will pass away in a moment."[17] The behavior of the raiders, some of them Christian, is contrasted with that of the Franks and other heathen peoples, who, when holding hostages, always respond to "holy men," who offer "many thousand solidi to ransom baptized captives."

Martin's most punishing encounter with civil authority issued from a theological dispute. Led by Ithacius, some Gaulish bishops denounced the questionable teachings of Priscillian, a Spanish Christian, who turned for support to the western imperial usurper Maximus, brutal former military commander of Britain. Concerned that the disagreement could lead to social unrest, Maximus had Priscillian tried before Evodius, Praetorian Prefect of Gaul. Found guilty of sorcery, the prisoner was executed. Martin was distraught, for the usurper had promised to spare the accused man.[18] He was especially perturbed because Bishop Ithacius and like-minded friends had supported the victim's prosecution. Hoping to induce emperor and prelates to admit the enormity of their deed, he refused to participate in celebrating the Eucharist at the inauguration of a new bishop of Trier.

[15] Patrick, *Letter to Coroticus*, 2; Bieler, 1.
[16] Patrick, *Letter to Coroticus*, 2–3, 14–15; Bieler, 41–42, 45.
[17] Patrick, *Letter to Coroticus*, 19; Bieler, 46.
[18] Sulpicius Severus, *Dialogues*, 2.11, n. 1; WF 133.

The logic of power made Maximus sure-footed. After vainly attempting to persuade Martin to celebrate with his fellow bishops, he threatened to persecute Priscillian's followers in Spain and execute others for whom the bishop had been interceding. Martin submitted, and "on that same day joined the bishops in communion, judging that to make this momentary concession was better than deserting the cause of those over whose heads a sword was hanging."[19] Shortly after Priscillian's execution, Ambrose was on a mission to the court of Maximus and encountered the bishops who had been denounced by Martin. His pointed avoidance of contact with them angered the emperor, who ordered him to leave at once. "I went," says Ambrose, "though several thought that I would not escape his ambushes." Refusing to be intimidated by the usurper, he "excluded him from communion" until he repented his misdeeds, which included murder.[20]

Later, Ambrose recognized that his stand against Maximus could have earned him the fate of the martyrs: "What opportunities I have had, and have been called back, almost from the goal."[21] In the year 390 he challenged a more powerful figure. Following the killing of the governor of Thessalonica during serious civil disorder in the city, Ambrose extracted a promise of pardon for the citizens from the eastern emperor, Theodosius, who then sanctioned the slaughter of seven thousand people gathered in an amphitheatre for the games. In a firm letter excluding the guilty ruler from "the assembly of the Church and participation in the sacraments," the bishop reminded him that he would be forgiven only through "tears and penance." On protesting that King David had committed adultery and murder, Theodosius was told, "As you imitated him in your transgressions, imitate him in his amendment." After several months' exclusion from communion, he was publicly absolved in Milan by Ambrose, who readmitted him to the fold at Christmas 390.[22]

With his noble background, wide learning, and former experience as civil governor, the bishop of Milan was adept at absorbing the shocks of public conflict. A decade after Ambrose's encounter with imperial power, John Chrysostom, bishop of Constantinople, attempted to reform his clergy and improve the moral climate at the court of Theodosius's successor, Arcadius. At this time Augustine was rebuking African ascetics

---

[19] Sulpicius Severus, *Dialogues*, 2.11–13; WF 133–37.
[20] Ambrose, Ep 10; FCh 26:62; Paulinus, *Life of Ambrose*, 19; WF 162–63.
[21] Ambrose, Ep 53; FCh 26:284.
[22] Ambrose, Ep 3; FCh 26:20–26; Paulinus, *Life of Saint Ambrose*, 26; WF 167–68.

who, "in the garb of monks, wander through the provinces, sent by no authority, never at rest, stable or settled." John denounced those who left their monasteries to engage in the social life of Constantinople.[23] He excoriated the rich and powerful, who neglected the plight of the poor, and applied church funds formerly lavished on entertaining visiting dignitaries to the support of the needy, the sick, and the neglected.

Caught in a web of church and court intrigue, but lacking the calm authority of Ambrose, John became the focus of a bitter enmity fanned by bishops Theophilus of Alexandria and Epiphanius of Salamis in Cyprus. His criticism of the empress Eudoxia and her circle finally provoked an alliance of secular and religious critics. Banished to the eastern reaches of the empire, John suffered the rigors of primitive provincial life for three years, with his one comfort the support of distant friends, Pope Innocent I among them. Finally, in 407, during a forced march to an even more remote region, he died. Renowned for his learning, holiness, and oratorical skills, John was defeated because he remained the uncompromising hermit who had once fasted and prayed in the mountains outside his native Antioch. His witness was in the tradition of the martyrs.

In an earlier episode of resistance to unjust authority, the redoubtable Basil of Caesarea had succeeded where John failed. On denouncing the promotion of Arianism by the emperor Valens, he was threatened with material deprivation and exile. His response, typically defiant, was that the loss of earthly possessions would signify nothing to one who owned only a cloak and a few books, and that the prospect of exile could not intimidate a bishop unconcerned with which part of God's world he inhabited. Were death itself the penalty, it would be "an act of kindness, for it will bring me closer to God, for whom I live, for whom I am created and toward whom I hasten."[24]

Basil's resistance was surely modeled on that of a bishop whom he revered, and whose friendship he enjoyed. Born in the final years of the third century, Athanasius was a student during the persecution instigated by Maximinus in 311. Appointed bishop of Alexandria, he was banished from his see on five occasions for defending apostolic teaching against the Arian error and denying the emperor's claim to dictate Church doctrine.

---

[23] Augustine, *On the Work of Monks*, 28.36; FCh 14:384; J.N.D. Kelly, *Golden Mouth: The Story of John Chrysostom, Ascetic, Preacher, Bishop* (London: Duckworth, 1995) 123–25.

[24] Quasten, *Patrology*, vol. 3, 206.

Though he died a confessor in 373 at the age of seventy-seven, Athanasius consistently acted in the spirit of the martyrs. In his *Life of Antony* he identifies martyrdom with asceticism when recording the hermit's return to the desert after supporting the persecuted Christians of Alexandria: "When the storm of persecution had died away and the blessed Bishop Peter had been crowned with a martyr's glory, Antony returned to his former cell and achieved a daily martyrdom of faith and conscience."[25]

Seventy years after the death of Athanasius, a Church father's defense of fellow Christians against a formidable military leader assumed an almost mythic significance in European history. In the year 452 there was panic in Rome as word spread that the Huns, led by Attila, were advancing on the city. Acting decisively, Pope Leo, the consul Arienus, and the ex-prefect Trigetius made their way to Attila's camp on the banks of the Mincio, where it flows into the Po near Mantua. Attila was persuaded to turn away. Just three years later, when Geiseric and his army crossed the Mediterranean and captured Rome, Leo's quiet authority induced the Vandal to spare the city and its people. The barbarian leader confined his soldiers to taking plunder.[26] A quarter of a century earlier, he and his forces were besieging the African town of Hippo when its bishop, Augustine, died.

A sermon preached by Leo in the autumn of 442 suggests why, in his writings, there is no reference to his own contribution to Rome's survival. Commemorating the sack of the city by Alaric in the year 410, he thanks God, who, on that occasion, protected it from slaughter, snatched it from captivity, and restored it to safety: "Let us attribute our deliverance not, as the pagans think, to the effects of stars, but to the inexpressible mercy of almighty God, who willed to soften the heart of raging barbarians."[27] By exhibiting moral courage in perilous times, and acting as shepherds, not hirelings, bishops like Leo, Ambrose, Patrick, and Martin were true to the spirit of Augustine's words to the people of Hippo on his dual responsibility: "We bishops, apart from being Christians, as which we shall render God an account of the manner of our lives, are also in charge of you, and, as such, will render God an account of our stewardship."[28]

---

[25] Athanasius, *Life of Antony*, 47; ECL 38.

[26] Grisar, Hartmann, *History of the Popes in the Middle Ages*, vol. 1 (London: Kegan Paul, Trench, Trubned, 1912) 94.

[27] Leo, S 84.2; FCh 93:361.

[28] Augustine, S 46.2, from *Image of the Good Shepherd as Source of the Ministerial Priesthood* (Rome: Gregorian University Press, 1997) 187.

When the martyrs died they were acclaimed by Christians and their tombs became places of pilgrimage. Recognized as the "new martyrs," the ascetics were similarly honored by the people. In his church at Primuliacum, between Toulouse and Narbonne in southern Gaul, Sulpicius Severus placed relics of Clarus, "Martin's companion in meditation and now his partner in praise."[29] Martin himself died in 397 while attempting to settle a quarrel in Candes, a village thirty miles from Tours. Immediately afterward, there was a "contention" between Poitiers and Tours about his place of burial. The men of Tours succeeded in conveying Martin's remains down the rivers Vienne and Loire to their city. The bishop's funeral was attended by a multitude of ordinary people, nearly two thousand monks, and many consecrated virgins. It differed greatly from a worldly ceremony, says Severus, who adds, "Let others drive before their chariots captives with hands bound behind their backs; Martin's body was followed by those who, with him for their leader, have overcome the world."[30]

Writing in the last decade of the seventh century, Muirchú describes how, with death imminent, Patrick attempted to reach Armagh but was told by an angel to return to Saul. On his passing, a "dreadful conflict" which erupted over the destination of his remains was quelled by a miraculous flooding of the sea into an inlet near Saul. He was buried at Dun Lethglaisse, now Downpatrick.[31] Germanus of Auxerre, whose name was so often associated with Patrick's, died at Ravenna in Italy in 448, having gone there to intercede with the emperor on behalf of the people of Brittany. His last request was that "his dust should return to his native soil." Before the final journey, there was some disagreement over the division of his possessions, with even the empress and the local bishop anxious to receive something associated with him. His body was then brought the 550 miles to Auxerre. Great respect was shown by the inhabitants of towns and villages on the way.[32]

When John Chrysostom died in 407, an exile from his see, he was buried in a remote corner of what is now eastern Turkey. Thirty years later his remains were brought to Constantinople and placed with great ceremony in the Church of the Apostles. As John's relics were received

[29] Paulinus of Nola, Ep 32.6; ACW 35:139–41.

[30] Sulpicius Severus, Ep 3; WF 60.

[31] Muirchú, *Life of Saint Patrick*; De Paor, 197.

[32] Constantius of Lyons, *The Life of Saint Germanus of Auxerre*, 42–44, trans. F. R. Hoare, *The Western Fathers* (London: Sheed and Ward, 1954) 318–19.

at the waterside, the emperor paid tribute, praying that his parents be forgiven "for their ill-advised persecution of the bishop."[33] Jerome recorded the memorable funeral of his friend Paula, abbess of the women's monastery in Bethlehem, who died in 404. Her bier was carried by bishops to the Church of the Nativity. Dedicated virgins and desert monks came from far and wide. The widows and the poor "showed the garments she had given them, while the destitute cried aloud that they had lost a mother and a nurse." Psalms were chanted in Greek, Latin, and Syriac, not just for the three days of funeral ceremonies, but throughout the week. Jerome had an inscription placed in the church, beside Paula's tomb:

> Seest thou here hollowed in the rock a grave,
> 'Tis Paula's tomb; high heaven has her soul.
> She Rome and friends, riches and home gave up,
> Here in this lonely spot to find her rest.
> For here Christ's manger was, and here the kings
> To him, both God and man, their off'rings made. [34]

Since the burial place of each martyr or ascetic became a place of prayer and intercession, Christians approaching death often asked to be interred at the sacred site. On one occasion Paulinus asked Augustine's advice about a lady's request that her son be buried near the shrine of the martyred Saint Felix at Nola. He received a typically detailed and thoughtful reply. It is good to pray for the dead, concludes Augustine, especially by assisting in celebration of the Eucharist, and prayers are more important than location. However, the fact that one chooses such a holy place to bury a relative increases devotion, just as the physical gestures made by Christians enhance the fervor of their prayer.[35] Throughout Ireland, the graves clustered around ancient shrines of spiritual leaders still witness to that early respect for the saints who lie there. The Gaelic word for cemetery, "reilig," confirms the antiquity of the custom.

---

[33] Quasten, *Patrology*, vol. 3, 427.

[34] Jerome, Ep 108.34; NPNF 6:212.

[35] Augustine, *The Care to be Taken for the Dead*, 4–5, trans. John A. Lacy, FCh 27 (Washington, DC: CUAP, 1969) 358–61; *Retractions*, 2.90, trans. Mary Inez Bogan, FCh 60 (Washington, DC: CUAP, 1968) 265; Augustine, *City of God*, 12.10; Bettenson, 1048–49.

# 5

# HUMILITY AND TRUTH
## TESTAMENTS OF FAITH

Inspired by the ascetic ideal and committed to exclusive service of God and neighbor, the fathers of the fourth and fifth centuries renounced all worldly aspirations, whether social, political, or academic. However, some still felt burdened by the legacy of their liberal education, believing that its emphasis on pagan poets and philosophers was at variance with the Gospel message. Jerome recorded his own experience of this troubled state of being. Following conversion at Trier, he aspired to a life of simple Christian service but was plagued by guilt through his continued attachment to the pagan classics. In 373, on the way to Syria to become a desert hermit, he stayed at the home of Evagrius in Antioch, where he contemplated the painful final step in renunciation. It entailed rejection of his precious library of classical literature for what he regarded as the uncultured language of the Bible.

Racked by guilt and laid low by a dangerous fever, Jerome had a vivid dream in which he was at the point of death. Dragged before a tribunal, he saw a figure seated on a throne. Bathed in a terrifying light, surrounded by an accusing multitude and not daring to look up, he flung himself to the ground. Asked his profession, he replied that he was a Christian. "You are lying!" said the one on the throne. "You are a Ciceronian and not a Christian! Where your treasure is, there is your heart also." As he was severely beaten, Jerome begged for mercy. Only on vowing to reject his secular books was he released.[1] For some time after, the scholar refused to return to the works of even the greatest pagan

---

[1] Jerome, Ep 22.30; NPNF 6:35; see Matt 16:21.

authors. He never again read them for their own sake but applied his secular learning to God's service.

Despite his good intentions, the mercurial monk never quite shrugged off the pride that dogged his great talent. Though aware that writers who can "charm the popular ear by the finish of their style" often conclude that "every word they say is the word of God," he remained vulnerable to the lure of intellectual vanity and was ever ready to vaunt his literary skills or bridle at the slightest hint of criticism.[2] Indeed, his *On Illustrious Men*, which contains details of the works of eminent Christians, opens with those of the apostles and ends with his own.

Jerome was not alone in taking a less than saintly pride in his literary prowess. Noted for its felicities of style, the immensely popular *Life of Martin*, written by Sulpicius Severus, opens with a conventional protestation of the author's reluctance to submit his efforts to the world's judgment "for fear that an all too unpolished diction should prove displeasing to the reader." There is also an assertion that "the Kingdom of God comes not by eloquence, but rests upon faith." Shortly after the book's publication, Severus, through a character in his *Dialogues*, bragged that it was being read from Gaul to Rome and from Carthage to Alexandria. So popular was it in Rome that "the booksellers are in raptures."[3]

Representing a brilliant galaxy of accomplishment, the learned fathers of the fourth and fifth centuries produced works of theology and philosophy, scriptural translations and commentaries, sermons and letters, all directed to the glory of God and the transmission of his word. Possidius, first biographer of Augustine, is conscious of the importance of that part of the bishop's legacy to the Church, which includes "libraries containing his own books and discourses and those of other holy men." In these, he says, Augustine "will always be alive and faithful."[4] The bishop of Hippo has always been most alive to Christians in his *Confessions*, acclaimed as the first intimate portrayal of a writer's spiritual life and a supreme expression of personal indebtedness to God's goodness and mercy.

Patrick was alone among the humbler bishops and ascetics of that era in leaving an account of his spiritual life, in the brief *Confession* which

---

[2] Jerome, Ep 53.7; NPNF 6:99.

[3] Sulpicius Severus, *Dialogues*, 1.23; WF 96; *Life of Saint Martin*, dedication; WF 10–11.

[4] Possidius, *Life of Saint Augustine*, 31.8, trans. Matthew O'Connell, Augustinian Series, vol. 1 (Villanova, PA: Augustinian Press, 1955) 130.

was published several decades after Augustine's death in 430. He was fulfilling a long-held desire to express a lasting heartfelt tribute to God's glory and mercy. Having hesitated for fear of exposing his ignorance to "lordly men of letters," he ruefully recounts the circumstances which inhibited his academic progress. Confinement in a non-Roman country had denied him the important third level of education which entailed the study of rhetoric. Earlier, he had willfully neglected the second stage, devoted to literature and the structure of language. Finally, during his years as bishop, while old acquaintances "thoroughly drank in the law and the Holy Scriptures" and continued to perfect their Latin, he was speaking the language "of a foreign people."[5]

Patrick feared the strictures of the critics, but no Church father would have questioned his fitness for the task of evangelizing the Irish through spoken word and pen. Though Augustine felt that communicators of God's word should speak with elegance, spirit, and wisdom, he concluded that there are eloquent individuals whose lack of wisdom produces "no more than an abundant flow of empty words." It is sufficient that the person who lacks skills of expression speak plainly and wisely, drawing on the words of Scripture where possible.[6]

Ambrose, a famed preacher who, in his youth, was a brilliant advocate at the court of the Praetorian Prefect, had few illusions about the worth of rhetoric in conveying eternal truths. His preference was for the plain speech of the apostolic man who, "holding fast to the true faith," does not seek after ornamental diction and brilliant arguments.[7] "Away with the finery and paint of words, which weaken the force of what is said," he exclaimed.[8] Ambrose's facility with words was a stepping-stone to Augustine's conversion. Having attended the bishop's church to savor his renowned oratory, the proud young rhetor of the imperial court left it pondering the eternal truths to which he had been exposed: "As I opened my heart to appreciate how skillfully he spoke, the recognition that he was speaking the truth crept in at the same time, though only by slow degrees."[9]

---

[5] Patrick, *Conf*, 9–10; Bieler, 23–24.

[6] Augustine, *On Christian Instruction*, 4.8–10, trans. John J. Gavigan, FCh 2 (Washington, DC: CUAP, 1966) 187–92.

[7] Paulinus, *Life of Saint Ambrose*, 5; WF 152.

[8] F. Homes Dudden, *Life and Times of Saint Ambrose*, vol. 1 (Oxford: Clarendon Press, 1935) 11.

[9] Augustine, *Conf*, 5.14.24, trans. Maria Boulding, ed. John E. Rotelle (Hyde Park, NY: New City Press, 1997) 132.

Patrick's determination to write, despite his incapacity, was fortified by Saint Paul's assurance that "the kingdom of God depends not
on talk but on power." From the apostle he learned that it is sufficient
to speak the plain truth, not with "lofty words or wisdom," but simply
to tell "what God has prepared for those who love him."[10] It is not only
the power of discourse or argument that brings others to the faith, but
a spiritual conviction that comes from the heart. This assurance finally
convinced Patrick that, though "fearful of what the critics would say,"
he had a duty "to cry out aloud and render something to the Lord for
his great benefits here and in eternity, benefits which the mind of man
cannot fathom."[11] Presenting himself, like Paul, as "a letter of Christ for
salvation to the utmost part of the earth," he assures the Irish people
that, while he cannot claim to be "an eloquent letter," he is "firmly and
powerfully written in your hearts, not with ink, but with the spirit of
the living God."[12] Determined to "exalt and praise God's wonders before
every nation under the heaven," Patrick resolves to "make known the
gift of God and his everlasting consolation."[13] Challenging those who
"wish to laugh and scorn," he defiantly exclaims, "I will not be silent."[14]

Patrick wrote his spiritual testament in old age. Augustine published
the *Confessions* in 398, just over a decade after being baptized by Ambrose. In charting their separate odysseys toward the fullness of faith,
each writer celebrates the divine mercy. Augustine is grateful that, in the
"terrible dangers" through which he wandered, "God's faithful mercy
hovered over me, but from afar," finally bringing deliverance from "my
most wicked ways." Thankful that God "had mercy on my youth and
ignorance, and watched over me before I knew him," Patrick acknowledges the one who "opened my unbelieving mind, so that even at that
late hour I should remember my sins and turn with all my heart to the
Lord my God."[15]

Celebrating the one true God who keeps faith with his creatures,
however faithless they have been, Augustine announces his epic theme
in a sonorous invocation of the divine majesty: "You are great, O Lord,

[10] 1 Cor 4:20; 2:1, 9.
[11] Patrick, *Conf*, 12; Bieler, 24.
[12] Patrick, *Conf*, 11; Bieler, 24; see 2 Cor 3:1–3; Acts 13:47; Isa 49:6.
[13] Patrick, *Conf*, 3, 14; Bieler, 21, 25.
[14] Patrick, *Conf*, 45; Bieler, 35.
[15] Augustine, *Conf*, 3.3.5; Ryan, 80; Patrick, *Conf*, 2; Conneely, 63.

and greatly to be praised; great is your power, and to your wisdom there is no limit." He asks God to "accept the sacrifice of my confession," then begs him to "heal all my bones and let them say, 'Lord, who is like to you?'" There follows a song of praise in which the need to find God is effortlessly suggested through an image of the human being "carrying the evidence of his sinfulness" as he wanders on a seemingly fruitless search. It is not Augustine's own gifts, but the divine promptings, that will enable him to reach his goal: "You have made us for yourself, and our heart is restless until it rests in you."[16]

Patrick opens his *Confession* with a characteristic expression of lowliness: "I am Patrick, a sinner, unlettered, the least of all the faithful and held in contempt by a great many people." His celebration of the divine goodness, simply expressed, remains rooted in the only life he knows, his God-given mission to the Irish. It embraces a truth discovered in adversity, that there is One who "so often pardoned my lack of wisdom and my negligence, and who on more than one occasion held back from vehement anger with me."[17] God's grace led him to renew his faith and is the continuing source of his zeal in preaching the Gospel. Enabling him to surmount the many dangers associated with his mission, grace engenders a confidence "in proportion to the faith which I have received from the Trinity."[18]

Augustine's fertile genius is manifest as he contemplates the recovery of those details of his life which will illuminate his theme. Surveying the densely populated "fields and vast mansions" of memory, he finds all the required images at his command. Some are "pursued for a time and dug out from remote crannies." Others come "tumbling out in disorderly profusion and leap into prominence as though asking, 'Are we what you want?' when it is something different that I am asking for and trying to recall." Then there are the pliant memories that come "easily and in orderly sequence as soon as they are summoned, the earlier ones giving way to those that follow and returning to their storage-spaces, ready to be retrieved the next time I need them."[19]

Patrick's prose, largely plain and unadorned, rarely takes flight, with his most potent images drawn from Scripture. Finding inspiration in

---

[16] Augustine, *Conf*, 1.1.1, 3.3.5, 5.1.1; Ryan, 43, 79, 113; see Pss 145:3, 147:5.
[17] Patrick, *Conf*, 2, 46; Conneely, 63, 73.
[18] Patrick, *Conf*, 1, 10, 14; Conneely, 1, 63, 65.
[19] Augustine, *Conf*, 10.8.12; Boulding, 244–45.

Paul, he rejoices that, having been a slave to sin, then slave to a pagan master, he finally became "the Lord's little slave."[20] Relishing the paradox that, through subjection to God, he has been empowered to bring salvation to a pagan people, he claims that if he, uneducated, unworthy, and despised, has achieved so much, it is surely proof of God's power. He is deeply grateful for gaining "such great favors and so great a grace" in the land of his captivity.[21]

While incidents recorded by Patrick are tantalizing in their brevity, Augustine confidently charts a dramatic journey from sin and unbelief to the fullness of truth. Writing the *Confessions* at the age of forty-five, he does not spare his younger self, revealing in vivid detail how, in boyhood, he willfully took "the great loads of fruit, not for our own eating, but to throw to the pigs." He confesses that, "going against the commands of parents and teachers," he preferred to enter contests and attend the adult games. His soul was at even greater risk during higher education in Carthage, "where a cauldron of shameful loves seethed and sounded about me on every side." All the while, he was searching for a truth which eluded him in Carthage, Rome, and Milan because he had turned his back to the light and his face "towards the things upon which the light fell."[22]

Patrick simply presents his early sufferings as retribution for his own and his companions' neglect of God and refusal to listen to their bishops, "who used to admonish us for our salvation." Without embellishment, he tells how God's anger scattered them among many peoples, "even to the uttermost parts of the earth."[23] A slave in Ireland, "an unlettered exile," and not knowing how to "provide for the life hereafter," he was "daily herding flocks." With the dawning of enlightenment came love and fear of God. Faith began to flourish and he turned to prayer. The brief, stark pictures, presented without stylistic artifice, are moving in their simplicity.[24]

Augustine paints captivating portraits of those who made his journey possible. There is praise for his mother Monica, so concerned for

---

[20] Patrick, *Conf*, 15; Conneely, 66; *ut hoc servulo suo concederet. Servulus*: young slave or servant; see 1 Cor 9:19.

[21] Patrick, *Conf*, 13, 15; Conneely, 63, 66; see Rom 6:17.

[22] Augustine, *Conf*, 2.4–10, 3.1.1, 4; 16.30; Ryan, 69–76, 78; 111.

[23] Patrick, *Conf*, 1; Conneely, 63; see Acts 13:47; Isa 49:6.

[24] Patrick, *Conf*, 12, 16; Conneely, 65–66.

his spiritual welfare, a "woman in outward form but endowed with virile faith, uniting the serenity of an elderly person with a mother's love and Christian devotion." There are friends like his former student and "heart's brother," Alypius, to whom he was first drawn because of his "great nobility of character." Above all, there is Ambrose, "known throughout the world as one of the best of men," whom Augustine revered from a distance and who baptized him at Easter 387.[25] Patrick supplies scant details of parentage and place, leaving the reader longing to know more about those who helped him on his spiritual way. However, while personalities are vaguely sketched and the road to faith is traversed in his book's earliest pages, the author's simple directness is so disarming that the bare bones of human experience suffice.

Woven into each man's story is the journey motif so popular with the fathers. Though Patrick's passage to the fullness of faith was swift, Augustine's was prolonged and tortuous. Nine of the thirteen books of the *Confessions* chart a restless and fitful movement from darkness to light, from error to truth, from sin to repentance and forgiveness. While the philosopher in Augustine fruitlessly sought truth through unaided intellect, God's grace was leading him inexorably toward it. He turned first to Manichaeism, seduced by its vision of devotees guided by reason in a world driven by competing forces of good and evil. Spurning the Scriptures, which, to his proud eyes, "seemed unworthy of comparison with the nobility of Cicero's writings," he wandered far from truth, "carried about with every wind."[26] Later, neoplatonism, with its belief in a transcendent deity, had its attractions, but by then he had fallen under the benign influence of Ambrose.

Augustine was supported on the final step to conversion by Simplicianus, who had baptized Ambrose and would succeed him as bishop. From the old priest, the youthful philosopher heard the story of Victorinus, professor of rhetoric in Rome. That renowned Platonist, who had been a "worshipper of idols and a communicant in sacrilegious rites," was so esteemed by the Romans that they had erected his statue in the forum. On deciding to become "a child of Christ and a newborn infant at the font," the aged scholar was given the opportunity of making a private profession of faith. Refusing, he insisted on standing in the sight of all

[25] Augustine, *Conf*, 9.4.8, 6.7.11, 5.13, 23; Boulding, 214, 144–45, 131.
[26] Augustine, *Conf*, 3.5.9, 4.14.23; Ryan, 82, 107.

and reciting the creed.[27] The lesson in humility was readily absorbed by Augustine. The proud young Platonist and master of rhetoric later observed how "an immature, perverted love of reason" can cause some to "consider it beneath their dignity to begin with faith."[28]

Augustine's quest for truth ended in a garden, where he heard the words of a child at play: "Take up and read, take up and read." Obeying, he opened the formerly despised Scriptures, and found the answer to his quest in Paul, from whom he learned that he must "put on the Lord Jesus Christ and make no provision for the flesh and its concupiscences."[29] The early pride proved to be a happy fault, for contemplation of his tardy progress toward faith inspired the *Confessions*. There, readers share the author's insights into the process of conversion and savor the eloquent celebration of his belated discovery, through God's grace, of the ultimate truth:

> Too late have I loved you, O beauty so ancient and so new, too late have I loved you! Behold, you were within me, while I was outside; it was there that I sought you and, a deformed creature, rushed headlong upon those things of beauty which you have made. You were with me, but I was not with you. They kept me far from you, those fair things which, if they were not in you, would not exist at all. You have called to me, and have cried out and have shattered my deafness. You have blazed forth with light, and have shone upon me and you have put my blindness to flight![30]

In Ireland, enlightenment came readily to Patrick, unimpeded by pride, the intellectual sin which caused Augustine to keep truth at bay for so long. In old age, in a remote land bounded by the Atlantic, the bishop is grateful that, as a man "truly unlearned," a sinner and "least of all the faithful," he, an unworthy individual, has, like the prophets, been singled out by God to be a light for the Gentiles, bringing "salvation to the uttermost parts of the earth." The belief that he has been selected for a special mission is reinforced by Isaiah: "Islands, listen to me, pay attention, remotest peoples. Yahweh called me before I was born, from my

---

[27] Augustine, *Conf*, 8.2.3–5; Ryan, 183–85.

[28] Augustine, *On the Trinity*, 1.1, trans. Stephen McKenna, FCh 45 (Washington, DC: CUAP, 1963) 3.

[29] Augustine, *Conf*, 8.12.29; Ryan, 202; see Rom 13:13–14.

[30] Augustine, *Conf*, 10.27.38; Ryan, 254.

mother's womb he pronounced my name."[31] It is a conviction confirmed by Jeremiah, who, like Patrick, doubted his fitness for a God-given task but found it impossible to deny the will of One who said, "Before I formed you in the womb I knew you; before you came to birth I consecrated you; I have appointed you as prophet to the nations."[32] Augustine's insight into his own destiny finds similar expression: "Before ever I was, you were; I did not even exist to receive your gift of being; yet, lo! Now I do exist, thanks to your goodness. Over all that I am, both what you have made me and that from which you made me, your goodness has absolute precedence."[33]

Patrick's humility had brought early conversion. Augustine was doubly repentant for his lengthy period in darkness. Convinced that his intellectual prowess would lead unerringly to the truth, he had been betrayed by human learning. "Full of words and folly," he had fallen among "glib men," Manichaeans, who were always saying, "Truth! Truth!" while their hearts were empty of it. Listening to them, hearing nothing but falsehoods, he "fed on phantoms."[34] During those lost years he, a learned man, disdaining his mother's simply held faith, had "floundered in the mud of the deep and the darkness of deception."

His journey neared its end when, hearing of the two young men in Trier who abandoned promising careers to serve God, Augustine turned to Alypius and exclaimed, "What is this? What did you hear? The unlearned rise up and take heaven by storm and we, with all our learning, but empty of heart, see how we wallow in flesh and blood! Are we ashamed to follow just because they have taken the lead, yet not ashamed of lacking the courage even to follow?"[35] Finally finding true wisdom in the pages of Scripture, he praises the spiritual insight of his mother, through whom, down the years, the words of God had been "singing in my ears . . . yet none of them sank deep into my heart."[36]

Patrick embraced the fullness of faith at sixteen; Augustine, at thirty-three. Through their spiritual testaments, both bishops sought to edify

[31] Patrick, *Conf*, 12; Conneely, 65; see Jer 16:19–21; Isa 49:6; Acts 13:47.

[32] Patrick, *Conf*, 2; Conneely, 63; *Letter to Coroticus*, 6; Conneely, 78; see Jer 1:4–5; 16:19–21.

[33] Augustine, *Conf*, 13.1.1; Boulding, 342.

[34] Augustine, *Conf*, 3.6.10; Ryan, 82–83.

[35] Augustine, *Conf*, 3.11.20, 8.8.19; Ryan, 91, 195; see Matt 11:12.

[36] Augustine, *Conf*, 2.3.7; Ryan, 68.

by sharing their experience of God's goodness and mercy with others. In one of his last works, the *Retractions*, Augustine recalls that, by recounting his deeds, good and evil, he had hoped to "lift up the understanding and affection of men" to God. In the *Confessions* he prays to the divine physician that his work will "stir up the heart" of each reader, trusting that, like him, people will come to know the truth about themselves and turn to God, "the eternal wisdom," as the only way to happiness.[37] Because Patrick had not known "the true God" in his youth and has been the victim of lies into old age, he is eager to give "an honest account" of his relationship with his Creator.[38] Recalling his "debt to God," to whom he is bound to give "unceasing thanks," he calls on "all who believe and hold God in reverence," to bear witness to his utter dependence on his Creator. Patrick's *Confession* is "a legacy to my brethren and sons whom I have baptized in the Lord, so many thousands of people."[39]

Augustine's profound insights and assured command of literary expression brought his spiritual testament vividly to life. Patrick's *Confession* owed its faltering genesis to the confidence gained from reading scriptural mentors like Jeremiah, who, chosen like him as a witness to the nations, humbly said, "Ah Lord Yahweh; look, I do not know how to speak: I am a child." Touching his lips, God reassuringly responds, "There, I am putting my words into your mouth."[40] Patrick also treasures Isaiah's assurance that, when the Savior comes, "the man who stammers will at once speak peace." He even invokes the divine promise to Moses, who, on receiving the call, protests that he has never been a man of eloquence, but "a slow speaker and not able to speak well."[41]

The Irish hailed Patrick as their Moses, who, despite enslavement in their country, brought them to the promised land of faith. Just over two centuries after his death, his biographer found a parallel, "although in a different manner," between his early flight to freedom and the divine release of Moses from slavery in Egypt. In Muirchú's *Life* Patrick not only learns of his imminent demise through a vision of a burning bush, but, like the prophet, dies at the age of 120. Thus, while one entry in the

---

[37] Augustine, *Conf*, 10.3.3–4; Ryan, 230–31.

[38] Patrick, *Conf*, 6, 14, 47; Conneely, 64–65, 73.

[39] Patrick, *Conf*, 14, 62; Conneely, 65, 76.

[40] Patrick, *Conf*, 38; Conneely, 71; *Letter to Coroticus*, 6; Conneely, 78; see Isa 49:6; Jer 1:4–10, 16:19; Acts 13:47.

[41] Patrick, *Conf*, 11; Conneely, 65; see Isa 32:4; Exod 4:10–17.

*Annals of Ulster* names 461 as the year of his passing, another echoes the Mosaic theme by proffering the alternative date of 492, over a century after his birth.[42]

Even when Augustine found faith and won acclaim as a spiritual teacher, the memory of his lengthy path to truth continued to humble him. In the *Confessions* he recalls that, on his search, he had first turned to Cicero and Plato, the great names of classical antiquity, who had led him to a wooded mountain peak from which he enjoyed a tantalizing glimpse of the land of peace but failed to reveal the way. In the last phase of his quest, he "seized upon the sacred writings of your Spirit, and especially the apostle Paul," and found the true path by attending to the words of "that least of your apostles." It is a way "guarded by the protection of the heavenly commander, where no deserters from the heavenly army lie in wait like bandits." Augustine remained aware that he had attained the ultimate truth only when, turning to God, he "meditated upon your works, and trembled at them."[43] It was the moment at which the proud man of learning, who had spurned Scripture because of its "humble style," discovered that the path to truth was open to the "unlearned" but closed to the learned until they were open to God's grace.

Writing the *Confessions* ten years after his baptism, Augustine acknowledges that only through the interaction of faith and God's grace can he attain the enlightenment necessary for the fulfillment of his mission. Consequently, long "burning with desire" to meditate on the law of the Creator, and wishing to convey its mysteries to his people as they encounter their earthly trials, he seeks divine enlightenment by invoking the imagery of the psalms:[44]

> Hear me as I cry from the depths,
> for unless your ears be present in our deepest places
> where shall we go and whither cry?
> Yours is the day, yours the night,
> a sign from you sends minutes speeding by;
> spare in their fleeting course a space for us
> to ponder the hidden wonders of your law:

---

[42] Muirchú, *Life of Patrick*; De Paor, 177, 194, 195; *Annals of Ulster*; De Paor, 119.

[43] Augustine, *Conf*, 7.21.27; Ryan, 179–80; see 1 Cor 15:9.

[44] Augustine, *Conf*, 9.2.2; Boulding, 285; see Ps 1:2.

shut it not against us as we knock.[45]
Not in vain have you willed so many pages to be written,
pages deep in shadow, obscure in their secrets;
not in vain do harts and hinds seek shelter in those woods,
to hide and venture forth,
roam and browse, lie down and ruminate.
Perfect me too, Lord, and reveal those woods to me. . . .[46]
Let me confess to you all I have found in your books;
let me hear the voice of praise,
and drink from you
and contemplate the wonders of your law,[47]
from the beginning when you made heaven and earth
to that everlasting reign when we shall be with you in your
    holy city.[48]

---

[45] See Ps 74:16; Matt 7:7–8.
[46] See Ps 29:9.
[47] See Pss 27:2; 119:18.
[48] Augustine, *Conf*, 11.2.3; Boulding, 286.

# 6

# BROTHERHOOD AND BETRAYAL

T he knowledge that, through faith, they share the same Father and enjoy the brotherhood of Christ is a profound source of comfort for Christians. The vision of God's kingdom as a community of faith moved the earliest believers so profoundly that they chose to live together, owning "all things in common; they would sell their possessions and goods and distribute the proceeds to all, as any had need."[1] The fathers consistently reminded fellow Christians that, through baptism, they made their pilgrim journey as a single community, whose unity was enhanced by participation in the Church's liturgy. A truth central to Augustine's *City of God*, it is enshrined in the "greatest commandment," which is the dynamic of God's kingdom.

Familiar, through their classical education, with Cicero's celebrated work on friendship, the fathers ensured that their relationships were grounded in faith and directed to God's glory. In the year 386, while preparing for baptism, Augustine, accompanied by his closest friends, retreated to Cassiciacum, outside Milan. The group included Monica and his son Adeodatus, with whose mother he had lived for seventeen years. After baptism, Augustine saw that his new life of faith bound him even more firmly to Monica and his deceased father. Those who had been "my parents in this passing light" now became "my brethren under you our Father in our Catholic mother, and my fellow citizens in that eternal Jerusalem."[2] When he returned to Africa, Augustine went to his old home in Thagaste, where several friends joined him "in God's service," fasting, praying, and "meditating on God's law day and night."[3]

---

[1] Acts 2:44–45.
[2] Augustine, *Conf*, 9.13.35; Ryan, 228.
[3] Possidius, *Life of Saint Augustine*, 3.1–2; WF 197.

In the peace, order, and harmony of monastic life Augustine found a true community of faith.[4] Summoned to Hippo and ordained priest by Bishop Aurelius, he established a monastery on cathedral grounds. In a letter to the bishop he referred to "the whole company of brethren which has begun to grow up together beside me . . . a flock committed to you . . . your help in times of need."[5] This sense of spiritual kinship extended beyond the immediate context of his life and work, even transcending national boundaries. Writing in 398 to Abbot Exodius in far-off Italy, he addressed him as a brother. The abbot's fellow monks are "brethren" to whom "Augustine and the brethren who are here send greeting." The distant ascetics are told that all are "one body under one head, so that you share our toils and we share your repose." Since they are "more lively and undistracted" in prayer than Augustine, a busy bishop whose prayers are interrupted "by the darkness and confusion arising from secular occupations," they are asked "to be mindful of us in your holy intercessions."[6]

On first visiting Martin's monastery, Sulpicius Severus was overcome by his kindness, particularly in "fetching the water for me to wash my hands and, in the evening . . . washing my feet."[7] Paulinus of Nola, another disciple of Martin, was a great connoisseur of spiritual kinship. Claiming the friendship of Sulpicius, Ambrose, Augustine, Jerome, and others, he was convinced that their comradeship was superior to even the noblest natural relationship. His friend Sulpicius is "my loving brother, the better part of me in Christ." Paulinus's relationship with the monk Pammachius, a former Roman senator like himself, is not a worldly one, "born more often of hope than of faith," but a friendship that has "sprung from the fatherhood of God."[8] With Bishop Victricius, who is yet another disciple of Martin's, he celebrates "the pleasure of our brotherly comradeship in the sacred ministry," and fondly reminds him of the occasion on which they were entertained by "my blessed father Martin." In a letter to Augustine in Africa, Paulinus claims kinship because "we tread the same path, we dwell in the same house."[9]

---

[4] Augustine, *City of God*, 19.14; Bettenson, 872–74; see Mark 12:28–34; Matt 22:34; Luke 10:25; Rom 13:9.

[5] Augustine, Ep 22.1; NPNF 1:239.

[6] Augustine, Ep 48.1; NPNF 1:294.

[7] Sulpicius Severus, *Life of Saint Martin*, 25; WF 41.

[8] Paulinus of Nola, Epp 5.10, 13.2, 11.1–6; ACW 35:60, 119, 90–95.

[9] Paulinus of Nola, Epp 18.9, 6.1–2; ACW 35:176, 71.

Paulinus's appreciation of spiritual friendship transcended the rigid social barriers of the time. Writing to Sulpicius in the year 400, he professed sincere regard for "brother Victor," who had brought a letter all the way from Gaul to Nola, twenty miles east of Naples. Seeing "the pattern of the blessed Martin and Clarus" in him, he praises the virtues of the ex-soldier, who "comes in God's name," and welcomes the "spiritual comradeship" they share. In another letter to his Gaulish friend, the bishop calls Victor "our joint pledge of affection, our faithful attendant, our regular consolation" and apologizes for detaining him for some weeks beyond the intended time.[10] As a messenger, he says, Victor is untiring, "a true victor over the longest journeys," undeterred by any obstacles.

In the year 406 this valued messenger was prevented from returning to Gaul by the onset of winter. He fell ill and was "rescued from death's door" by Paulinus, who confesses that, during Victor's illness, he himself "endured in affliction of heart and sympathy of mind the suffering which my dear friend sustained in body."[11] When the Gaul recovered, he joined his host on the annual pilgrimage to Rome for the feast of Saints Peter and Paul. It is an impressive example of brotherhood, with the bond between Victor and the highly cultivated former Roman senator as firm as Paulinus's relationship with peers like Severus or Ambrose. In relation to this indefatigable messenger, an intriguing possibility is suggested by the correspondence between Paulinus and Sulpicius. Since the letters of the fathers were open books, liable to be copied and circulated far and wide, those written by Paulinus would have been read by many in Gaul. Victor, who carried them "in God's name," must have been known to churchmen there, not least because he had been a close companion of Martin's.[12]

The conjunction of Patrick's time in Gaul with the still-circulating story of Paulinus's favorite letter-carrying monk may provide the source for that other Victor who came to the young man "in a vision of the night with countless letters," one of which transformed his life. Patrick too had spiritual brethren. It was to confirm their faith that he gives "an honest account" of his life in the *Confession*. He trusts that, by reading it, they will "know the sort of man I am" and that, in following him, they will "strive after greater things, and do more excellent deeds." Those whom he regards as brethren are not confined to Ireland, for he harbors

[10] Paulinus of Nola, Epp 23.3, 28.1; ACW 35:4, 93.
[11] Paulinus of Nola, Ep 43.1–2; ACW 35:227–28.
[12] Paulinus of Nola, Ep 23.3; ACW 35:4–5.

a fervent desire to "go as far as Gaul to visit the brethren and see the face of the saints of my Lord." It is a poignant longing, for Patrick knows that it will remain unrealized.[13]

The spiritual comradeship of the fathers could be built on long-established relationships. Alypius, a student of Augustine's in Carthage, later became his close friend. Both left Africa to pursue careers in Rome. Converted together in Milan, they were baptized by Ambrose. On their return to Africa, they became monks, then priests and bishops. Always generous in his praise of Alypius, Augustine told Jerome that "anyone who knows us may say that we are two only in body, so great is the union of our heart, so firm the intimate friendship subsisting between us."[14] Gregory of Nazianzen was equally appreciative of his friend Basil, recalling that, during their student days in Athens, they shared all things in common "and became a single soul, as it were, which was bound together in our two distinct bodies."

But even the friendships of the fathers could be severely tested. In 370, the contemplative and naturally retiring Gregory complained bitterly when the energetic and resourceful Basil appointed him to the see of Sasima, a lawless and violent town. Appalled, the sensitive ascetic fled, leaving an unappealing portrait of the place: "There is dust all around, the din of wagons, lamentations, groans, tax officials, implements of torture and public stocks. The population consists of casuals and vagrants."[15] There are other examples of patristic friendships put to the test. "I grow tired of inviting and awaiting you," lamented Paulinus in 398, alleging that Severus had neglected to visit him for two years. He estimates that the time taken for a single visit would have been less than that expended by Severus on "repeatedly travelling in Gaul all these years, visiting Tours and more distant places, often more than once, within the same summer."[16] The threatened rupture was followed by reconciliation, for two years later Paulinus voices appreciation of the sincere efforts made by his friend, "with such regular letters to compensate me for your absence."[17]

---

[13] Patrick, *Conf*, 14, 23, 43, 47; Conneely, 65, 67–68, 72, 73.

[14] Augustine, Ep 28.1; NPNF 1:251.

[15] Gregory of Nazianzen, *Poem on His Own Life*, 225–36, 440–45, trans. Denis Molaise Meehan, FCh 75 (Washington, DC, 1987) 83–84.

[16] Paulinus of Nola, Ep 17; ACW 35:163–66.

[17] Paulinus of Nola, Ep 23.1; ACW 35:176.

Jerome, sensitive in the extreme to slights on his scholarship or literary gifts, made as many enemies as friends. In the early years his exits from a variety of places were determined by the breakdown of his relationships. He had been closest to a fellow student, Rufinus, to whom he was "inseparably tied by brotherly love."[18] Eventually differing over theology, particularly the teachings of Origen, they became bitter rivals. In a letter to Jerome, Augustine expresses his distress that such tragic discord should have arisen between friends "once so loving and so intimate, formerly united by the bonds of friendship."[19] The breach between men as close as Jerome and Rufinus, he says, could lead one to fear any friend as a possible enemy.

Ironically, Augustine himself felt Jerome's wrath. Writing to Jerome for the first time, and acclaiming their brotherhood, "bound together in the Lord by unity of the spirit," but, unaware of the older man's extreme sensitivity, he proceeded to question the validity of his commentary on the disagreement between Peter and Paul in Antioch.[20] The communication was misdirected, copied, and read by many before a version of it reached Jerome several years later. Jerome's irritation pervades his response, which opens with a complaint that a letter meant for him was first copied and read by "most of the Christians in Rome and throughout Italy." Jerome has even heard rumors that the original had contained challenges aimed at winning fame for the writer at his expense. With characteristic bluntness, he asks Augustine to "send me an identical letter signed by you or desist from annoying an old man, who seeks retirement in his monastic cell." He concludes by demanding that, in future, "I am the first to receive whatever you may write to me."[21]

Even as they disagreed over Galatians, Augustine and Jerome would have been aware of a biblical example in Paul's painful and lasting estrangement, "following a disagreement [that] became so sharp," from his close companion Barnabas.[22] In their own case, a series of exchanges saw Augustine employing considerable tact to mend the breach. At one point he articulates, for Jerome's benefit, his vision of the true worth of spiritual fellowship: "Upon the love of such friends I readily cast myself

---

[18] Jerome, Ep 4.2; NPNF 6:6–7.
[19] Augustine, Ep 73.9; NPNF 1:332.
[20] Augustine, Ep 28.1–3; NPNF 1:251–52; see Gal 2:11–14.
[21] Jerome, in Augustine, Ep 72.1–5; NPNF 1:328–29.
[22] Acts 15:36–40.

without reservation, especially when chafed and wearied by the scandals of this world; and in their love I rest without any disturbing care: for I perceive that God is there, on whom I confidingly cast myself and in whom I confidingly rest."[23]

Augustine succeeded in establishing trust with the sensitive monk. However, when Jerome suggested that, as the price of "brotherliness," they should in future "exchange letters, not of controversy, but of mutual charity," his friend insisted that such a bond could not survive if it was at the expense of "the liberty . . . of frankly stating to the other whatever seems to him open to correction."[24] This sane suggestion prevailed. Thereafter, the two pursued their common spiritual interests in a spirit of amity. Augustine's bond with the biblical scholar, whom he never met, was largely forged through acquaintance with his writings. Certain that physical presence was not essential to the growth of their kinship, he assured him that never was the face of anyone more familiar to another "than the peaceful, happy and truly noble diligence of your studies in the Lord have become to me."[25]

Jerome lost allies as readily as he gained them, while Augustine considered himself blessed in all his friendships. In Ireland, Patrick lived with the memory of rejection by his peers and betrayal by a close friend. So bitter was his experience that the *Confession*, his song of praise and thanksgiving, serves also as an apologia, a passionate defense by one who had been cruelly wronged. In earlier days, hostile clerics tried to subvert his mission, and plotted against his appointment as bishop: "I was tested by some of my seniors, who came to cast up my sins as unfitting me for my laborious episcopate." Through one whom he twice calls "my best friend," those enemies had "found occasion for their charge" against him by revealing a boyhood misdemeanor confessed to the betrayer, "a man to whom I had entrusted my very soul."

The offense had been the product of a time when Patrick did not yet "believe in the living God, nor had I believed in him from childhood." He "grieves" for the man who might have been the instrument of his total humiliation had not his truest friend, the Lord, intervened, coming "powerfully to my aid when I was being walked upon, so that I did not fall unhappily into discredit and disgrace." Patrick prays that his suffering

---

[23] Augustine, Ep 73.10; NPNF 1:332–33.
[24] Augustine, Epp 81, 82.36; NPNF 1:349, 361.
[25] Augustine, Ep 28.1; NPNF 1:251.

at the hands of his fellows should not "be accounted to them as a sin." His sense of injustice is ameliorated only by the conviction that, though men have rejected him, God will support him to the end.[26]

Martin of Tours was similarly wronged by opponents who resented his appointment to the episcopate. A powerful minority, which included some bishops, claimed that he was "a despicable individual" who was unfit for office, "what with his insignificant appearance, his sordid garments and his disgraceful hair." His biographer wonders that so good a man should be so hated by churchmen. Like Patrick, Martin may have been the victim of more sophisticated and influential clerics unhappy with the elevation of an individual who, in their eyes, lacked learning and social standing. Martin's forays into the deep countryside of Gaul in search of converts from paganism and Patrick's stubborn conviction that God wished him to choose exile for the sake of the Irish could have sharpened the hostility. Opposition may have been provoked by both men's advocacy of the relatively novel practice of monasticism, which in various countries was being resisted by some clergy.

It is fitting that, after enduring similar humiliations, the two bishops enjoyed vindication through the word of God. As Martin's chief detractor, a bishop named Defensor, prepared to condemn him at a crucial meeting, there was a delay when the designated lector failed to appear. In the ensuing confusion, someone opened a psalter and "plunged" into the first verse he saw, which began, "Out of the mouths of babes and sucklings you have brought praise to perfection, to destroy the enemy and the defender."[27] With all present convinced that they had heard God speak on Martin's behalf, the unfortunate Defensor and his supporters were routed. Patrick was similarly justified by the divine word, following a humiliating betrayal by one who had not only promised to support him but even insisted that he "must be raised to the episcopate." He turned to God, who, "in a vision of the night," became his true defense. So reassuring was the revelation that he can express its import only in biblical terms: "He who touches you is one who touches the apple of my eye."[28]

Patrick's broken friendship left him with a sense of loss. Arriving in Ireland as he was approaching his "declining years," he never again en-

---

[26] Patrick, *Conf*, 26–27, 32; Conneely, 68–69.

[27] Sulpicius Severus, *Life of Saint Martin*, 9; WF 23; see Ps 8.

[28] Patrick, *Conf*, 29; Conneely, 69; see Zech 2:8, 32.

joyed an intimate friendship with a peer. Most of his new brethren would have differed from him in age and background and he reveals that, in his adopted country, he has always endeavored "in some measure to keep my reserve, even from the Christian brethren and the virgins of Christ and the religious women." Toward the end of the *Confession*, in expressing a desire to make final journeys to cherished places, he intimates that he has lost all contact with former friends in his native land. While a visit to Gaul would enable him to meet the brethren, one to Britain would fulfill his desire to see only "my homeland and my family."[29]

That enemies continued to harass Patrick to the end is manifest in the defensive tone of much of the *Confession*. The bishop's vehement denial that he has taken gifts of money in exchange for religious services suggests an accusation of simony:

> But when I baptized so many thousands of people, did I perhaps look for even half a screpall from any of them? Give me the evidence, and I will restore it to you. Or when the Lord ordained clerics everywhere through my insignificant person and I shared the ministry with them for nothing, if I demanded from any of them so much as the price of even my shoe, testify against me and I shall restore it to you.[30]

Patrick was not alone in his consciousness of the injustice caused by the malicious whispers of opponents. To ensure that the distribution of alms collected by him was seen to be beyond reproach, the cautious Paul sent two of the brothers, and a third, so "that no one should blame us about this generous gift that we are administering, for we intend to do what is right not only in the Lord's sight but also in the sight of others."[31]

The otherworldly Martin was also alert to the necessity of accepting money only when its use was clearly specified. Offered a hundred pounds weight of silver, he allocated it to the ransom of captives, resisting his brethren's suggestion that some of it be used to buy much-needed food and clothing.[32] The fathers were particularly averse to the sin of Simon Magus, who had attempted to buy from Peter something sacred, the

---

[29] Patrick, *Conf*, 28, 43, 49; Conneely, 69, 72, 73–74.
[30] Patrick, *Conf*, 50; Conneely, 74.
[31] 2 Cor 8:20–23.
[32] Sulpicius Severus, *Dialogues*, 2.14; WF 138.

power to bestow the Holy Spirit.[33] Allegations of simony must have been both common and difficult to disprove, leaving the accused under a cloud. So reviled was Jerome by enemies during his time in Rome that he was forced to leave the city. Part of the problem undoubtedly lay in the fiery ascetic's temperament, but his support for Paula and her friends had caused greatest friction. Subjecting those responsible to the lash of bitter words, he asks, "Have I taken anyone's money? Have I not disdained all gifts, whether small or great? Has the chink of anyone's coin been heard in my hand? No!"[34]

Even the universally admired Ambrose had suffered criticism. After breaking up and selling his church's sacred vessels to ransom men, women, and children from the Goths, he was accused of sacrilege. His reply was unequivocal: "Is it not better to save the poor than to preserve gold . . . better to preserve living vessels than gold ones. . . . The sacraments do not need gold. . . . The glory of the sacraments is the redemption of captives." In the knowledge that some of the vessels had been used in the celebration of the Eucharist, he ended with the potent and daring claim that through his action the blood of the Lord attains a twofold redemption.[35] Augustine later followed Ambrose's example, ordering some sacred vessels to be melted down "for the benefit of captives and of as many of the poor as possible." Predictably, it was done "against the all too human judgment of some."[36]

Rejecting the allegations against him, Patrick calls on his "brethren and fellow servants" in Ireland to confirm his claim that all donations received by him have been wisely distributed. Much of the money has gone as tribute to kings, who permitted him to travel through their territories "so that you might have the benefit of my presence and I might always have the joy of your presence before God." He has also paid the kings' sons, who escorted him from place to place. He is still spending and will spend even more. By doing so he will be able to baptize and confirm many people and ordain clerics to care for them. He assures his people that all is done "for the sake of your salvation."[37]

---

[33] Acts 8:18–20.
[34] Jerome, Ep 45.2; NPNF 6:59.
[35] Ambrose, *Duties of the Clergy*, 2.28; NPNF 10:64–65.
[36] Possidius, *Life of Saint Augustine*, 24.15–16; WF 224.
[37] Patrick, *Conf*, 52; Conneely, 74.

Ambrose and Augustine were widely revered in their time. Martin and Patrick endured criticism to the end. Sulpicius Severus regrets that Martin, though loved by the people, was pursued, even after death, by some critics among the clergy. Worst of all, says Severus, "Oh grievous and lamentable scandal, nearly all his calumniators were bishops."[38] However, he insists that Martin was immune to all hostility. It was otherwise with Patrick, who, in old age, was still smarting from the injustices he had endured. He reveals that it was not only enemies who had opposed his desire to go to Ireland. Well-meaning people, concerned about his meager education, had "tried to forbid this mission of mine." Even friends and religious superiors had implored him not to go, questioning his insistence on "thrusting himself into danger among a hostile people who do not know God." In attempting to dissuade him, many offered gifts, but "with weeping and tears and I gave offence to the givers," among whom were "some of my seniors."

Despite all, Patrick persevered, working even in "the remotest parts beyond which no one lived and whither no person had ever come to baptize, or ordain clerics or confirm the people." He thanks God for sustaining him and helping him to "act in accordance with what I had been shown and what the Spirit was prompting me."[39] He acknowledges his indebtedness to Saint Paul, who had overcome a sense of inadequacy caused by his converts' preference for the polished style of Apollos, a colleague. Paul's consolation is that the world's standard of judgment is not God's, for he has shamed the wise in choosing those who are foolish by human reckoning and shamed the strong by choosing the weak, "things that are not, to reduce to nothing things that are." Invoking Scripture, "I will destroy the wisdom of the wise, and the discernment of the discerning I will thwart," the apostle asks, "Where is the one who is wise? Where is the scribe? Where is the debater of this age?" Patrick likewise professes himself "a fool for the sake of Christ," and asks his worldly-wise critics, "Who was it that roused me, a fool, from the midst of those that are wise and learned in law and skilled in speaking and general affairs; and inspired me, me whom this world rejected."[40]

Augustine would have sympathized with Patrick, for even he encountered resistance when selected to succeed Valerius as bishop of

---

[38] Sulpicius Severus, *Life of Saint Martin*, 27; WF 43–44.

[39] Patrick, *Conf*, 37, 46, 51; Conneely, 70, 73.

[40] 1 Cor 1:4–10, 27–29, 19–20; Patrick, *Conf*, 13; Conneely, 65.

Hippo. Megalius, bishop of Calama, led the critics. In a letter written shortly after the death of Megalius, Augustine observes how readily human weaknesses like anger, when habitually cherished, can lead to hatred. He appreciates the difficulties which will inevitably be placed in the way of the person who, taking up his own cross, tries to follow Christ faithfully: "Many will contradict him, try to stop him, or dissuade him, even those who call themselves Christ's disciples."[41]

The bishop of Hippo never ceased to enjoy the confidence and support of a wide circle of brethren. It is therefore fitting that the genesis of the *Confessions* can be traced to the interest shown by one of his friends in the life of another. In the course of correspondence with Alypius, now bishop of Tagaste, Paulinus of Nola asked for a "slight sketch" of his personal history. It was a request common among churchmen who might never meet. In 395 Paulinus received a reply, not from Alypius, but from Augustine, who offered to undertake the task because of his fellow bishop's unwillingness to write about himself. He promised to provide a "good description" of his friend.[42]

The *Confessions* evolved from Augustine's portrait of Alypius, who had been present at important junctures in his own life. The author's affection for his friend is manifest in the stories of his former student's youthful "madness for the circus" in Carthage and later addiction to gladiatorial shows in Rome. There is a glimpse of the dangers of the time in the revelation that Alypius, once a prominent legal figure in Rome and now a highly esteemed bishop in Africa, had been arrested while he was a student in Carthage. Apprehended after lifting an axe abandoned by a fleeing thief, in one terrifying moment the young man experienced the volatility of an angry mob and learned the lesson that in judicial cases "no man ought to be condemned with rash credulity by another."[43]

The *Confessions* were completed in 398. Fittingly, in that very year, Paulinus, progenitor of the book, received from his friend Sulpicius a copy of the just published *Life of Saint Martin*. In response, he first thanks Sulpicius, then reflects on their relationship with their saintly mentor and with each other. Finally, he characteristically draws on Scrip-

---

[41] Serge Lancel, *Saint Augustine*, trans. Antonia Nevill (London: SCM Press, 2002) 184; Augustine, Ep 38.2; NPNF 1:271.

[42] Augustine, Ep 27.5; NPNF 1:250.

[43] Augustine, *Conf*, 6.9.14; Ryan, 146.

ture to give a just description of the nature of the spiritual friendships shared by the fathers: "Nothing can be compared to a faithful friend. For the consolation of your love is like the medicine of life, and your words like a honeycomb. As cold water to thirsty souls are good tidings from a far country to me when it concerns you."[44]

---

[44] Paulinus of Nola, Ep 11.1; ACW 35:90; see Prov 16:23–24; Sir 6:14–16.

# 7

# THE SACRAMENTAL LIFE

A t one in celebrating the divine goodness and mercy, fathers and
ascetics preached a faith nourished by the spiritual benefits of
the sacraments, whose power to bind believers to God and fellow
Christians enables them to persevere on their journey. In the fourth and
fifth centuries the term sacrament was applied to actions as diverse as
the *symbolum*, prayer, exorcism, sign of the cross, and even to the ritual
in which catechumens were seasoned with salt. However, then, as now,
the Christian body's primary sources of spiritual initiation and growth
were identified in the major rites of baptism, confirmation, forgiveness
of sin, the Eucharist, and marriage. The priestly ministry was also seen
as an essential element in the sacramental life of the Church.

Called by Augustine "the sacrament of the faith," baptism offered
entry to the new life of salvation. Buried with Christ in the waters, believers enjoyed rebirth as members of the community of faith.[1] Like other
bishops of his time, Augustine personally catechized his catechumens
and describes, in an Easter Sunday sermon, how those "seeking together
the kingdom of heaven" presented themselves as *competentes*, candidates
for baptism. They were so called, he says, because they were "beating
against their mother's womb, seeking to be born." Baptized, newly born
to Christ, "they are now called *infantes*."[2] Instructed in the essential elements of Christian belief during the weeks before Easter, catechumens
learned the *symbolum*, "the creed of the most holy martyrdom which is
our rule of salvation." As they prayed, fasted, and engaged in almsgiving
through the Lenten season, they were reminded that "these forty days

---

[1] Augustine, Ep 98.9–10; NPNF 1:410; see Rom 6:4.
[2] Augustine, S 228.1–2; FCh 38:199.

are sacred, and at the approach of Easter the entire universe, which God reconciles to himself in Christ, celebrates them with laudable devotion."[3]

The sacrament of initiation into the Christian life has always centered on Easter, the annual culmination of the Church's celebration of Christ's redemptive actions. In early times, those about to be baptized at the Easter vigil first professed their faith before the entire congregation. They then entered the baptistery, where they were questioned on their belief in the Trinity, the incarnation and redemption, the Church, the remission of sins, and the resurrection of the body.[4] The response on each occasion was "I believe." The baptismal water was poured in the name of each member of the Trinity. Affirming the power of the sacrament, Ambrose observes that "in that water, all sin is washed away, all disgrace is buried."[5] Augustine is equally emphatic: "When you rise from these waters, you will be without sin."[6] Immediately after the baptismal ceremony, new Christians were confirmed by the laying on of hands and the anointing. They received the gifts of the Holy Spirit, identified by Ambrose as "wisdom, understanding, counsel, fortitude, knowledge, and piety," together with "the spirit of holy fear."[7]

The *infantes* or neophytes, the newly born, donned white linen garments in token of their new life of grace. In Ambrose's words, they had become "members of Christ's Church and beautiful through grace."[8] Their baptismal night was rich in a symbolism which, says Augustine, intensifies the experience of the spiritual, just as the movement of a lighted torch causes the flame to burn more brightly.[9] When they returned to the church, which was illuminated by lights drawn from the Paschal fire, the entire congregation, with whom they were now fully united, sang in celebration. An early fourth-century Easter hymn captures the essential joy of the baptismal night:

> O night, brighter than day! O night, more radiant than the
> sun! O night, whiter than snow! O night, more dazzling than

---

[3] Augustine, S 209.1–2; FCh 38:95–96.

[4] Ambrose, *On the Mysteries*, 2, trans. H. De Romestin, NPNF, vol. 10 (Grand Rapids, MI: Eerdmans, 1997) 318.

[5] Ambrose, *On the Mysteries*, 5.28; 3.11, trans. Roy Joseph Deferrari, FCh 44 (Washington, DC: CUAP, 1977) 15, 9.

[6] Augustine, S 213.8; FCh 38:128.

[7] Ambrose, *On the Mysteries*, 7.42; NPNF 10:322.

[8] Ambrose, *On the Mysteries* 7.38; NPNF 10:322.

[9] Augustine, Ep 55.11.21; NPNF 1:310.

lightning! O night, more shining than torches! O night, more precious than paradise! O night, freed from darkness! O night, filled with light! O night, which banishes sleep! O night, which teaches to watch with angels! O night, terror of demons! O night, longing of the year! O, night, which brings the bridegroom to the Church! O night, mother of the newly baptized![10]

Patrick claims to have baptized thousands during his ministry in Ireland, having answered the call to become "a fisher of men" and "make disciples of all nations."[11] Celebrating the goodness of God, who has supported his efforts, he finds in Saint Paul and the prophet Hosea the words which define his achievement: "Those who are not my people I will call 'my people,' and in the very place where it was said, 'You are not my people,' they will be called 'sons of the living God.'" He associates his work with that of the apostles by echoing Peter's words at Pentecost: "I will pour out my spirit upon all flesh, and your sons and your daughters shall prophesy, and your young men shall see visions, and your old men shall dream dreams; yes, and even on my slaves, male and female, in those days I will pour out my Spirit."[12]

Sadly, the paschal tone of rejoicing is lacking in Patrick's sole reference to a particular baptismal ceremony, in a letter condemning fellow Briton Coroticus and his warriors for killing many of the newly baptized and abducting the survivors. Having "begotten and confirmed" the victims, their bishop deplores the assault on "white-robed neophytes who had been anointed with chrism which was still fragrant on their foreheads." His anguish and sense of helplessness are palpable: "O my fairest and fondest brothers and sons, whom beyond numbering I have begotten in Christ, what shall I do for you?"[13]

Struggling to find words to convey his revulsion at a deed "so horrendous, so unspeakable," by men who have become "the devil's agents," Patrick turns to Scripture: "For it is written: Weep for those who weep; and again: If one member suffers, let all the members suffer with it."[14] Coroticus has "stained his hands with the blood of children of God." He and his soldiers

[10] Asterius, *Homily*, 11.4, *History of the Church*, vol. 1, ed. Hubert Jedin and John Nolan (London: Burns Oates, 1980) 273.

[11] Patrick, *Conf*, 38, 40; Conneely, 71; Matt 28:19–20.

[12] Patrick, *Conf*, 40; Conneely, 71; see Rom 9:25–26; Hos 2:1, 23–24; Acts 2:17–18.

[13] Patrick, *Letter to Coroticus*, 2, 3; Conneely, 77.

[14] Patrick, *Letter to Coroticus*, 15, 16; Conneely, 80.

are "bloodstained men bloodied in the blood of innocent Christians, whom I have begotten in countless numbers unto God, and have confirmed in Christ." The victims' pastor can barely conceive that, among the guilty, there are some who "received one and the same baptism" as their victims. They even mocked a "holy priest," taught by Patrick "from his infancy," who presented them with a letter demanding the return of the captives.[15]

There is an awful irony in the neophytes' abduction and murder during the traditional eight days of rejoicing, when they continued to wear white garments, receive religious instruction, live simply, and attend the Eucharist daily. On the eighth and final day it was Augustine's custom to warn them: "You are *infantes*, children entered upon a new life, reborn unto eternal life. You must now return to the people, mingle with the faithful. Beware of imitating wicked believers, those who are believers by their profession, but unbelievers by their evil lives."[16]

Patrick's converts were all too quickly overwhelmed by evil. Personal experience of slavery sharpens his apprehension at the possible fate of the innocents taken as "booty" to be shared out among these "rebels against Christ." He can only "wail and weep for those sons and daughters . . . deported and exported to distant lands where grave sin openly and shamelessly abounds."[17] There is some solace in the eternal truths imbibed by the dead during their preparation for the sacrament. Implicit in the feast which has just passed, these center on Christ's resurrection and the happiness it brings to those who persevere in faith. The victims' baptism ensures that, despite the unspeakable injustice of their passing, they no longer endure "night, or mourning or death." Happy with God, they will "skip for joy like calves loosed from their bonds."[18]

Patrick would have been further comforted by the knowledge that participation in the Easter rites ensured that those who were about to die had received not one, but three, sacraments. Through administration of the chrism, they were confirmed in their faith. They had also participated fully in the Eucharist, receiving the consecrated elements which signified their integration into the body of the Church. As catechumens, the new Christians had previously withdrawn from the Eucharist at the *missa*, or dismissal, which followed the scriptural readings and homily.

---

[15] Patrick, *Letter to Coroticus*, 2–3, 16; Conneely, 77, 80.
[16] Augustine, S 260; FCh 38:377–78.
[17] Patrick, *Letter to Coroticus*, 15; Conneely, 80.
[18] Patrick, *Letter to Coroticus*, 17; Conneely, 80; see Mal 2:10; 4:2.

As neophytes they remained, carrying the offerings to the altar for the first time. So charged with meaning was this point of entry into the heart of the Eucharist that the terms *missa* and "offering" were applied to the entire rite, the latter becoming *aifreann* in the Irish language.

Augustine's Easter Sunday sermon to the newly baptized on the "sacrament of the Lord's table" reveals how grievously the eucharistic action had been undermined by Coroticus. Reminding his listeners that the consecrated elements are indeed the body and blood of Christ, he records Paul's words on the sacrament's unifying power: "The bread is one; we, though many, are one body." Just as the many grains of the harvest become a single loaf, Christians achieve unity with Christ and fellow believers by worthily receiving the "sacrament of the Lord's table." Through this bread, says Augustine, believers learn how they ought to cherish unity.[19]

Ambrose too affirms that those who, for the first time, "hasten to the altar of God" to receive the "living bread, which came down from heaven" achieve unity and will never die, "for it is the body of Christ."[20] From the earliest times Christians celebrated this unifying action of the Eucharist, which had been signified in the ritual of the last supper when Jesus prayed that his followers "may all be one."[21] At the beginning of the second century, the author of the *Didache* prayed that, as the broken bread, "scattered on the mountain tops after being harvested, was made one, so let thy Church be gathered together from the ends of the earth into thy kingdom."[22] On his way to martyrdom, Ignatius of Antioch urged the Philadelphians to "observe one common Eucharist, for there is but one flesh of our Lord Jesus Christ, and one chalice that brings union in his blood. There is one altar of sacrifice, as there is one bishop with the priests and deacons, who are my fellow workers."[23]

Patrick is alive to Paul's words on the power of the Eucharist to unite Christians to the true God and to their fellows: "The blessing-cup that we bless is a communion with the blood of Christ, and the communion that we break is a communion with the body of Christ." The apostle's

---

[19] Augustine, S 227; FCh 38:195–98; see 1 Cor 10:14–17.

[20] Ambrose, *On the Mysteries*, 8.43–47; NPNF 10:323; see John 6:49–58; 17:21; Ps 42:4.

[21] John 17:21.

[22] *Didache*, 9; FCh 1:179.

[23] Ignatius, *Letter to the Philadelphians*, 4, trans. Gerald G. Walsh, FCh 1 (Washington, DC: CUAP, 1981) 114.

accompanying warning that, by sacrificing to demons, Christians can divorce themselves from the table of the Lord underlies the suggestions of subversion of the heavenly feast by a diabolical substitute that pervade the letter to Coroticus. In the abduction and murder of his neophytes Patrick perceives disruption of the harmonious heavenly repast by an orgy of violence. The life-enhancing eucharistic meal, presided over by a bishop, has been followed by an evil banquet in which men seduced by the devil have "gobbled up the people of the Lord like bread on the table."[24]

Patrick extends this image of a sacred meal subverted by contrasting the oblation offered on the altar with the tainted gifts which the evil-doers will offer from their plunder. Anyone, he says, would shrink in horror from "enjoying a banquet in their company." Even their friends and children will suffer, for, on returning to their homeland, the guilty men will bring "deadly poison as food."[25] Invoking Job, the bishop insists that Coroticus will not benefit from his savagery, for "the riches which he gathered unjustly will be vomited up from his belly; the angel of death will drag him away." Meanwhile, though his victims can no longer participate in the Eucharist, they now sit "at table with Abraham and Isaac and Jacob in the kingdom of heaven." Patrick celebrates their reward: "My baptized believers, you have gone from this world to paradise." There they will "banquet with Christ, judge nations and rule over wicked kings forever and ever." Outside will remain "the dogs, the sorcerers and the murderers." The sorrowing bishop addresses the guilty: "Woe to those who fill themselves with what is not their own. And what does it profit a man if he should gain the whole world and suffer the loss of his soul?"[26]

In the *City of God* Augustine considers how the sacrificial elements in the life of a believer, acts of compassion, self-control, duty to family and society, works of mercy, and devotion to God, are drawn together when the entire Christian body, through Christ, becomes a sacrificial offering to God "in the sacrament of the altar."[27] This is the sacrifice of Christians, who "are many, making up one body of Christ." Patrick has emulated Christ by sacrificing all for the salvation of the people of Ireland. His converts had given up their old ways for the new life of faith.

[24] Patrick, *Letter to Coroticus*, 5; Conneely, 77; see 1 Cor 10:14–21.

[25] Patrick, *Letter to Coroticus*, 13; Conneely, 79.

[26] Patrick, *Letter to Coroticus*, 8, 17–18; Conneely, 77, 80; see Matt 8:11–12; Job 20:14–16; Wis 3:8; Rev 22:15.

[27] Augustine, *City of God*, 10.6; Bettenson, 379–80; see Rom 12:3.

The evil-doers have sacrificed others to further their ambition and greed. "The man who offers a sacrifice from the property of the poor is like one who slays a son in sacrifice before his father's eyes," exclaims Patrick.[28] As a pastor-father forced to witness the death and abduction of his spiritual sons and daughters, he deplores the change wrought in "evil-minded Coroticus" and his "band of robbers" by their cruel sacrilege.[29]

Conscious that the mockery which greeted his request for release of the prisoners came from one "who has no reverence for God or his bishops," from a man through whom Satan has been able to "give vent to his malice," Patrick accuses Coroticus of overthrowing justice and undermining God's harmonious law, "which in these last times he had successfully and graciously planted in Ireland, and had grown up by the favor of the Lord." Invoking his moral and spiritual authority as bishop, he declares to "every God-fearing person" that the Christians among the aggressors are "excommunicate from me and from Christ my God for whom I am an ambassador." His authority to deny them participation in the sacramental life of the Church rests on no "false claims," but is shared by fellow bishops, whom God has called "to preach the Gospel amid no small persecutions unto the farthest part of the earth." All have been granted "the highest, divine, sublime power, that those whom they "bind on earth would be bound also in heaven."[30]

Excommunication was a rarely invoked power. Leo recommended that no Christian should be lightly excluded from the sacraments, particularly by bishops acting in anger. It is a penalty which a thoughtful judge should inflict unwillingly, and, as it were, with sorrow, and in order to punish a serious offense, not for trivial reasons.[31] Reproving a young bishop who has applied it rashly, Augustine is emphatic that only in the most extreme circumstances should a person be deprived of the sacraments.[32] Ambrose had employed the sanction against two emperors. Augustine was a member of the African episcopate when, in 418, it encouraged Pope Zosimus to excommunicate Pelagius. Later,

---

[28] Patrick, *Letter to Coroticus*, 8; Conneely, 78; see Sir 34:21–24.

[29] Patrick, *Letter to Coroticus*, 12; Conneely, 79; see Acts 20:29; Pss 14:4; 53:5.

[30] Patrick, *Letter to Coroticus*, 5–7; Conneely, 77–78; see Matt 16:19; 18:18.

[31] Leo, *Letters*, 10.8., trans. Charles Lett Feltoe, NPNF 12 (Grand Rapids, MI: Eerdmans, 1997) 11–12.

[32] Augustine, Ep 250, trans. Wilfrid Parsons, FCh 32 (Washington, DC: CUAP, 1965) 242.

he told Pope Celestine how he had barred Antonius of Fussala from communion until he made full restitution for the extortion of which he was guilty.[33] Like Patrick, Augustine finds the source of this power in the words "Whatever you loose on earth will be loosed in heaven; whatever you bind on earth will be bound in heaven."[34]

Patrick does not doubt the justice of his action, but sorrow, anger, and concern are mingled as he reflects on the guilt of the raiders and its implications for their final destiny: "Hence I do not know for whom I should grieve the more: whether for those who have been slain, those taken captive, or those whom the devil has grievously ensnared." While denouncing the crime committed by the abductors, he asks for penitence and amendment from men in whom he sees the image of the man who would seek "to gain the whole world and suffer the loss of his own soul."[35] Fearing for their eternal fate, he assures them that, if even at "a late hour" they repent their "impious deed," they can be "made whole here and in eternity," thus rejoining the community of the faithful.[36]

Similarly anxious that exclusion from participation in the sacraments should encourage sinners to repent, seek forgiveness, and rejoin their fellow Christians in worship, Augustine trusted that, through being deprived of the fellowship of the altar they, "having despised God by sinning, are able to appease him, not just in profitable regret, but by the sacrifices of mercy."[37] At the time of the fathers, the ritual of repentance which marked the return of the contrite sinner to full communion was enacted in public. It was as a public penitent that the emperor Theodosius had been readmitted to communion by Ambrose during the Eucharist celebrated on the feast of the nativity in the year 390. Patrick is adamant that Coroticus and his warriors can be reunited with the Christian community only if, "through rigorous penance, unto the shedding of tears, they render satisfaction to God and free the menservants of God and the baptized maidservants of Christ, for whom he died and was crucified."[38]

---

[33] Augustine, Ep 209; FCh 32:32.

[34] Augustine, Ep 250; NPNF 1:589–90; *Divjak Letters*, 1*, trans. Robert B. Eno, FCh, vol. 81 (Washington, DC: CUAP, 1989) 10–13; Matt 18:18; Jedin and Nolan, vol. 2, 259.

[35] Patrick, *Letter to Coroticus*, 4, 8; Conneely, 77, 78; Matt 16:26; Luke 9:25.

[36] Patrick, *Letter to Coroticus*, 21; Conneely, 81.

[37] Augustine, Ep 153.6; FCh 20:292.

[38] Patrick, *Letter to Coroticus*, 7; Conneely, 78.

# 8

# THE POWER OF PRAYER

Since apostolic times Christians have communicated their gratitude and needs to a caring and generous Creator who chose to share their nature and their plight. In the earliest surviving patristic letter Clement of Rome intoned a hymn of praise, asking God to teach all Christians "the full knowledge of the glory of his name, which is the source of all creation." Three centuries later Augustine, encouraging the widow Proba to pray for all her needs, reminded her of Paul's desire that believers should pray also for "that life of happiness which is nothing if not eternal," and ask it of him "who alone is able to give it." Seeing the soul illumined by contemplation of the divine as one's eyes are illuminated by light, John Chrysostom taught that life itself becomes a prayer when directed toward the glory of God. He envisaged the Christian's prayerful life as the protective roof of a secure house built of faith, humility, justice, generosity, and good works.[1]

Meditating on the Lord's Prayer in the mid-third century, Cyprian of Carthage, responding to Paul's call for Christians to "pray without ceasing," concluded that it is the believer's destiny to pray at all times, "even at night."[2] Augustine praised the widow Anna, whose constancy in prayer led her to "serve God in fastings and prayers night and day." Encouraging Eustochium, daughter of Paula, in her choice of the ascetic way, Jerome instructed her in the monastic observance of the fixed hours of prayer, day and evening. He told her that, since prayer can be found

---

[1] Clement, Ep 1.58–61; ECW 55; Augustine, Ep 130.9; 18; NPNF 1:462; 465; John Chrysostom, Homily 6, *On Prayer*, http://www.vatican.va/ documents/ spirit_20010302_giovanni-crisostomo_it.html.

[2] 1 Thess 5:17; Cyprian, *On the Lord's Prayer* 36, trans. Alister Stewart-Sykes (Crestwood, NY: Saint Vladimir's Seminary Press, 2004) 92.

in every aspect of life, "let us, in every act we do, in every step we take, trace the Lord's cross."[3] In this way, said Jerome, "we pray without ceasing." Ever practical, Augustine noted that "the brothers in Egypt" use certain very brief prayers which, recited often, "dart forth like arrows so that the alert attention does not fade."[4] The fathers' own lives became extended prayers of praise, penitence, intercession, and thanksgiving.

Sulpicius Severus lauded Martin's "capacity for night vigils and prayer," coining a memorable image to convey the ascetic bishop's ability to mingle prayer and action: "Blacksmiths have a way of striking on their anvils while working, as a kind of relief from the strain; that was precisely how Martin, when he seemed to be doing something else, was praying all the time."[5] Patrick was sustained by a similar spirit of prayer when, a slave in Ireland, he turned to God for assistance many times a day, and in all seasons: "even while I was staying in the woods and on the mountain; and before daylight I used to be stirred to prayer, in snow, frost and rain." Though very young, he "felt no ill effects from it, nor was there any sluggishness in me." As he prayed, he grew in faith and experienced "the love and fear of God."[6]

From apostolic times, prayer was seen as a sure support in time of trial. Paul prays that the recipients of his letters may enjoy "the grace of the Lord Jesus Christ, the love of God and the fellowship of the Holy Spirit." He assures those whose devotions are faltering that the "Spirit intercedes with sighs too deep for words."[7] Ambrose advises a fellow bishop not to despair if he cannot pray, for the Spirit who "pleads for us with unutterable groaning . . . also helps the weakness of our prayer."[8] Augustine too invokes Romans when recapturing that visionary moment before his mother's death at Ostia, at which he was bound up with "the first fruits of the Spirit."[9]

Patrick remembers with gratitude that, even when failing in prayer, he was protected by God, whose Spirit prayed with him and within him, "with sighs." Through his pleas for divine help, he was able to surmount

---

[3] Jerome, Ep 22.37; NPNF 6:38–39; see 1 Thess 5:17.
[4] Augustine, Ep 130.18–20; NPNF 1:465; see Luke 2:36–37.
[5] Sulpicius Severus, *Life of Saint Martin*, 26; WF 43.
[6] Patrick, *Conf*, 16; Conneely, 66.
[7] Rom 8:26–27.
[8] Ambrose, Ep 53; FCh 26:283–84; see Rom 8:24.
[9] Augustine, *Conf*, 9.10.24; Ryan, 221–22; see Rom 8:23.

the most formidable challenges. On his escape from slavery, when he and the pagans were starving after journeying for twenty-eight days, he "confidently" advised them to turn to the true God, "because nothing is impossible to him." Writing about his harrowing experience of betrayal by friends, he gives "unwearying thanks to my God, who kept me faithful in the day of my trial."[10]

In his letter to Proba, Augustine dwells on the necessity of prayer for those who "walk by faith and not by sight" but reminds her that "other good and necessary works" also contribute to the worship of God.[11] One of these, almsgiving, inseparable from prayer and fasting, was referred to by Jesus when he taught his disciples how to pray.[12] Augustine links the three in a vivid and appropriate image: "Let us by our prayers add the wings of piety to our almsdeeds and fasting so that they may fly more readily to God."[13] In Italy, Paulinus presented the alms table in his church as "the table which the Lord has placed in church for the poor," while Ambrose emphasized that fasting, when serving a Christian purpose, "is the refreshment of the soul, the food of the mind, the life of angels, the end of guilt . . . and the remedy of salvation."[14] He also reminded his listeners that the process not only enables individuals to overcome vice and support virtue but benefits their physical health.[15]

Both John Chrysostom and Pope Leo saw fasting as "food for virtue" and a means of drawing closer to God. Together with prayer and almsgiving, it is a remedy for those injuries incurred in the clash with evil. Simple and frugal living also provides opportunities to help those in need, with the compassion shown mirroring "the kindness and thoughtfulness of God." It is a compassion that shows concern for widows, orphans, the sick, and the oppressed.[16] Both bishops were practical in their approach and organized collection and distribution of alms during Lent and Advent.[17]

---

[10] Patrick, *Conf*, 19, 25, 34; Conneely, 67, 68, 70; see Rom 8:26–27.

[11] Augustine, Ep 130.5–18; NPNF 1:461–65; see 2 Cor 5:6–7.

[12] Matt 6:1–13.

[13] Augustine, S 206.2; FCh 38:87; *Expositions on the Book of the Psalms*, 43.7, trans. Cleveland Coxe, NPNF, vol. 8 (Grand Rapids, MI: Eerdmans, 1996) 140.

[14] Dudden, *Life and Times of Saint Ambrose*, vol. 1: 108–9, n. 10.

[15] Paulinus of Nola, Ep 34.1–2; ACW 35:162–64; see Prov 19:7; Paulinus, *The Life of Saint Ambrose*, 38; WF 177.

[16] Leo, S 13; S 15; FCh 93:54; 56.

[17] Leo, S 6; FCh 93:35; John Chrysostom, Homily 10.1–7, trans. Robert C. Hill, *Homilies on Genesis*, vol. 74 (Washington, DC: CUAP, 1986) 127–31.

The fathers' promotion of the relationship between duty to God and social responsibility was enhanced by their recognition of the communal nature of prayer. Saint Cyprian taught that, in beginning with the words "Our Father," the prayer which Jesus gave his followers is a reminder that "our prayer is common and collective; and when we pray, we pray, not for one, but for all the people, because we are all one people together." In this great prayer, says Cyprian, Jesus did not ask the faithful to say "I," "me," and "my," but "we," "us," and "our."[18]

Cyprian's words provide a key to understanding why, next to celebration of the Eucharist and the other sacramental liturgies, antiphonal singing of the psalms became a favored means of engaging in Christian worship. Paul called on the Colossians to "sing psalms, hymns, and spiritual songs to God."[19] Even the pagan administrator Pliny, writing from Asia Minor to the emperor Trajan around AD 111, noted the Christian practice of assembling before daylight to sing, in alternating groups, hymns in honor of Christ.[20] Ambrose's familiarity with the writings of the Greek fathers inspired him to introduce this practice to the west. On the psalms chanted in his basilica four times daily, he comments: "What human being would not be ashamed to end the day without the festal recital of psalms, when even the tiniest birds observe the beginning of day and night with solemn devotion and sweet song?" What could be more natural than to sing the psalms, he asks, for "from the singing of men, women, virgins, and children, there results a harmonious volume of sound, like that produced by the waves of the ocean." In being sung by young and old, male and female, these hymns bring unity, "softening even the stoniest heart."[21]

"Keenly affected by the voices of the sweet-singing Church," Augustine wept when he attended Ambrose's church after being baptized. On his mother's death at Ostia, he was comforted by a psalm-like evening hymn, "God, creator of all things, ruler of the sky."[22] It was composed by Ambrose, as was another favored by Augustine, "Eternal Author of All," sung to welcome the coming of dawn. The psalms provided not

[18] Cyprian, *On the Lord's Prayer*, 8; Stewart-Sykes, 69; see Matt 6:1–13.

[19] Col 3:16.

[20] Pliny, *Letters*, 10.96–97, J. Stevenson, *A New Eusebius* (London: SPCK, 1980) 14.

[21] Dudden, *Life and Times of Saint Ambrose*, vol. 1, 294; vol. 2, 444; Paulinus, *Life of Saint Ambrose*, 13; WF 158–59.

[22] Augustine, *Conf*, 9.6.14, 9.12.32; Ryan, 214, 226.

only endless food for spiritual thought but support in the trials attendant upon leading the Christian life. In them Augustine hears "the voice of Christ . . . head and body." Sung by "the whole body of Christ," they encourage unity, "and since all are in his body, as it were one man speaks; and he is one who is also many."[23] In the first verse of the short Psalm 133,

> How good, how delightful it is
> for all to live together like brothers,

Augustine finds a source of the monastic brotherhood. "These same words of the psalter, this sweet sound, that honeyed melody," he says, "did even beget the monasteries." In the simple verse he hears "a trumpet, which, sounded through the whole earth, has summoned the brethren to live together."[24]

Fathers and ascetics immersed themselves in the psalms, whose rhythms sounded through their lives. In them, Patrick found the theme of his spiritual testament, with Psalm 116 providing the primary refrain of the *Confession*, "Let me make return to the Lord then, for his bounty to me."[25] He joins the psalmist in praising God's generosity "before every nation under the whole heaven" and vowing to "exalt and glorify" the divine name "among the nations."[26] Grateful for the grace that came through his providential enslavement, Patrick turns to another psalm to declare that "before I was humbled I was like a stone lying in deep mire; and that he who is mighty came and in his mercy lifted me up; and more than that, truly raised me aloft and placed me on top of the wall."[27]

In the *Confessions* Augustine repeatedly invokes the psalms. He recalls that, in his twenties, his world assumed an aspect of unreality on the death of a close friend: "To myself I was a great riddle and I questioned my soul as to why it was sad and why it afflicted me so grievously."[28] He turns to the sacred songs in confessing that, following a false trail and far from God, the hope of his youth, he had "walked in darkness, and upon a slippery way, and I sought for you outside myself, but I did not find you, the God of my heart. I went down into the depth of the sea, and I

---

[23] Augustine, Ps 131:1; *Expositions on the Psalms*, NPNF 8:614.
[24] Augustine, Ps 133:2; *Expositions on the Psalms*, NPNF 8:622.
[25] Patrick, *Conf*, 3; Conneely, 11–12.57; see Ps 116:12.
[26] Patrick, *Conf*, 3, 34; Conneely, 64, 70; see Pss 25:4–5; 70; 47.
[27] Patrick, *Conf*, 12; Conneely, 65; see Ps 113:7–8.
[28] Augustine, *Conf*, 4.4.9; Ryan, 98; see Ps 42:5–6, 11.

lost confidence, and I despaired of finding the truth."[29] At the culmination of his spiritual quest, as he falls under the fig tree and weeps, he penitently presents his tears as "an acceptable sacrifice" to God, asking, with the psalmist, "And you, O Lord, how long? How long, O Lord, will you be angry forever? Remember not our past iniquities."[30] At one of the most moving points in his testament, he recollects that, just before the burial of his mother Monica, his friend "Evodius took up the psalter and began to sing. The whole household responded, 'I will sing of mercy and judgment unto you, O Lord.'"[31]

As a Manichaean, Augustine had neglected the Scriptures. Now a baptized Christian, he finds in the psalms of David an antidote to the pride which had barred his path to truth: "What cries did I send up to you when reading those psalms! How was I set on fire by them and how did I burn to repeat them, if I could, throughout the whole world, as a remedy against mankind's pride."[32] Revisiting with gratitude the moment at which he experienced the fullness of truth, he again finds inspiration in the psalter:

> In a spirit of thankfulness let me recall the mercies you lavished on me, O my God; to you let me confess them. May I be flooded with love for you until my very bones cry out, "Who is like you, O Lord?" Let me offer you a sacrifice of praise, for you have snapped my bonds. How you broke them I will relate, so that all your worshippers who hear my tale may exclaim, "Blessed be the Lord, blessed in heaven and on earth, for great and wonderful is his name."[33]

Through the words of the psalms Patrick is able to articulate his anguish at the brutal treatment inflicted on his people: "Lord, the wicked have destroyed your law." In twin psalms he finds words which convey the full weight of the atrocity: "Parricides! Fratricides! Ravenous wolves gobbling up the people of the Lord like bread on the table."[34] To his brethren and others familiar with these songs Patrick is saying, "We are

---

[29] Augustine, *Conf,* 6.1.1; Ryan, 133; see Pss 71:5, 35:6, 68:22.

[30] Augustine, *Conf,* 8.12.28; Ryan, 202; see Pss 50:19, 6:3, 79:5, 8.

[31] Augustine, *Conf,* 9.12.31; Ryan, 225; see Ps 101:1.

[32] Augustine, *Conf,* 9.4.8; Ryan, 210; see Ps 19:1–13.

[33] Augustine, *Conf,* 8.1.1; Boulding, 184; see Pss 86:13, 35:10, 116:16–17, 135:6; 72:6.

[34] Patrick, *Letter to Coroticus,* 5; Conneely, 78; see Pss 119, 126, 14:4, 53:4.

dealing with godless men," for each psalm begins with the words, "The fool says in his heart, 'There is no God.'" The psalms also enable him to express his confidence that, through God's justice, the "wretched temporal kingdom" built by these miscreants will pass away in a moment, "as a cloud of smoke that is scattered by the wind." Implicit is David's call on God to scatter his enemies: "Let those who hate him flee before him! As smoke disperses, they disperse."[35]

In the sufferings of the psalmists Patrick perceives his own painful experiences. Through their words he reminds God of his promise: "Call upon me in the day of your trouble and I will deliver you, and you shall glorify me."[36] He is especially sensitive to the song of the just man's subjection to insults by people who dare to "slander their own brother" and "bring down misery" on him "with their malicious tongues." With its portrayal of enemies baying at the just man, Psalm 55 resonates for one who has been reviled by many and betrayed by his best friend:

> It is not enemies who taunt me—
>     I could bear that;
> it is not adversaries who deal insolently with me—
>     I could hide from them.
> But it is you, my equal,
>     my companion, my familiar friend,
> with whom I kept pleasant company;
>     we walked in the house of God with the throng.[37]

Toward the end of the *Confession* Patrick returns to this psalm. For one who has experienced the pain of betrayal there is comfort in the words of a fellow sufferer mourning a friendship forsworn. Surveying the surrounding dangers, he avows that he fears nothing because he has cast himself "into the hands of almighty God" and reaffirms his confidence by concluding with the prophet, "Cast your care upon God and he will sustain you."[38]

Patrick's language is energized by the words of the psalmists because his experiences so closely resemble theirs. Threatened on all sides by evil, apparently about to fall, he and they are supported by God. Sunk

---

[35] Patrick, *Letter to Coroticus*, 19; Conneely, 80; see Pss 37:20, 68:1.

[36] Patrick, *Conf*, 5; Conneely, 64; see Ps 50:15.

[37] Patrick, *Conf*, 27, 32; Conneely, 68, 69; Ps 55:12–14.

[38] Patrick, *Conf*, 55; Conneely, 75; see Ps 55:22.

in the mud, buried in the dust, stranded on a dunghill, or mired in the hatred of others, he and they are extricated by the divine power. In facing the final trials of old age, Patrick once again turns to them for succor. Grateful that he has been faithful to God since youth, he appreciates his continuing need of divine help while "I am in this body of death." He is echoing the psalmist, who begs God "not to reject me now I am old, or to desert me now that my strength is failing."[39]

Augustine advised evangelists lacking rhetorical skills to turn to the riches of Scripture for support.[40] Frequently lost for words, Patrick finds in the psalter a unique source of praise, intercession, and penitence. In the psalms Augustine sees a new song, worthy of being intoned by those reborn through baptism. Sung from the heart, the psalms can even enable Christians to move beyond words. In explaining that to sing from the heart with true joy is to realize that words can never communicate adequately what has been experienced by the worshipper, Augustine reaches for an image drawn from his knowledge of rural Africa. There, "singers in the harvest, or the vineyard, or at some other arduous toil, express their rapture to begin with in songs set to words; then, as if bursting with a joy so full that they cannot give vent to it in set syllables, they drop actual words and break into the free melody of pure jubilation."[41]

He again affirmed the worth of the psalms when writing to certain rebellious monks, who wished to modify their vows in the belief that, for them, worship without work was sufficiently pleasing to God. Asking them to earn their bread by the work of their hands, the bishop reminded them that labor in the fields truly glorifies God, and that the burden can be lightened by intoning the canticles, "at the divine call, as it were."[42] Augustine further suggests that the psalms be intoned not just in church, "when we are chanting these very words," but carried in the soul, through the day, when at work, in eating and in drinking. Envisaging their power suffusing the entire being of the individual involved, he adds, "When you sleep, let your soul praise the Lord."[43]

[39] Patrick, *Conf*, 44; Conneely, 72; see Ps 71.

[40] Augustine, *Christian Instruction*, 4, 8, trans. John J. Gavigan, FCh 2 (Washington, DC: CUAP, 1966) 187–92.

[41] Augustine, Ps 32:2, 8; *Discourse on the Psalms*, vol. 2, trans. Scholastica Hebgin and Felicitas Corrigan, ACW 30 (London: Longmans and Green, 1961) 111–12.

[42] Augustine, *On the Work of Monks*, 17.20; FCh 14:362–63; *Retractions*, 2.47; FCh 60:162.

[43] Augustine, *Expositions on the Psalms*, 103.1; NPNF 8:503.

# 9

# DEFENDERS OF THE FAITH

I n endeavoring to spread the Gospel and support the faith of fellow Christians, the fathers of the Church resisted any attempt to dilute or distort the apostolic message. They were conscious that, even from earliest times, there had been false teachers who, in Peter's words, would "secretly bring in destructive opinions" and "deny the Master who bought them," leading others to "follow their licentious ways."[1] When Timothy was ministering in Ephesus, Paul urged him to "instruct certain people not to teach any different doctrine." Mindful of the presence of "false prophets," John exhorted Christians to be watchful lest they be led astray.[2] The invocation of the incarnation, "the Word became flesh," in the prologue to his Gospel, was an implicit rebuke to the Gnostics, who taught that the material world is intrinsically evil.

The activities of such deceivers prompted Paul's plea from prison to the Ephesians: "I, therefore, the prisoner in the Lord, beg you to . . . maintain the unity of the Spirit in the bond of peace. . . . There is . . . one Lord, one faith, one baptism, one God and Father of all, who is above all and through all and in all." The apostle begs pastors to defend their flock against individuals who would emerge, even from their own ranks, "distorting the truth in order to entice the disciples to follow them." He insists that the fullness of revelation is in Christ, to whom believers are bound through his Church, "because we are members of his body."[3] Paul's image of the unity of belief echoes Christ's prayer for the com-

---

[1] 2 Pet 2:1–2.
[2] 1 Tim 1:3–4; 1 John 4:1.
[3] Eph 4:1–6; Acts 20:28–30; Eph 5:29–30.

munity of the faithful: "As you, Father, are in me and I am in you, may they also be in us, so that the world may believe that you have sent me."[4]

The fathers continued this work of fostering unity. On his journey to martyrdom in AD 107, Ignatius of Antioch cautioned the Ephesians against certain strangers who "hold bad doctrine," prudent men, full of worldly wisdom, who would undermine faith in the humanity of Christ. He advised Christians to maintain unity by participating in the Eucharist.[5] Irenaeus, who wrote prolifically against the Gnostics and died in AD 200, urged Christians to observe the binding force of the Church's unified teaching, "for the languages of the world are different, yet the import of the tradition is one and the same." Disunity would be avoided only if believers remain close to their bishops who, as inheritors of the apostolic tradition, are primary guardians of the faith.[6]

Ignatius had already reminded the Smyrneans that unity could not be maintained if this bond was broken: "Where the bishop is to be seen, there let all his people be; just as wherever Jesus Christ is present we have the world-wide Church."[7] In hailing the successful transmission of the undivided faith, Irenaeus noted that, though "this preaching and this faith" which the Church has received is scattered through the whole world, "she preserves it carefully, as if occupying but one house." She believes it "as if she had but one soul and one and the same heart" and she proclaims and hands it down "with perfect harmony, as if she possessed only one mouth."[8]

Gnosticism, a product of pagan philosophy popular among the educated classes, was a persistent snare for certain believers, who were drawn by the promise of an esoteric knowledge confined to privileged initiates. The Gnostic spirit was foreign to the openness and generosity evident in the faith of Christians. Its dark view of the material world was vigorously challenged by the earliest fathers, who taught the goodness of God's creation, which, solely because of sin, was in need of the redemption gained through Christ's obedience to the Father. Though reared a Christian catechumen by his mother, Augustine was a Manichaean by his twentieth year. After his conversion and baptism, he concluded that,

[4] John 17:21.
[5] Ignatius, *Letter to the Ephesians*, 9, 18–20; FCh 1:90–91, 94–95.
[6] Irenaeus, *Against Heresies*, 1.10.2; 3.3.1; ANF 1:331; 415.
[7] Ignatius, *Letter to the Smyrnaeans*, 8; ECW 121.
[8] Irenaeus, *Against Heresies*, 1.10.2; ANF 1:331.

by feeding their fantasies, certain individuals divorce their followers from the saving embrace of the universal Church and thrust them into a "small party," where they abandon their interest in the promises of God.[9] Another critic of doctrinal division was Augustine's fellow countryman Cyprian, martyred bishop of Carthage, who, in his *Unity of the Catholic Church*, wrote, "This sacrament of unity, this bond of concord inseparably connected, is shown when, in the Gospel, the tunic of the Lord Jesus Christ is not at all divided and is not torn." He concluded that the bishops are responsible for the continued unity of the Church.[10]

Jerome first witnessed the scandal of divided Christianity in the year 374. Arriving in the east, he found a community "shattered by long-standing feuds, tearing into shreds the seamless robe of Christ." Feeling that it was his duty "to consult the chair of Peter and turn to a church whose faith has been praised by Paul," he sought the support of Pope Damasus, exclaiming, "While the arian frenzy raves there are three factions, each eager to seize me as its own." The experience confirmed Jerome's belief that unity of faith is fundamental to the well-being of the Church.[11] Around the same time, Damasus received a similar letter from Basil, who spoke of the "terrible storm and tempest" agitating the Church in the east. Basil rejoiced that, though separated by distance, orthodox believers in east and west were "bound in a union of love into one harmonious membership in the body of Christ."[12]

The error decried by Jerome and Basil had its source in Alexandria, where, in 318, the priest Arius claimed that, since the Son was born of the Father, he was not consubstantial and coeternal with the first person of the Trinity.[13] Concluding that the Arian teaching implied that Jesus had died in vain, bishops assembled at Nicaea in modern Turkey in 325 and condemned the heresy. At this first ecumenical council of the Church they affirmed the orthodox teaching that the Son is "eternally begotten of the Father, God from God, Light from Light, true God from true God, begotten, not made, of one substance with the Father, through whom all things were made."

---

[9] Augustine, *Conf*, 3.7.12; Ryan, 85.

[10] Cyprian, *The Unity of the Church*, 5–7; FCh 36:99–102; see John 19:23–24.

[11] Jerome, Ep 15.1; 16.2; NPNF 6:18; 20.

[12] Basil, Ep 70; FCh 13:168–70.

[13] J. N. D. Kelly, *Early Christian Doctrines* (London: Longman, 1976) 226–31.

Despite the success of Nicaea, the error persisted, since it won the favor of Constantius, son and successor of Constantine. Athanasius of Alexandria, its most resolute opponent, had attended the council as adviser to his predecessor as bishop. His own prolonged resistance to the heresy brought exile from his see on five occasions, for seventeen years in all, with the greatest trials coming during the reign of Constantius. Athanasius was sent to Trier as early as 336, when the Arian prelate Eusebius of Nicomedia gained the approval of Constantine himself. Returning in 345 from a seven-year stay in Rome, he was able to live in relative peace for a decade. Then, harassed once more, he was in hiding till the death of Constantius in 361.

Athanasius's writings against the heresy included the *Incarnation of the Word*, in which he argues for the necessity of the Word of God assuming human nature if mankind was to be saved. Among prominent western fathers who wrote in support of the true teaching was Hilary of Poitiers, mentor of Martin of Tours. Exiled for a time to Phrygia, in the east, Hilary wrote an influential work on the Trinity.[14] Martin himself had two encounters with Arianism. Some time after being baptized, he returned to his old home to convert his pagan parents. On confronting Auxentius, Arian bishop of the region, he was forced to leave Pavia. Pausing on the journey back to Gaul, he built a hermitage outside the city of Milan, but was again expelled by Auxentius.[15]

Even when Ambrose succeeded Auxentius in 376 the error persisted among Gothic members of the army based in Milan. Justina, Arian mother of the new western emperor, a minor, whose court was in the city, had a prelate of her own persuasion appointed in opposition to Ambrose. Resisting an imperial demand for the surrender of one of Milan's basilicas, Ambrose encouraged the faithful to occupy the building. In a letter to his sister Marcellina, he describes how he refused to "hand over the temple of God." Insisting that his people would remain peaceful, he appealed to the military "to direct their weapons all on me, and slake their thirst with my blood." The imperial army withdrew on Holy Thursday. Threatened with death after his triumph, Ambrose replied, "May God grant that you fulfill your threat, for I shall suffer what bishops suffer." Later, quoting the words of Saint Paul, "When I am

---

[14] Hilary of Poitiers, *The Trinity*, trans. Stephen McKenna, FCh 25 (Washington, DC: CUAP, 1968).

[15] Sulpicius Severus, *Life of Saint Martin*, 6; WF 18–20.

weak, then I am strong," he presented the incident as a confrontation between earthly force and spiritual power.[16]

In the *Confessions* Augustine claims that his mother Monica was one of the "devout people" who participated in the resistance, singing hymns and canticles "so that they would not become weak through the tedium and sorrow." Both he and Ambrose's first biographer, Paulinus, reveal that, during the siege, the bishop introduced the eastern practice of "antiphonal chanting of the psalms, the singing of hymns and the chanting of the night office."[17] It is noteworthy that, while Ambrose was achieving this victory, his eastern counterpart, Basil, was successfully withstanding the Arian emperor Valens. Shortly before, Basil had sent Ambrose the relics of Dionysius of Milan, who had been martyred while exiled in Cappadocia, and encouraged him to persist in his defense of the faith.[18]

Basil died in 379. In the same year, his diffident friend, Gregory of Nazianzen, was invited to minister in Constantinople, which was dominated by Arians. Before his consecration as bishop of the city in 380, Gregory won many people back to orthodox belief by delivering five powerful orations on the Trinity. In them he reflected on those paradoxes of Christ's life which illustrate that he is both God and man:

> He was baptized as man, but he remitted sins as God. . . . He was tempted as man, but he conquered as God . . . he hungered, but he fed thousands; yes, he is the bread that gives life, and that is of heaven. He thirsted, but he cried, "If any man thirst, let him come to me and drink." Yes, he promised that fountains should flow from them that believe. . . . He was wearied, but he is the rest of those that are weary and heavy laden.[19]

A year after Gregory's appointment, his teaching was confirmed at the Council of Constantinople. Ratifying Nicaea and buttressing its creed, the council condemned the teachings of Arius and the error of Apollinaris of Laodicaea, who had questioned Christ's humanity.

---

[16] Ambrose, Ep 60; FCh 26:374–75; see 2 Cor 12.

[17] Augustine, *Conf*, 9.7.15; Ryan, 215; Paulinus, *Life of Saint Ambrose*, 13; WF 158–59.

[18] Basil, Ep 197; FCh 28:42–45; see n. 1, p. 42.

[19] Gregory of Nazianzen, *Third Theological Oration: On the Son*, 19–20, trans. Charles Gordon Browne and James Edward Swallow, NPNF, Second Series, vol. 7 (Grand Rapids, MI: Eerdmans, 1996) 308–9.

Repelled by the dissension that marked Church circles in the eastern capital, the sensitive Gregory resigned the see despite his decisive victory. It was during Gregory's brief tenure that Jerome reached Constantinople while returning to Rome from Syria. Reflecting on his experiences in the city during that tumultuous time, the ascetic scholar, who was generally so reluctant to praise others, named Gregory as "my catechist in the Holy Scriptures" and "my teacher."[20]

Assaults on the faith like those encountered by Basil, Jerome, Gregory, and Ambrose engendered the early creeds, some of which are still recited. The most succinct of the fourth- and fifth-century creeds was the *symbolum*, or rule of faith. Encapsulating the essence of Christian belief, its profession was a necessary step in the baptismal rite. In it Augustine saw a bond, a pact of fidelity, not to be written, but sufficiently short to be memorized, "held, and cherished in memory," a covenant "to be written on the heart of Christians."[21] He was following Paul in maintaining that faith demands a duty of heart and tongue: "For one believes with the heart and so is justified, and one confesses with the mouth and so is saved."[22] With its ritual of initiation centered on the Trinity, baptism was the point at which the new Christian gave profound consideration to the content of belief. Initiates recited the *symbolum* before receiving the sacrament.[23]

Augustine was especially conscious of the life-enhancing nature of faith. Remote from it in his youth, he had wandered even further during his vain quest, while his mother, "by that spirit of faith which she received from God," never lost hope that he would find happiness. Later, looking back to the dark days of pride and unbelief, he contritely recalls that Ambrose, "when he saw me, would often break forth in her praise, and congratulate me on having such a mother. But he did not know what sort of son she had, for I doubted all things, and thought that the way to life could not be found."[24] Following his baptism, Augustine, happy to share the faith of humble fellow Christians, accepted that learned believers may be led astray by the false reasoning of philosophers who do not know that "the foolishness of God is wiser than men." However,

---

[20] Jerome, Epp 50.1, 52.8; NPNF 6:80, 93.
[21] Augustine, SS 212, 214; FCh 38:117, 130; see 2 Cor 3:2–3.
[22] Rom 10:10.
[23] J. N. D. Kelly, *Early Christian Creeds* (London: Longman, 1976) 33.
[24] Augustine, *Conf,* 6.2.2; Ryan, 135.

he did not abandon "the God-given faculty which makes us superior to all other living beings." While accepting the difficulty of contemplating and comprehending God and the mysteries surrounding him, and agreeing with Paul that the greatness of God "can be known only in a dark manner," he urged Christians to advance as far as possible along the road of reason. However, faith must come first to cleanse the heart, so that it can "receive and bear the light of reason," for, "unless you believe, you will not understand."[25]

This conviction colored Augustine's initial reaction to the Donatist error, which had persisted in Africa since the reign of Constantine. Spurning clergy and prelates whose orders derived from bishops who had been reinstated after lapsing during persecution, Donatists deemed Catholic baptism invalid. Preoccupation with religious purity alone separated them from other believers. Coercive laws had been enacted against them by Constantine, but Augustine initially chose to "act only by words, fight only by arguments and prevail by force of reason." He debated with Donatist bishops, trusting that they would return to "the communion of the whole world" and look to the "lineal succession of the bishops" and especially to the figure of Peter.[26] Later, he acquiesced in the application of law and what he called the medicine of "moderate severity of exile and fines" to recalcitrant religious leaders.[27]

Though his attitude in this matter was uncompromising, Augustine resolutely rejected more punitive treatment in these and other circumstances, and in 412 asked the tribune Marcellinus to ensure that Donatist militants called Circumcellions, who were on trial for the murder of one priest and the maiming of another, should, if found guilty, be left "alive and physically unmutilated." He argued that the "medicine of repentance" for the guilty was preferable to the extreme punishments then reserved for serious crimes. Healing the wounds of sinners, not revenge, should motivate the judges. Retaliatory punishment of the malefactors would bring only shame on "the sufferings of the Catholic servants of God."[28]

[25] Augustine, *Faith and the Creed*, 1.1; NPNF 3:321; Ep 120, trans. Wilfrid Parsons, FCh 18 (Washington, DC: CUAP, 1966) 301–2; *Expositions on the Psalms*, 8.6; NPNF 8:29; see Ps 105:4; Gal 3:11; Col 2:3.

[26] Augustine, Epp 43.27, 53.1–2, 93.17; NPNF 1:285, 298.

[27] Augustine, Epp 93.4–10, 17; NPNF 1:383–85, 388.

[28] Augustine, Ep 133; NPNF 1:470–71.

Augustine's difficult personal path to the fullness of faith enabled him to meet the major challenge of Pelagianism in his later years. A heresy which originated in the first decade of the fifth century, it saw in grace not a necessary support from God, but a form of enlightenment that comes with baptism. Pelagians believed that, since the baptized were not disposed to break God's law, they could freely choose between good and evil and readily lead simple, devout lives. After building a following in Rome, Pelagius, a native of Britain, fled the sack of the city in 410, going first to Africa, then to Palestine, where his teaching was denounced by Jerome. Shocked by the claim that one could live without sin through the power of the human will alone, the old warrior wrote to Augustine. The bishop, who had already initiated his assault on the heresy, likened Pelagians to the foolish virgins, who seek to "establish their own justice." He noted that this parable instructs Christians on the grace of the New Testament, whose many enemies refuse to "attribute to God the fact that they are good, but take the credit themselves."[29]

Augustine wrote in similar vein to the mother of Demetrias, a Roman girl of noble family who was contemplating a dedicated life. The young woman had received a letter from Pelagius assuring her that, though earthly rank and wealth come through her relatives, "your spiritual riches no one can have conferred on you but yourself." Demetrias should disregard such pernicious words, says Augustine, and listen to Saint Paul's: "We are only the earthen vessels that hold this treasure, to make it clear that this overwhelming power comes from God and not from us."[30] On Pelagius's sanguine claims for the human capacity to overcome evil without the support of grace, he quotes Saint John's warning that, by denying human sinfulness, "we deceive ourselves and truth is not in us."[31] Augustine asks the Pelagians why, if what their mentor claims is true, Jesus gave his followers the Lord's Prayer, in which they ask God not to abandon them to evil. Freedom of will, insists Augustine, is not destroyed by being helped; it is rather helped because it is not destroyed. In the Pelagian refusal to envision this he detects the sin of pride.

When Pope Innocent I condemned the heresy in 417, Sixtus, a high-ranking Roman priest who had initially been sympathetic to Pelagius, wrote to Aurelius, bishop of Carthage, affirming his orthodoxy. He was

[29] Augustine, Ep 140.37; FCh 20:133–34; see Ps 21.
[30] Augustine, Ep 188.4–6; NPNF 1:549–50; see 2 Cor 4:7.
[31] Augustine, Ep 157.1; FCh 20:319; see John 1:8.

answered by Augustine, who identified the bearer of the Roman's letter as "the acolyte Leo," future pope and another defender of the faith. Commending Sixtus on the "transparent soundness" of his views, Augustine asked him to proclaim his faith openly, particularly to those who still saw him as a supporter of their error.[32]

In a second letter, Augustine carefully defined his thoughts on the primacy of grace, concluding that there is no place for it in the teaching of Pelagius.[33] He also rejected the Pelagian claim that grace is not freely received, but comes "in accordance with our merits."[34] This is given the lie, he said, by the words of Paul: "For the good which I will, I do not; but the evil which I will not, that I do . . . unhappy man that I am, who shall deliver me from the body of this death? The grace of God, by Jesus Christ our Lord." Augustine's words were fortified by the recollection of his own futile struggle to turn to God while being held by an enemy who "had control of my will, and out of it fashioned a chain and fettered me with it." Only through God's grace had he been able to break the chain.[35]

As for Jerome, *Against the Pelagians*, the last of his controversial works, demonstrates that, even in extreme old age, he reveled in the fight. Exploiting his extensive knowledge of Scripture to refute the same erroneous teachings, he mocks those who are supposedly "insensible to the attraction of sin." In a short letter, written a year before his death, he urged Augustine to continue to defend the faith. "The heretics abhor you," he exclaims with his customary pungency. "They persecute me also with equal hatred, seeking by imprecation to take away the life which they cannot reach with the sword. May the mercy of Christ the Lord preserve you in safety and mindful of me, my venerable lord and most blessed father."[36] Jerome ends *Against the Pelagians* with an uncharacteristically generous tribute to his younger friend. Commending Augustine's writings against the heresy, he adds, "If we wished to say something fresh, we should find our best points anticipated by that splendid genius."[37]

Augustine was forced to resist Pelagianism until his death. Ironically, his most implacable foe, Julian of Eclanum, a young bishop in the south

[32] Augustine, Ep 191; NPNF 1:554–55.
[33] Augustine, Ep 194; NPNF 1:554, n. 8.
[34] Augustine, *Retractions*, 1.8; FCh 60:33.
[35] Augustine, *Conf*, 8.5.10–12; Ryan, 188–90; see Rom 7:19–25.
[36] Jerome, Ep 195; NPNF 6:556.
[37] Jerome, *Against the Pelagians*, 3.19; NPNF 6:482.

of Italy, was a relative of his old friend, Paulinus of Nola. Following Pope Innocent's action against the error in 417, Julian, with seventeen other bishops, rejected the orthodox teaching. Deprived of his see, he moved to the east and continued to argue his case. Showing scant respect for his African colleague's advanced age and position, the aristocratic prelate loftily dismissed him as a "detestable punic quarrel-seeker" and a "punic Aristotle." He even claimed that Augustine's earlier writing on freedom of the will had "pleaded the cause" of his present adversaries.[38]

In *Against Julian*, Augustine invokes "those brilliant catholic advocates," the fathers, who, as faithful spiritual leaders, had propagated and defended the faith in the past, contrasting them with Julian and Pelagius, who have plunged some believers into the "pelagian darkness" of error. Among those "instructors" are "Irenaeus, Cyprian, Hilary, Basil, and Jerome." Last named is the bishop's hero, Ambrose, "whose books I have read and whose words I have heard from his own lips." On three occasions Augustine presents the same "famous and brilliant teachers of the catholic truth," to whom Christians can turn for support and inspiration, as guarantors of the continuity of the faith. In their achievements he sees the hand of God who, in his wisdom, has distributed them, as his stewards, in different ages, times, and places. It has been through "such planters, waterers, shepherds, and fosterers" that the Church has grown since the time of the apostles.[39]

Patrick reached maturity and later ministered during the period in which the Pelagian debate raged. He shared Augustine's conviction on the bond of faith, "written on the heart, with the Spirit of the living God." As bishop, he baptized many catechumens, who would have been familiar with the elements of the short and carefully structured profession of faith recorded in the *Confession*.[40] Patrick's immunity to the error was reinforced by an enduring conviction of his own need for grace. In the opening lines of the *Confession* he tells of God employing "the wrath of his anger" to scatter so many careless Christians in a strange land, where he opened a young man's "unbelieving mind," bringing him back to knowledge of the truth. It is an experience suggestive of Augustine's "prevenient grace" which enables a person to take the first

---

[38] Augustine, *Retractions*, 1.8; FCh 60:33.
[39] Augustine, *Against Julian*, 2.10.36–37; FCh 102–3.
[40] Patrick, *Conf*, 4–5, 11; Conneely, 63–64, 65.

step to goodness, a grace illuminated by his assertion that we could not love God unless he first loved us.[41]

In old age Patrick gives thanks that, through grace, he has achieved so much, and, "till now, by the favor of the Lord," has kept faith.[42] Confessing that "my own self I do not trust as long as I am in this body of death," he prays that God will grant him final perseverance "and keep me a faithful witness to him until I die, for the sake of my God." This is a gift, says Augustine, for which all Christians must pray, especially when saying the Lord's Prayer, which is concerned throughout with that disposition, so necessary for salvation.[43]

As Patrick brings his *Confession* to an end, he insists more urgently on the need for grace. Adamant that he will continue to "make return to the Lord for all his bounty," he asks, "But what shall I say, or what shall I promise my Lord, for I am unable to do anything unless he himself enables me."[44] With the last lines of his apologia comes a final affirmation of what he owes to God's grace:

> And now, to all who believe and hold God in reverence, should one of them condescend to inspect and accept this writing put together by Patrick, a mere unlettered sinner, this is my prayer: that if I have accomplished or brought to light any small part of God's purpose, none shall ever assert that the credit is due to my own uneducated self, but regard it rather as a true fact to be firmly believed that it was all the gift of God. And that is my confession before I die.[45]

In 427, just three years before his death, Augustine learned from Prosper of Aquitaine, an enthusiastic supporter living in southern Gaul, that certain monks there did not agree with his teaching on grace. At the same time, he heard that the brethren at the monastery of Hadrumentum, not far from Hippo, had read a copy of the letter to Sixtus and concluded

---

[41] Patrick, *Conf,* 1–3; Conneely, 64; Augustine, *Free Choice of the Will,* trans. Robert Russell, FCh 59 (Washington, DC: CUAP, 1968) 288–89; see John 15:5; 6:44; 8:36; Rom 9:14ff.

[42] Patrick, *Conf,* 44; Conneely, 73.

[43] Patrick, *Conf,* 58; Conneely, 75; see Phil 1:4–6; 29–30; Augustine, *Retractions,* ch. 93; FCh 60:272.

[44] Patrick, *Conf,* 57; Conneely, 75.

[45] Patrick, *Conf,* 62; Conneely, 76; see Ps 116.

that the case for grace had been argued so trenchantly that it left little room for the strenuous personal effort demanded by their vocation. In response, Augustine wrote *On Grace and Free Choice* and *On Admonition and Grace*. He assured Abbot Valentinus that his teaching did not exclude freedom of will. In the *Retractions*, completed shortly before his death, he recalls the ascetics' misunderstanding of his writings: "Thinking that free choice is denied when the grace of God is defended, they defend free will in such a manner as to deny the grace of God, by affirming that it is bestowed according to our merits."[46] His final works, *On the Predestination of the Saints* and *On the Gift of Perseverance*, strongly affirm his teaching that God's grace, freely given, supports every good deed.

For one distinguished monk there was a painful sequel to the Pelagian controversy. Shortly after Augustine's death, the indefatigable Prosper claimed to have detected error in the thirteenth book of the *Conferences* of John Cassian of Marseilles.[47] In a brief passage of this work, the respected authority on monastic life attempted an accommodation between his monks' fears and Augustine's robust words on grace by carefully defining a place for free exercise of the will. Emphatic that one's own exertions can do nothing without God's aid, he adds that the grace of God "always works together with our will on behalf of the good."[48] Seeing "in us the slightest glimmer of good will, which he himself has in fact sparked from the hard flint of our hearts, God fosters it, stirs it up, and strengthens it with his inspiration." Cassian adds that the very beginnings of a good deed can arise in a person, to be completed only by being "guided by the Lord."[49] The two are in harmony, not opposed.

Cassian continued to be highly regarded in the Church, particularly by ascetics like Saints Benedict and Gregory the Great. His writings on monasticism and spirituality are still read with benefit by Christians who accept that, in seeking to temper the severity of the words on grace wrung from Augustine by his opponents, the monk drifted into a mild form of Pelagianism.

---

[46] Augustine, *Retractions*, 2.92; FCh 60:268.
[47] Prosper, *Against Cassian*, 2.1–5, trans. P. De Letter, ACW 32 (London: Longmans, Green, 1963) 72–76.
[48] Cassian, *Conf*, 13.13; ACW 57:481.
[49] Cassian, *Conf*, 13.7; ACW 57:472.

# 10

# LEO THE GREAT
## FAITH AND VISION

I n 430, the year of Augustine's death, the deacon Leo was one of
Pope Celestine's most trusted advisers. Long residence in Rome
and his acknowledged ability had brought him to the heart of papal
decision making. In his youth Leo had witnessed the sack of the city by
Alaric. He may have met Augustine, who in 418 identified him as bearer
of the letter from former Pelagian sympathizer Sixtus to the bishops of
Africa. As a younger man he befriended John Cassian, who in the year
404 had moved to Rome from Constantinople in search of support for
the exiled John Chrysostom. Pope Celestine benefited from Leo's support during his ten-year struggle against the Pelagians. In 428 the pope
again turned to the able deacon on learning from Cyril of Alexandria
that Nestorius, newly appointed bishop of Constantinople, was refusing
to acknowledge Mary's title of Theotokos, mother of God or God-bearer.

Through his action, Nestorius seemed to signal his denial that there
was a true union of the divine and the human in the person of Jesus.
That the Church's teaching on this matter firmly united east and west is
seen in a late fourth-century letter from the normally pacific Gregory
of Nazianzen. Gregory not only anathematized those who claimed that
"the flesh of Jesus comes from heaven" but declared that the person
who does not believe Mary to be the mother of God is "severed from
the Godhead." He added that anyone asserting that Jesus is not "at once
divinely and humanly formed in her is in like manner Godless."[1]

---

[1] Gregory of Nazianzen, *Letters*, 1.101, trans. Charles Gordon Browne and James
Edward Swallow, NPNF, Second Series, vol. 7 (Grand Rapids, MI: Eerdmans, 1996) 439.

In 429 Leo assembled the documents necessary for a rebuttal of the error and sent them to John Cassian, asking him to compose a refutation.[2] The outcome was Cassian's *On the Incarnation of Our Lord.* Recalling how Leo, "my esteemed and highly regarded friend," had dragged him from "the obscurity of silence," Cassian demonstrates that, in claiming that the Savior "was born a mere man," Nestorius is "repeating what the Pelagians had said before him," thereby subverting belief in the redemption. Indeed, his followers are claiming that Christ came, not to redeem mankind but merely to give an example.[3]

Nestorianism was condemned at a Roman council in 430. A year later, the Council of Ephesus affirmed that the two natures of Christ reside in the single person born of Mary. The council also rejected the Pelagian error.[4] Meanwhile, in the very year of Leo's urgent request to Cassian, there was a dramatic encounter in Patrick's native land between Pelagianism and orthodox belief. The facts are detailed by Prosper, who was not only an admirer of Augustine but an enthusiastic chronicler of Church affairs. In attempting to break down the Church's defenses with the "pelagian battering ram," a certain Agricola had so "insidiously corrupted the churches of Britain with his teachings" that, in 429, Celestine, "through the negotiation of the deacon Palladius," sent Bishop Germanus of Auxerre to that country.

An additional dimension to the story is provided by Constantius, biographer of Germanus, who writes of "a deputation from Britain telling the bishops of Gaul that the heresy of Pelagius had taken hold of the people over a large part of the country and that help ought to be brought to the Catholic faith as soon as possible."[5] The deacon Palladius gained Pope Celestine's blessing for the mission. Arriving in Britain in autumn, the Gauls preached throughout the countryside, refuting the Pelagians' false doctrines in public debate, so that "everywhere faithful Catholics were strengthened in their faith and the lapsed learned the way back to the truth."[6] Prosper expresses the outcome more forcefully, rejoicing that, following "the expulsion of the heretics," Germanus led the Brit-

---

[2] Jedin and Nolan, 2:101.

[3] John Cassian, *On the Incarnation: Against Nestorius*, preface 1, 1.1–5, trans. Edgar C. S. Gibson, NPNF 11 (Grand Rapids, MI: Eerdmans, 1998) 548.

[4] Jedin and Nolan, 2:103–21.

[5] Constantius, *Life of Saint Germanus*, 12; WF 295.

[6] Constantius, *Life of Saint Germanus*, 12, 14; WF 296–97.

ons back to the Catholic faith.[7] Celestine freed their country from the "disease," he says, when he rid it of those "enemies of the grace of God" who had "taken possession as in the land of their birth."[8]

During his stay in Britain, Germanus discovered that there were Irish Christians in need of spiritual leadership. At that time there was a large Irish settlement in what is now southwest Wales. Ogam grave inscriptions in that region and related incisions on grave stones in southeast Ireland confirm accounts of large population movements eastward across the Irish Sea during the fourth and fifth centuries.[9] Germanus would have learned that the faith had reached Ireland through communication between kinship groups in that western part of Roman Britain and their homeland. The many Roman Britons abducted by raiding parties constituted another element of Christian presence in Ireland. Irish trade links with countries like Gaul, Spain, and Britain would also have contributed. Informed of these believers' spiritual needs, Celestine acted promptly.

Prosper records that in 431, just a year after Germanus returned to Gaul, Palladius the deacon was ordained bishop by the pope and sent "to the Irish who believe in Christ as their first bishop." Within a year of this appointment, the enthusiastic Prosper envisaged Celestine's action bringing Ireland, "this pagan nation, to the Christian fold."[10] Celestine's decision and the circumstances surrounding it would have opened the way for many priests to become part of a great spiritual enterprise. With threats to orthodox belief in Britain so recent, Palladius would have been accompanied by clerics whose faith was sound. Patrick was acquainted with the language and customs of the Irish. He was untainted by error. In this novel and unexpected context his lack of education would not have been an insurmountable obstacle. To a humble individual who had long believed that he had been called to serve God in Ireland, it would have represented a heaven-sent opportunity.[11] Writing at the close of the

---

[7] Prosper, *Chronicles*, trans. Liam De Paor, *Saint Patrick's World: The Christian Culture of Ireland's Apostolic Age* (Dublin: Four Courts Press, 1993) 79.

[8] Prosper, *Against Cassian*, 21.1–2; ACW 32:134.

[9] K. H. Jackson, *Language and History in Early Britain* (Edinburgh: University Press, 1971) 154, 21; T. T. M. Charles-Edwards, *Christianity in Roman Britain* (Cambridge: University Press, 2000) 158–76; F. J. Byrne, *Irish Kings and High-Kings* (Dublin: Four Courts Press, 1973) 182–83.

[10] Prosper, *Against Cassian*, 21.2; ACW 32:134.

[11] For differing views on Saint Patrick's dates: R. P. C. Hanson, *Saint Patrick, His Origins and Career* (Oxford: Clarendon Press, 1968) 171–88; David Dumville, ed.,

seventh century and drawing on living tradition, biographer Muirchú claimed that Patrick had been at Auxerre in the time of Germanus and his saintly predecessor, Amator.[12] Both bishops were prayerful and austere, shared a missionary instinct, and promoted monasticism as a means of converting pagans by example.[13]

A patrician link with Gaul is by no means improbable, for it was then customary for individuals to travel vast distances in pursuit of spiritual fulfillment. Martin was born in what is now Hungary, grew up in northern Italy, and died in Gaul in 397. John Cassian, born in Scythia, modern Romania, spent many years as a monk in Bethlehem, lived with the ascetics of the Egyptian desert, was ordained deacon in Constantinople by Saint John Chrysostom, and ended his days in Marseilles. Before arriving in Gaul, he had been in Rome, where he befriended Leo. At Marseilles he established two religious houses, one for men and one for women.

During the time at which Patrick is said to have been at Auxerre, it was common practice for individuals of varied nationalities to populate the monasteries of Gaul. In the year 410 Saint Honoratus headed a famed foundation at Lérins, in the south. A community of men "assembled around him from all parts of the earth through a desire for the service of God, and, differing as much in habits as in language, loved him with one accord. All called him master, all called him father and reckoned that, in him, country, kinsmen and all else were restored to them together." The monks of Lérins were led by a man who, says his biographer, eagerly obeyed the words "sell all you have, give to the poor and then come, follow me."[14] The presence farther north, in Auxerre, of a bishop similarly dedicated to the ascetic ideal would have represented an irresistible attraction for the young Patrick.

It may be presumed that Leo played some part in organizing the missions to Britain and Ireland. Indeed, preoccupation with the Pelagian affair in Britain could explain his plea in 429 for Cassian's assistance in preparing the documentation used to combat the teaching of Nestorius.

---

*Saint Patrick, AD 493–1993* (Woodbridge, Suffolk: Boydell Press, 1993) foreword, 29–50.

[12] Muirchú, *Life of Saint Patrick*; De Paor, 178.

[13] Constantius, *Life of Saint Germanus*, 6; WF 290.

[14] Hilary of Arles, *The Life of Saint Honoratus*, 4.19–21; WF 264–66; see Mark 10:21.

It was fitting, therefore, that when Celestine died in 432, this vigorous and decisive churchman should be found beside the pope's successor, Sixtus III. It was the same Sixtus whose letter had been delivered to the African bishops by Leo fifteen years before, and who had been the recipient of Augustine's letter on Pelagianism. Leo was at his side when, as pope, he received a request from Augustine's former antagonist, the Pelagian Julian of Eclanum, for reinstatement to his see. Prosper the chronicler, who was to become a confidant of the deacon on his accession to the papacy in 440, pointedly notes that, "urged on by the deacon Leo," Sixtus rejected the plea of the still unrepentant Julian.[15]

Leo's commitment to orthodoxy of belief and his continuing influence on Sixtus may account for two further gestures by the pope. When restoring the church of Saint Mary Major, which had suffered in the Visigothic attack of 410, Sixtus commissioned mosaics celebrating the victory over Nestorianism. As an earnest of his faith in the power of baptism to remit sin, a key point of contention between Pelagius and Augustine, he repaired Constantine's baptistery at the Lateran, where he inscribed the metrical inscription extolling grace and baptism which, to this day, continues to affirm his orthodoxy. Among the verses are:

> Here is the source of the water of life
> Which takes away the sins of the world;
> Which springs from the wounded side
> Of our dying Savior.
>
> Here a divine seed gives birth to a holy tribe;
> the spirit of God breathed upon the water and became its
> creator. . . . Those born again to new life are no longer separated by a dividing wall.
> One font, one Spirit and one faith make them one also.[16]

Elected pope on the death of Sixtus in 440, Leo was confronted by further dangers to faith. In Rome itself there were Manichaeans who denied Christ's humanity. "Because they do not believe in his true nativity," said Leo, "they do not accept his true passion. As they do not confess that he was truly buried, they refuse to acknowledge that he is truly

---

[15] Prosper, *Chronicle*, 439; De Paor, 81.
[16] Hartmann Grisar, *History of Rome and the Popes in the Middle Ages*, vol. 2 (London: Kegan Paul, Trench, Trubner, 1912) 24.

risen."[17] Meanwhile, in Constantinople, the monk Eutyches challenged his bishop, Flavian, by teaching the Monophysite doctrine that, since the humanity of Jesus has been absorbed into his divinity, he has one nature only. Flavian sought the support of Rome and in 449 Leo sent him a letter, or tome, condemning the error and defining the true teaching.

To the pope's consternation, a council which assembled at Ephesus reinstated Eutyches, condemned Flavian, and rejected the tome. Denouncing it as the "robber council," Leo resolutely disputed the flawed doctrine. The conflict was resolved in 451 at the Council of Chalcedon, which effectively proclaimed the teaching defined in the pope's letter of 449.[18] Leo observed that the error occurred because those who thought that they were seeking truth had recourse, not to the prophets or apostles or "the authority of the Gospels," but to themselves. By doing so, they ignored the words of the creed which state that Jesus, the only Son of God, "was born eternal, of the Holy Spirit and the virgin Mary."[19]

Containing no theological innovation, Leo's tome is remarkable for its comprehensive yet succinct fidelity to Scripture and tradition. Regarding the incarnation, it encapsulates the Christian belief that in the person of Christ, there are two natures, and that Christ is true Son of God and, as son of Mary, true man; that he is substantially one with the Father in divinity and truly human in all things except sin. The pope clearly identifies the patristic sources of his teaching. On Christ as true God and true man he quotes Hilary of Poitiers, Athanasius, and Ambrose. John Chrysostom and Augustine are cited on Jesus as mediator and savior. Cyril of Alexandria and Gregory are his authorities on the incarnation. It is Chrysostom who enables Leo to express his wonder at what this teaching means for man: "Fragile nature, contemptible nature, and nature shown to be completely inferior overcame all, conquered all and on this day merited being found superior to everything." Indeed, on this day human nature was seen on the throne of God, "ablaze with immortal glory."[20]

It can be readily appreciated why Leo shares with Pope Gregory the distinction of being named "the Great." He was a pastoral bishop whose

---

[17] Leo, S 24.4; FCh 93:95.

[18] Leo, Ep 28; NPNF 12:38–43.

[19] Leo, Ep 28.1–2; NPNF 12:38–39.

[20] Leo, Ep 129.2; NPNF 12:96; Leo, Ep 117; 165; Testimonia 1–25; 18, n. 31, trans. Edmund Hunt, FCh, vol. 34 (Washington, DC: CUAP, 1963) 165, 273–74, 275–88, 282.

sermons centered on the essentials of faith: creation, the fall of man, the incarnation, death and resurrection of Christ, and the coming of the Holy Spirit at Pentecost. He presents a high ideal for human beings, who have been made in God's image "so that they might imitate their creator."[21] Encouraging reflection by Christians on the redemption won by the Son of God, who assumed human nature so that humans, brought low by the fall, would be restored to God's image, Leo asks them to shun the darkness and embrace the true light "which enlightens everyone coming into this world."[22] They can return thanks by loving God but cannot fulfill that duty if they despise their neighbors, who are made in the image of God.

In sermons preached on major feasts of the Church's year, Leo dwelt on creation, the fall of man, and the story of salvation. Convinced that faith should issue in action, he encouraged a response which encompassed concern for the aged, the ill, and the poor. As times of preparation for the feasts of the incarnation and redemption, Advent and Lent were presented as opportunities for generosity and forgiveness.[23] Paul's assurance that "God loves a cheerful giver" was echoed in Leo's statement that by feeding the hungry, clothing the naked, and caring for the sick the kindness of the servant becomes "the gift of" the God who supports suffering human beings through the actions of their fellows.[24] When imitating their creator in this way, creatures become "executors of divine work." Indeed, through their works of mercy, they minister to Christ himself.

Like the generation of fathers who preceded him, Leo prized the ascetic life. No so far from Saint Peter's Basilica he established a monastery named for Saints John and Paul.[25] Preaching on the first beatitude, Leo reminds his listeners that the disciples, after their conversion, in imitation of the Lord, offered an example of "magnanimous poverty," and that many in the early Church followed them by disposing of goods and possessions and leading simple lives. Such faithfulness to the Gospel

---

[21] Leo, S 12.1; FCh 93:49–50.

[22] Leo, SS 25.5, 27.6; FCh 93:102–3, 114–15; see John 1:9.

[23] Leo, SS 12.2–3, 89.5; FCh 93:50–52, 378.

[24] Leo, S 43.4; FCh 93:189; see 1 Cor 16:2; 2 Cor 7–9.

[25] *The Book of Pontiffs (Liber Pontificalis): The Ancient Biographies of the First Ninety Roman Bishops to AD 715*, trans. Raymond Davis (Liverpool: Liverpool University Press, 1989) 38.

requires similar exemplary service from bishops and priests, whose duty is "to have an unbiased care for everything that benefits both learned and unlearned" in the Church.[26] Leo is echoing the teaching of earlier fathers like Jerome, who, in quoting Paul's assertion that "he who desires the office of bishop desires a good work," adds that it is the glory of a bishop to be humble and "provide for the needs of the poor."[27]

Augustine too is emphatic that the name of bishop is "the name of a task, not an honor."[28] Though his works brought him fame in his lifetime, Augustine's primary concern, in his see of Hippo, was to share the message of the Gospel with his people and fulfill his "onerous duties" as bishop.[29] Ever aware of the need for exemplary service, Leo tells bishops not to "depart from that rule of faith which was outspokenly maintained by your ancestors and ours," but to teach what "the fathers of revered memory taught." He asks Proterius of Alexandria to exhort the people and clergy to make progress in the faith, "in such a way that you are teaching nothing new."[30] Leo also warns that unworthy churchmen endanger the Lord's flock, "for the integrity of the rulers is the safeguard of those who are under them." Even where a prelate's life is beyond reproach, if his appointment involves intrigue, it is "pernicious from the mere example of its beginning."[31]

Leo spoke of his "grief and vexation" that the bishops of Mauretania in Africa were bowing to social pressures and appointing unworthy candidates to the episcopate. There was a rebuke for the bishops of Campania, who were performing baptisms without due preparation.[32] The bishop of Aquileia was told that every priest should persevere in the place for which he was ordained and not be "drawn away by ambition, seduced by greed or corrupted by the influence of men." When the highly respected Hilary of Arles, biographer of Honoratus of Lérins, caused dissension by meddling in the affairs of other sees, Leo disciplined him and denied his claim to metropolitan rights.[33] Reproving Anastasius of Thessalonica for exacerbating divisions in his diocese, Leo asked for

[26] Leo, SS 95.3, 94.1; FCh 93:396–97, 391.
[27] Saint Jerome, Ep 69.8; NPNF 6:147.
[28] Augustine, *City of God*, 19.19; Bettenson, 880; see 1 Tim 3:1.
[29] Augustine, *On the Work of Monks*, 37.29; FCh 14:385–86.
[30] Leo, Ep 129.1.2; NPNF 12:96.
[31] Leo, Ep 12.1; NPNF 12:12.
[32] Leo, Epp 12.1–2, 168; NPNF 12:12–13, 112.
[33] Leo, Epp 1.5, 10.2; NPNF 12:2, 9.

urgent efforts to heal them. Were the disagreements to become so bitter as to defy resolution, "all must be referred to us, with the minutes of your proceedings attested, that all ambiguities may be removed, and what is pleasing to God decided."[34]

Following the tradition of the fathers, Leo was conscious of the spiritual authority exercised by the episcopate. It was as bishop that Augustine asked his people to attend to his "commands, admonitions, and entreaties."[35] Jerome noted that the Greek term *episkopos* represents the protective and guiding oversight possessed by each prelate, observing that neither wealth nor poverty makes a person more or less a bishop, for "all alike are successors of the apostles."[36] Theirs is the power to ordain, and "the Holy Spirit descends at the bishop's prayer."[37] The humble Patrick, "God's ambassador in my lowliness," asserted his episcopal status to Coroticus by declaring, "I believe with complete certainty that it is from God that I received what I am."[38] So confident is he of his spiritual authority that he adds, "It is not my words that I have set forth in Latin, but the words of God and of his apostles and prophets, who have never lied."[39]

As bishop of Rome, Leo claimed the episcopal primacy which comes from Peter, who first occupied the see of Rome.[40] In doing so he encouraged and supported bishops who were suffering opposition or disillusionment. He sympathized with Rusticus of Narbonne, whose vexations closely resembled Patrick's. Threatened by "the perversity of the disobedient and the barbs of slanderers," Rusticus wished to resign his see. Attempting to restore his resolve, Leo counseled fortitude. He likened the bishop to a helmsman without whom the ship cannot be guided through the waves, a shepherd whose absence would leave the sheep vulnerable to wolves, or a watchman whose presence deters robbers and thieves. His episcopal advice was firm and inspiring:

[34] Leo, Ep 14; NPNF 12:19.
[35] Augustine, S 196.4; FCh 38:47.
[36] Jerome, Ep 146.1; NPNF 6:289.
[37] Jerome, *Dialogue against the Luciferians*, 9, trans. W. H. Fremantle, NPNF, vol. 6 (Grand Rapids, MI: Eerdmans, 1996) 324.
[38] Patrick, *Conf*, 56; Conneely, 75; *Letter to Coroticus*, 1; Conneely, 77.
[39] Patrick, *Letter to Coroticus*, 20; Conneely, 81.
[40] Leo, Ep 56.1; NPNF 12:57–58.

One must abide, therefore, in the office committed to him and in the task undertaken. Justice must be steadfastly upheld and mercy lovingly extended. Not men, but their sins must be hated. The proud must be rebuked, the weak must be borne with . . . above all, if the worst comes, let us not be terror-stricken as if we have to overcome disaster through our own strength, since both our counsel and our strength is Christ, and while through him we can do all things, without him we can do nothing.[41]

Rusticus was reminded that "all who live Godly lives shall suffer persecution," and that, for a bishop, the direst persecution is often inflicted by "persistent disobedience and the barbs of ill-natured tongues." The letter was written around the time that Patrick was suffering similar adversity. Its contents suggest that, had Leo been informed of that bishop's plight, he would have reproved the proud prelates and clerics who had so cruelly humiliated a man whom they deemed unfit for office. Unlike the spiteful clerics, the pope would not have regarded Patrick's lack of learning as an impediment to consecration. Reflecting on the qualities required in emissaries of Christ, Leo recalls Saint Paul's observation that Jesus, when preparing to call all nations to the light of faith, did not choose his apostles "from among philosophers or orators, but from the lowly and from fishermen." It is not the "wisdom of words" that is needed to preach the "foolishness" of the cross, but "the power of God."[42]

Leo's words, so pauline in tone, are drawn from the very passage of Corinthians that most comforted Patrick, who, on reading them, was able, "in awe and reverence," to work uncomplainingly for the people whom he would "humbly and sincerely serve to the end."[43] A sympathetic reader of the Confession must harbor the hope that word of the injustices suffered by the lowly bishop reached the ears of a spiritual leader who was so well informed on conditions in the universal Church, and that an entry in the Annals of Ulster for the year 441 represents the pope's considered rebuke to his enemies: "When Leo was ordained forty-second bishop of the Roman church, Patrick the bishop was approved in the Catholic faith."[44]

---

[41] Leo, Ep 167.1–2; NPNF 12:108–9; see 2 Tim 3:12.
[42] Leo, Ep 164.2; NPNF 12:106; see 1 Cor 1:17–25; Patrick, Conf, 11–13; Bieler, 25.
[43] Patrick, Conf, 13; Bieler, 25.
[44] Annals of Ulster, 441; De Paor, 118.

# 11

# THE CHURCH AND THE PAGANS

Throughout the patristic period, the good news of salvation was preached with vigor and assurance, but the Church of the time tended to confine its ministry to the inhabitants of an empire under constant pressure from without. This did not signify rejection of Christ's call to convert all peoples, but recognition that much of the Roman world remained firmly pagan. Indeed, when Pope Gregory initiated the conversion of the English a century and a half after Leo's death, he was not opening a new mission field but was restoring the faith to a part of the old empire which had become pagan through invasion.

In the fourth and fifth centuries the primary concern of bishops was the spiritual welfare of Christians in towns and their immediate hinterland. The unbelievers in the more distant regions moved only gradually toward belief. Martin of Tours was one of the few who ventured into the remotest reaches of his see to challenge the traditional beliefs of the forest dwellers. His encounters with the idols of the Gauls led many to the faith. Sulpicius Severus recounts one hair-raising exploit, entailing the bishop's proposed destruction of a sacred tree. There was initial resistance, then a challenge that Martin demonstrate his faith in the power of God by lying before the tree while it was felled. As the huge pine toppled, he held up his hand, and, "after the manner of a spinning top, the tree swept round to the opposite side, to such a degree that it almost crushed the country people." In the wake of this risky triumph the brethren accompanying him understandably "wept for joy." Martin's biographer notes that almost all the pagans present decided to become catechumens.[1]

[1] Sulpicius Severus, *Life of Saint Martin*, 13; WF 26–28.

Martin was not alone in pursuing such conversions. The biographer of Germanus of Auxerre relates that, as pastor of a region infiltrated by barbarian tribes, the bishop provided them with "two roads to Christ." One involved the normal "ministrations" of the Church, the other a monastery, founded within sight of the town, so that the surrounding population "might be brought to the Catholic faith" by experiencing the good example of the brethren.[2] Germanus's approach to his mission represents a possible model for Patrick's promotion of the asceticism which drew many pagan Irish to Christian belief.

Another Gaulish bishop, Victricius, who, like Martin, was a former soldier, evangelized the pagans in his border see of Rouen. Paulinus of Nola lauded his successes: "In the land of the Morini, at the edge of the world battered by a deafening ocean with its wild waves, the people of those distant races . . . now rejoice in the light which, through your saintly person, has risen before them from the Lord." Paulinus marveled that land which was once pagan wilderness now harbored worshipping communities and monasteries "harmonious in peace and thronged by revered, angelic choruses of saintly men."[3] They are words reminiscent of Patrick's claim that, in pagan Ireland, "the flock of the Lord is flourishing so well that the sons of the Irish and the daughters of their kings who have become monks and nuns are beyond my power to number."[4]

In the course of the fourth and fifth centuries occasional instances of conversion in lands beyond the empire tended to arise from extreme circumstances such as war or invasion. Captivity in Ireland had engendered in Patrick a desire to evangelize its people. Germanus's discovery of Irish Christians in southwest Britain proved to be a stepping-stone to their cousins across the sea. Leo, as Celestine's deacon, would have played a part in organizing this mission. Later, as pope, he was alive to the providential conversion of barbarian peoples from darkness to the light of the Gospel message. Preaching on the feast of Saints Peter and Paul in the year 441, he rejoiced that, though pagan Rome had conquered many peoples, Christianity now prevailed over an area which was even greater than that of the empire. Triumphantly addressing Rome herself, he claimed that "what the labors of war have subjected to you is less than what the peace of Christ has subdued."

[2] Constantius, *Life of Saint Germanus*, 6; WF 290.
[3] Paulinus of Nola, Ep 18.4–7; ACW 35:170–74.
[4] Patrick, *Letter to Coroticus*, 12; Conneely, 79.

Grateful that, in his own time, the Church's mission is beginning to extend beyond the empire's bounds, Leo notes that Rome, whose conquest of so many nations had made their conversion possible, was herself "enslaved by the errors of them all" and had to be led to Christian belief.[5] Ten years later, in his *Call of All Nations*, Prosper of Aquitaine, now an intimate of Leo's, echoed the pope's sentiments. In the empire's expansion he saw God's providential means of bringing the fruits of Christ's redemptive actions to all peoples without distinction. Adapting Leo's words, he concluded:

> But the grace of Christianity is not content with the boundaries that are Rome's. Grace has now brought under the scepter of the cross of Christ many peoples whom Rome could not subject with her arms. Now Rome, by her primacy of the apostolic priesthood, has become greater as the citadel of religion than as the seat of power.[6]

Prosper and Leo could justly celebrate such missionary successes but would have acknowledged some disasters. One involved the conversion of the eastern Goths by Ulfilas. Son of Christian parents who had been captured by the barbarians, Ulfilas in the year 341 joined a Gothic mission to the eastern imperial capital, Constantinople. While there, he was consecrated bishop by Eusebius of Nicomedia, an ardent Arian and inexorable opponent of the orthodox Anastasius. Ulfilas became a successful missionary among his father's barbarian countrymen in Dacia, the Balkan region north of the Danube. When pressure from the Huns later forced the tribes across that river into territory controlled by Rome, the Goths brought with them the Arian faith in which their forebears had been instructed by Ulfilas. Later, with the disintegration of the empire, the heresy was carried by the invaders as far as Italy, Spain, and Augustine's Africa. One of the most prominent Arians was Auxentius, the bishop who preceded Ambrose in the see of Milan.

Despite such setbacks, the Church was able to celebrate her successes, one of them the ready reception of the Gospel message by the Irish. In exploring the mysterious ways in which God achieves his pur-

---

[5] Leo, S 82.1–2; FCh 93:352–54.
[6] Prosper of Aquitaine, *The Call of All Nations*, 16; trans. P. De Letter, ACW, no. 14 (London: Longmans, Green, 1952) 120.

pose, Prosper, in his *Call of All Nations*, presents some instances of the interaction of providence and grace spreading the Gospel. There are the barbarians serving in the Roman army who, becoming Christians, carry the faith back to their native lands. There are even "some sons of the Church, made prisoners by the enemy, who changed their masters into servants of the Gospel, and by teaching them the faith, became the superiors of their own wartime lords."[7] In Ireland, Patrick too saw God's grace at work, for by no other means could a former captive have brought salvation to those who had enslaved him. It enhanced the sense of destiny which caused him to tell Coroticus that he was a sharer with those "called and predestined to preach the Gospel."[8]

It is fitting that one who was close to Leo, and a chronicler of the mission of Palladius to the Irish, should make an observation so close to Patrick's account of his metamorphosis from slave to revered bishop of the Irish people.[9] Prosper believed, like Patrick, that "nothing can prevent God's grace from accomplishing his will, for he makes even of dissensions a bond of union and turns misfortunes into remedies; thus, where the Church feared danger, there she finds her expansion."[10] Perceiving in such paradoxes and ironies evidence of God's providential design, Leo followed his mentor Augustine in noting that, while the Roman Empire was founded on the blood of one brother spilled by another, the spiritual kingdom was built on truth.[11] He would have relished the contrast between Patrick's peaceful conquest of the Irish and that other victory briefly contemplated in the late first century by Agricola, pagan Roman Governor of Britain, who, according to his son-in-law, Tacitus, felt that Ireland could be taken by "a single legion and a fair contingent of irregulars."[12]

Patrick's mission was undertaken in the conviction that he was acting in concert with the apostles, who, like him, had responded to the words "Follow me and I will make you fishers of men."[13] In his youth he had been banished to the "uttermost parts of the earth," to which he later returned,

---

[7] Prosper of Aquitaine, *Call of All Nations*, 2.33; ACW 14:146.

[8] Patrick, *Letter to Coroticus*, 6; Conneely, 78; see Acts 13:47; Isa 49:6.

[9] Patrick, *Conf*, 15; Bieler, 25.

[10] Prosper, *Call of All Nations*, 2.33; ACW 14:146.

[11] Leo, S 82.1; FCh 93:353; Augustine, *City of God*, 3.6; Bettenson, 93–94.

[12] Tacitus, *Agricola*, 24, trans. W. Peterson (London: William Heinemann Ltd., 1980) 71.

[13] Patrick, *Conf*, 40; Conneely, 71; see Matt 4:19.

fulfilling the divine plan revealed in Acts and Isaiah: "I have set you to be a light for the Gentiles, so that you may bring salvation to the uttermost parts of the earth." He found confirmation of his providential role in the prophecy of Jeremiah: "To you the nations will come from the uttermost parts of the earth and say, 'Our fathers got for themselves worthless idols, and there is no profit in them.' "[14] The cost, willingly borne, was to "endure insults from unbelievers, to hear myself taunted for being a foreigner, to experience many persecutions unto bonds, and to surrender my free-born status for the benefit of others." By introducing himself to Coroticus as "God's ambassador," he identified with Paul, apostle to the Gentiles, who asked the Ephesians to pray that he, an ambassador of the Gospel in chains, might be able to speak without fear. Seeing God smile on his efforts, Patrick declared himself "exceedingly in debt" to the One who had granted him "so great a grace."[15]

The tenacity of faith and endeavor of humble ascetics like Martin and Patrick engendered a spiritual appeal which inexorably attracted unbelievers, as when Martin's approach to Chartres on one occasion brought "vast numbers of pagans, streaming from far and wide across the open fields," to meet him. After hearing his words, all became catechumens.[16] Patrick's witness won the "multitudinous people" whom he baptized and confirmed as a "hunter and fisher" for Christ. The successful missions of both bishops suggest the irresistible attraction of lives lived in Gospel simplicity and acceptance of God's will. Patrick puts it well: "We are gravely bound, therefore, to spread our nets, so that a great multitude and throng should be caught for God."[17] Sulpicius compares Martin to the apostles and prophets, "for the power of his faith and the works of power that he accomplished show him to have been like them in everything."[18] The same could be said of Patrick.

Commitment to God's service brought Martin and Patrick daily dangers which they faced with faith. Once, prompted by a dream, Martin set out for Italy to convert his pagan parents. On the way he was attacked by robbers, bound, stripped, and almost dispatched by an axe blow. He

---

[14] Patrick, *Conf*, 38; Conneely, 71; see Acts 13:47; Isa 49:6; Jer 16:19–21.

[15] Patrick, *Conf*, 37–38; Conneely, 71; *Letter to Coroticus*, 5; Conneely, 77; see Eph 6:19–20.

[16] Sulpicius Severus, *Dialogues*, 2.4; WF 107.

[17] Patrick, *Conf*, 38–40; Conneely, 71; *Letter to Coroticus*, 11; Conneely, 79.

[18] Sulpicius Severus, *Dialogues*, 2.5; WF 108.

not only survived but converted one of his attackers.[19] On another occasion, while walking along a country road in Gaul with his companions, he encountered a military convoy. At the sight of the approaching figure in monk's coarse tunic, "with black cloak swaying," the pack mules took fright and became entangled in the traces. The furious soldiers "proceeded to belabor Martin with whips and sticks." When his brethren found him, he was "lying almost lifeless on the ground, smeared with blood and with wounds all over his body." On coming to their senses, the attackers begged the bishop's forgiveness. It was granted at once.[20]

Patrick, in pursuing his mission, invariably gained the acquiescence and support of local rulers and was escorted by young noblemen as he moved from one petty kingdom to another, but even these precautions could be ineffective. Once he and his brethren were imprisoned by kings with whom he was negotiating. Death seemed imminent, but, "on the fourteenth day, the Lord freed me from their power." Patrick and his helpers were saved, he says, because "my time had not yet come." Even late in life he is adamant that no peril will ever deter him from serving God faithfully: "Daily I expect to be slaughtered, defrauded, reduced to slavery, or to any condition that time and surprise may bring." In all his travails, he claims, he has never suffered fear, nor will he, for he has cast himself "into the hands of Almighty God, who rules everywhere."[21]

Subject to such dangers, Patrick and Martin should have won praise from fellow churchmen, but their activities provoked the incomprehension of colleagues happy to confine their attention to believers within the empire. The rigors of their early lives would have prepared them for their challenging ministries, with Patrick being particularly inured to the hardships incidental to working among pagan peoples. Other members of the mission to Ireland would not have come to terms so readily with life in that remote, pre-urbanized society. Implicit in biographer Muirchú's description of Patrick's northward journey by sea from Inber Dee in the south, by way of Inis Padraig to Strangford Lough and Saul, is the danger of traveling through hostile and heavily forested terrain. Such an existence would have been barely tolerable to individuals accustomed to Roman roads and living conditions.

---

[19] Sulpicius Severus, *Life of Saint Martin*, 5; WF 17–18.
[20] Sulpicius Severus, *Dialogues*, 2.3; WF 105–6.
[21] Patrick, *Conf*, 52, 55; Conneely, 74, 75.

It is a factor that may account for the dearth of information about the mission of Palladius. Plucked by circumstance from a senior ministry on the European mainland, the former deacon and his entourage would have been ill-prepared for life in Ireland. In his biography of Patrick, Muirchú draws on a tradition that the Gaulish bishop spent only a short time in the country. Unable to endure life among "wild and obdurate people who did not readily accept his doctrine," he retreated across the sea, ending his life in the territory of the Britons, presumably among the Irish colonists of the southwest.[22]

It is ironic that, as news of occasional missionary successes in barbarian lands reached Rome in the fifth century, pagan superstitions and practices were persisting there. Even during Patrick's childhood and Augustine's early manhood the city had been a bastion of the old religions, with some of the great patrician families clinging to the ancient ways. It was the murmuring of these aristocratic pagans after the sack of Rome in 410 that caused Augustine to write the *City of God*. Earlier, paganism had suffered a setback when the emperor Gratian removed the altar and statue of the god of victory from the senate house. Priests and vestal virgins of the cult lost their privileges and financial support. There were protests from pagan senators. In 384 a petition was presented to Gratian's successor by Symmachus, prefect of Rome, who in the same year recommended the young Augustine for the position of public orator in Milan.

In a subtle and moving plea for restoration of pagan rites in the senate, the cultivated prefect begged the emperor to listen to Rome herself. She asked for nothing more, he claimed, than the reverence due her great age, recognition of her dominion over the whole world, and acknowledgment of her victories in so many battles, all of which had been due to her ancient worship. Asking that the native gods of Rome be spared, he concluded with persuasive rhetoric:

> We look on the same stars, the heaven is common to us all; we are embraced by the same world. Does it matter by what means each of us reaches for Truth? We cannot arrive at such a great secret by a single way. This argument rightly relates to persons who can pursue it. We now offer prayers, not arguments.[23]

---

[22] Muirchú, *Life of Saint Patrick*, De Paor, 179.

[23] James Stevenson, *Creeds, Councils and Controversies* (London: SPCK, 1989) 120–22.

When the petition reached the court in Milan, capital of the western empire, the city's bishop, Ambrose, hurriedly wrote a letter contesting Symmachus's case. Reminding Emperor Valentinian II that the Roman pagans had bitterly persecuted Christians, he claimed that no Christian ruler could, in conscience, erect a pagan altar in the senate house and force Christian senators to be present at worship.[24] The young emperor and his council ruled against Symmachus and the pagans.

By the early fifth century, Christianity was the sole religion recognized by the Roman state, yet the influence of the old beliefs persisted. Augustine occasionally engaged in discussion and debate, or communicated by letter, with educated adherents of the pagan cults. In the years 414 and 415 one such exchange, with Volusianus, a committed pagan and member of the highest nobility of Rome, was inconclusive.[25] However, just before his death in 437, while he was serving as ambassador to Constantinople, this learned Roman converted to Christianity.

The immediate concern of Augustine, as bishop, was the lingering pagan influence on the Christians of Hippo. His sermons are punctuated by warnings that believers should guard against the pernicious influence of ancient cults, especially when expressed in public spectacles. He even dwells on this danger in the *City of God*.[26] Before becoming bishop, Augustine had preached against the feasting and drinking which had intruded into the people's celebration of the local martyrs' feasts. Warning against pagan beliefs in general, he reminded his still vulnerable congregation that "God made the sun, but man, by fashioning an image of the sun, exchanges the truth of God for a lie."[27] In a letter to the citizens of Madaura, he regrets that, though crumbling, the pagan idols still find a place in their hearts. He asks them to look beyond, to the "Creator and First Cause," from whom "all things seen by us derive their being."[28]

Almost two decades after Augustine's death, the old superstitions and practices persisted in Rome. Preaching in "the basilica of the blessed apostle Peter" on Christmas Day 447, Pope Leo reminded his people that God's descent into human affairs had elevated them to the level of the divine, so that "iniquity turns back into innocence, oldness into

---

[24] Ambrose, Ep 8; FCh 26:37–51.
[25] Augustine, Ep 132, 135, 137; NPNF 1:470, 471, 473.
[26] Augustine, *City of God*, 2.26; Bettenson, 82–83.
[27] Augustine, S 197; FCh 38:52.
[28] Augustine, Ep 232.5; NPNF 1:586.

newness; strangers come into adoption and foreigners enter upon an inheritance." Conscious of his listeners' knowledge that, on the very day of their celebration of Christ's nativity, the pagans of the empire had formerly observed the Mithraic festival of the unconquered sun, he warned them against the traps that Satan, the "ancient enemy," would lay for them. By transforming himself into an angel of light, the evil one has the capacity to present evil as good and make attractive the very errors which they have renounced. Leo claims that there are even some Christians who, on coming to Saint Peter's basilica, "climbing the steps to the upper level . . . turning themselves around toward the rising sun, bow down to honor its shining disc." He deplores these remaining signs of the spirit of paganism. Exhibited at a place dedicated to the one true God, they represent a "damnable perversion."[29]

In the light of the pope's words, it is ironic that, even at that time, Rome's citizens were still celebrating the coming of spring by observing the Lupercalia, a pagan festival which was not discontinued till 494, in the pontificate of Pope Gelasius. These activities lent urgency to the fathers' efforts to foster the redemptive process. In Ireland, Patrick experienced daily the stark contrast between Christian and pagan beliefs, the gulf between Satan's malevolence and the grace of God, so vividly illustrated in the account of his escape from slavery. After a three-day sea crossing, he and his pagan companions made their way through a landscape devastated by war. With starvation imminent, Patrick's prayer for God's help led them to a herd of wild pigs.[30] As the pagans worshipped their gods in thanksgiving, the young man stood apart. Awakening in the night, Patrick, unable to move a limb, felt Satan fall on him "like a huge rock." It was then that, "ignorant in spirit," he called upon "Helios" and saw the sun rise in the heavens.

Representing a disturbing dual awareness of the presence of evil and the need for God, Patrick's dramatic experience was worthy of articulation by Augustine. Turning to the Scriptures as he recalls the incident, the aged bishop realizes that God had been protecting him: "And I believe that I was aided by Christ my Lord, and that his spirit was even then crying out on my behalf." It was not Helios, the sun, that he had invoked, but Elias, or Elijah, the prophet who, at his death, was met by

---

[29] Leo, S 27.2–5; FCh 93:111–14.
[30] Patrick, *Conf*, 19; Conneely, 67.

a chariot of fire and brought to heaven in a whirlwind. In the motion of the fiery chariot Patrick sees an image of his own journey to join the one true God, while Helios, perversely worshipped by heathens, remains a mere part of God's creation.[31]

Patrick is reminding his people of the parallels between Irish pagans and the biblical king Ahab, who worshipped Baal, the Canaanite god. Ahab's idolatry was so discredited by Elijah that its former adherents, falling on their faces, cried out, "The LORD indeed is God; the LORD indeed is God."[32] It is an appropriate image, for Patrick, like Martin and the apostles, is toppling the vain beliefs and natural idols of the pagans and replacing them with worship of the one true God.

Just over two centuries after Patrick's death, his biographer Muirchú presented another, better known, image of this triumph over evil. As the bishop was celebrating Easter by kindling the Paschal fire "truly bright and blessed," he was confronted by the contrasting darkness represented by the pagan priests of Tara. Blessed by him, the Easter light shone in the night, overcoming the murky flames kindled by the pagan priests, who had been summoned by Laoghaire, the Irish Nebuchadnezzar, to Tara, "their Babylon."[33]

Toward the end of the *Confession*, Patrick issues a warning that, by worshipping the sun, which, as part of God's creation, is essentially good, pagans transform it into a demonic symbol: "for that sun which we see rises daily at God's command for our sake; but it will never reign, nor will its splendor abide; but all who adore it will come, as unhappy men, unhappily to punishment." Harmony with God and nature can be attained only by those who put God first. The bishop reassures fellow Christians who have turned their backs on false beliefs and practices by reminding them that, though surrounded by people who still adore the sun, "we who believe in the true Sun, Christ, and adore him, will never perish. And neither will he who does his will; but he will abide for ever, as Christ abides for ever, he who with God the Almighty Father and with the Holy Spirit reigns before all ages, as now, and for ever and ever. Amen."[34]

---

[31] Patrick, *Conf*, 20; Conneely, 67; see 2 Kgs 2:11.

[32] 1 Kgs 18:39.

[33] Muirchú, *Life of Saint Patrick*, De Paor, 183.

[34] Patrick, *Conf*, 60; Conneely, 76; see Ps 104:4; Col 2:3.

# 12

# RENEWAL AND ASCETICISM
## GREGORY THE GREAT

L eo the Great was pope for twenty-one years. He had exercised his ministry against a backdrop of constant social strife. In the decades following his death in 461, barbarian invaders consolidated their hold on the west, forging new kingdoms from the ruins of the empire. In 475 the last western emperor was replaced by Odoacer, an Arian Ostrogoth, who became king of Italy. Theoderic, Odoacer's successor, brought relative stability till his death in 526. Although the eastern emperor Justinian reclaimed Italy from the Goths in 556, within fourteen years the Lombards were harrying and occupying extensive regions of the country. From the mid-fifth century, when Franks were replacing Visigoths as masters of Gaul, much of Spain was under Gothic rule. The African provinces were controlled by the Vandals until their defeat by Belisarius in 534.

Most invaders on the European mainland were Arian Christians. Some, like the Franks, were pagans. In the kingdom of the Franks, the baptism of Clovis in 496 brought neither peaceful ways nor regard for Church teaching as the king's successors were immersed in bloody internecine warfare, which persisted through several generations. Christian faith and practice suffered. Patronage of the Church by the new leaders brought further spiritual decline, as many churchmen succumbed to material inducements.

*On the Ruin of Britain*, by Gildas, a sixth-century churchman, paints a grim picture of his country's plight during that period. As Roman forces were withdrawn in the early fifth century, "hordes" of Irish and Pictish raiders had come "like dark throngs of worms that wriggle out of narrow fissures in the rocks when the sun is high and the weather grows warm."[1] Initially summoned as protectors, the pagan Saxons, like "wolves to the fold," noted their hosts' weakness and began to settle the country by force.[2] In prophetic mode, Gildas perceived divine retribution for the behavior of contemporaries who, like Simon Magus, did not hesitate to "purchase the office of bishop or priest for a worldly price."[3] Within a short time of Gildas's death in 570 the culture and religion of Roman Britain survived only in the western and northern fringes of a country which was awaiting its turn to be re-evangelized. However, in most countries, the Church, though battered and bruised by barbarian inroads, was achieving a precarious survival because many of the incoming regimes valued its contribution to the stability of the new order. The Roman system of law and administration was generally retained for the same reason.

Meanwhile, though the religious leaders in the east were enjoying the patronage of the emperor in Constantinople, religion there was not prospering. Its most serious reverses were caused by theological disputes and imperial interference. Even the monasteries were divided. Court circles were influenced by Monophysites, who recognized in the person of Christ only a single, divine nature. Bishops sympathetic to the error were appointed to important eastern sees. Then, through the intervention of Emperor Justinian, a weak and venal pope was forced to attend a council whose pronouncements caused a schism in the year 553.

Promise of recovery and renewal came in 590 when Gregory was elected to the see of Rome, where conditions were reminiscent of those which followed the city's fall in 410. In an early letter to the clergy of Milan, the pope responded to the magnitude of the crisis: "Thus we see before our eyes the evils which we long ago heard should come upon the world, and the very regions of the earth have become as pages of a book to us."[4] Reflecting in his *Dialogues* on the contemporary scene, Gregory records Bishop Redemptus's vision of the world's end, a vision which was shortly followed by the Lombards' descent on Italy. He paints a terrifying picture of a land whose population, "grown vast, like a rich

---

[1] Gildas, *The Ruin of Britain*, 19.1; trans. M. Winterbottom (London: Phillimore, 1978) 23.

[2] Gildas, 23.2; Winterbottom, 26.

[3] Gildas, 66–68; Winterbottom, 52–54.

[4] Gregory the Great, Ep 3.29; NPNF 12:129.

harvest of grain," was cut down to wither away. "Cities were sacked, fortifications overthrown, churches burned, monasteries and cloisters destroyed. Farms were abandoned and the countryside, uncultivated, became a wilderness. Wild beasts roamed."[5] The pope concludes by begging believers to shun the exclusively material and seek what is eternal.

That Gregory's apocalyptic language did justice to the awful realities of the time is confirmed by an independent account of his installation. Writing to Gregory of Tours, the deacon Agilulf painted a harrowing picture. With its walls already damaged by the Lombards, Rome was so devastated by floods that ancient churches had collapsed and the papal granaries had been destroyed. Plague and famine were ravaging the population. The pope moved quickly to reassure the citizens and assuage the panic that had seized them. Asking them to turn to God and remember the divine invitation to "call upon me in the day of trouble and I will deliver you and you will glorify me," he led them on an intercessory and calming procession through the streets.[6]

Gregory the Great was uniquely equipped to arrest the decline in Christian faith and practice. Of patrician parentage and with a good education, he had been a civil administrator before being appointed prefect of Rome. Around 573, at the age of thirty, he donated his family estates in Sicily to the Church, then founded and endowed seven monasteries. Selling his remaining property and possessions, and using the proceeds to support the poor, he entered the community of Saint Andrew's as a simple monk. Gregory of Tours expressed his admiration: "He who till then had been in the habit of processing through the city in silken robes sewn with glittering gems, now served at the Lord's altar in a fustian gown."[7] In 579 Gregory was ordained deacon and sent as the pope's representative to the imperial court at Constantinople.

Later, as bishop of Rome, Gregory saw the harmony of creation overthrown by man's negligence and sought a cure for the Church's many ills. A self-proclaimed follower of Augustine, he believed that renewal would come through the witness of a devoted clergy and the prayers of a dedicated ascetic brotherhood. With a spiritual mandate

---

[5] Gregory the Great, *Dialogues*, 3.38, trans. Odo John Zimmerman, FCh, vol. 39 (Washington, DC: CUAP, 1983) 186; Ep 3.29; NPNF 12:129.

[6] Gregory of Tours, *History of the Franks*, 10.1, trans. Lewis Thorpe (London: Penguin Books, 1983) 546.

[7] Gregory of Tours, *History*, 10.1; Thorpe, 544.

which embraced countries as far apart as Spain and Syria, he wrote the *Pastoral Care*, in which those who feel called to "the government of souls" are asked not to undertake that "art of arts" rashly. Individuals who have the gifts and are worthy of the office should accept pastoral responsibility. They must be firm in wisdom and patience, "gentle in the grace of loving kindness, strict and unbending in justice."[8]

It is the spiritual leader's duty to "touch the hearts" of his hearers as a skilled harpist creates a harmonious melody. As a physician of souls, he must heal a variety of spiritual ills. Gregory insists that bishops, the successors of the apostles, should willingly "set an ideal of living" by leading truly spiritual lives and rejecting all worldly prosperity.[9] He warns that no one does more harm in the Church than those who "trample on" the spiritual precepts they have studied with skill, belying by their conduct "what they teach by words." When such a pastor walks "through steep places, the flock following him comes to a precipice."[10]

Gregory himself set an example of pastoral concern. Endlessly patient, he found no detail of Church life unworthy of his attention. He promoted frequent diocesan meetings aimed at pastoral care and the correction of abuses. In his letters he reproved churchmen whose actions fell short of the Christian ideal. Maximianus of Syracuse was chided for excommunicating the aged and chronically ill Abbot Eusebius. On succeeding the recently deposed Anastasius, John of Corinth was asked to deal resolutely with the problems which he had inherited.[11] The bishop of Salona was rebuked for neglecting his pastoral duties and "giving himself to feasting."[12] Gregory showed constant concern for the wellbeing of others. Bishops facing difficulties, pastoral and personal, were offered support and sympathy. Advice, even prescriptions for fellow pastors' ailments, came from a man racked by chronic pain and severe digestive problems.

The first monk to be elected pope, Gregory accepted the responsibility of his new office but regretted what he had lost. During his early days in the office, "immersed in earthly cares," he looked back longingly

---

[8] Gregory the Great, *Pastoral Care*, 1.1, trans. Henry Davis, ACW 11 (Westminster, MD: Newman Press, 1950) 21.

[9] Gregory the Great, *Pastoral Care*, 1.5, 1.10, 3. Prologue; ACW 11:29–30, 38, 89.

[10] Gregory the Great, *Pastoral Care*, 1.2; ACW 11; 23–24.

[11] Gregory the Great, Epp 2.34, 5.52; NPNF 12:110–11, 181.

[12] Gregory the Great, Ep 2.18; NPNF 12:103.

to the life he had left behind: "Brought back into the world, I have lost the deep joys of my quiet." He confessed that, "tied by the chains of this dignity," he is stricken by such great sorrow that he can hardly speak.[13] However, like Augustine, who had also expressed a preference for a life of work, reading, prayer, and study of Scripture in a monastic setting, Gregory readily assumed the burden of being a bishop, while leading a semimonastic life.[14] The monks whom he later elevated to the episcopate could rely on the same sympathetic, yet firm, advice received by Cyriacus, bishop of Constantinople, who was so overcome by the pressures of office that he craved the quiet of contemplation. Told that, as pilot of a ship, he must remain steadfast, even in the midst of storms, Cyriacus was reminded that Gregory too once wished for monastic calm, but "seeing the divine counsels to be opposed to me, I submitted the neck of my heart to my Creator's yoke."[15]

Like his patristic predecessors, Gregory saw in the ascetic way a martyrdom without external suffering. He noted that, while Saint John died quietly when the Church was enjoying peace and Saint James suffered a violent death, both sons of Zebedee had answered affirmatively when Jesus asked, "Are you able to drink the cup that I drink?"[16] He is emphatic that, had the saintly individuals with whom he populates his *Dialogues* lived in times of persecution, they would have accepted martyrdom. By enduring the assaults of the devil, loving their enemies, and resisting carnal desires, they became "new martyrs," who, "sacrificing themselves to almighty God on the altar of their hearts," willingly bore the sufferings of a transitory world because there is a "true life" elsewhere.[17] Among Gregory's company of saints is Benedict, the great monastic founder, who died in the mid-sixth century. An entire book of the *Dialogues* is devoted to him.

Gregory planned to place the monasteries at the heart of his renewal of the Church. However, they were in disarray, their order and harmony disturbed even in Gaul, which had known the glories of Martin, Cassian, and Honoratus. The pope insisted on faithful observance of worship and the vow of poverty by which all is held in common. Embroiled in a dis-

---

[13] See Gregory the Great, Epp 1.5, 1.3; NPNF 12:75, 74.
[14] Augustine, *On the Work of Monks*, 29.37; FCh 14:385.
[15] Gregory the Great, Ep 7.4; NPNF 12:211.
[16] Mark 10:38.
[17] Gregory the Great, *Dialogues*, 3.26; FCh 39:160–61; see Mark 10:38.

pute about property, Abbot John of Syracuse was advised to appoint an agent to manage external affairs, give his whole attention "to the souls of the brethren," and devote adequate time to prayer and reading. He should also attend to hospitality and, "as far as you are able, give to the poor."[18] Abbot Eusebius, in conflict with his bishop, must realize that "it is no great thing for us to be humble to those by whom we are honored. Even worldly men do this; but we ought especially to be humble to those at whose hands we suffer." In Sicily, where barbarian invasions had scattered the monks, Subdeacon Peter was asked to provide them with a monastery in which they could devote themselves to uninterrupted worship.[19]

Though monasticism was in general decline when Gregory became pope, it was burgeoning in Ireland. Through the sixth century, that country's ascetics had been fulfilling Patrick's prayer that his people would "strive after greater things and do more excellent deeds" for God.[20] Their faith and devotion is evident in the litany of saintly sixth-century founders. By 530 Finnian had established the monastery of Clonard. In 550, a year after Finnian's death, Ciarán, a product of Clonard, founded Clonmacnoise, which became a noted center of learning and culture. Comgall of Bangor died at a great age in 602. Not far from Bangor, another Finnian was abbot of Moville. He died in 579, two years after Brendan of Clonfert, the voyager. Columba left Ireland for Britain in 563 and was abbot of Iona till his death in 597.

Brigid was among the earliest generation of Irish female ascetics. Monenna established a famed monastery at Killevy and another at Faughart, reputed birthplace of Brigid. In Munster, Íte overcame her father's opposition to lead a religious house for women at Killeedy.[21] In the early ninth-century *Martyrology* of Óengus, she is "the white sun of Munster's women," while Monenna of the mountain of Cuilenn is "a fair pillar, a hostage of purity and a kinswoman of holy Mary."[22] Brigid is described as "the fair, strong, praiseworthy chaste head of Erin's nuns."[23]

---

[18] Gregory the Great, Ep 3.3; NPNF 12:123.

[19] Gregory the Great, Epp 2.36, 1.41; NPNF 12:111, 87.

[20] Patrick, *Conf*, 47; Conneely, 73.

[21] Ryan, *Irish Monasticism: Origins and Early Development* (Dublin: Irish Academic Press, 1992) 134–40.

[22] Óengus, *Martyrology*, 15 January; 6 July, trans. Whitley Stokes (London: Henry Bradshaw Society, 1905) 36, 161.

[23] Óengus, *Martyrology*, 1 February, H.B.S., 58.

Gregory's vision of monastic renunciation as a form of martyrdom was shared by the Irish ascetics, some of whom embraced a further sacrifice as "exiles for Christ." Their spiritual journeying was inspired by the patristic teaching that, as members of God's kingdom, Christians are on pilgrimage to the heavenly Jerusalem.[24] Some made their way to regions of Ireland far removed from home and family. In a tribal society marked by strong ties to kin and locality, this represented a considerable degree of renunciation. Voluntary exile from their country brought an even sharper sacrifice. So many followed this path that, while Gregory was determining to restore monasticism to its exemplary role in the Church at large, monks from Ireland were eagerly promoting its practice beyond their own shores.

These monks had an exemplar in Patrick, who had been willing to "forsake homeland and family" and minister to their pagan ancestors, as "a stranger and an alien" in God's name.[25] Despite efforts to detain him, he had followed the will of God, who "in all things gave me strength and did not hinder me from the journey I had decided on."[26] The ascetics' consciousness of being at one with Patrick in self-denial and devotion to God is evident in the most ancient Irish hymn *Audite Omnes Amantes*, contained in the *Bangor Antiphonary*.[27] It celebrates the saint's tireless dedication to

> preaching to the people of God with both words and deeds
> that he might, with a good act, inspire the one whom his words
>     did not move.[28]

A "model to the faithful," he inspires others, because, like the martyrs, he follows the Master,

> bearing in his righteous flesh the mark of Christ
> and carrying his cross, in which alone he glorifies.[29]

In the year of Gregory's accession to the papacy, Columban of Bangor sailed for Gaul, ensuring his lasting recognition as a contributor to

---

[24] Augustine, *City of God*, 19.17; Bettenson, 877.

[25] Patrick, *Conf*, 26; Conneely, 68; *Letter to Coroticus*, 1; Conneely, 77.

[26] Patrick, *Conf*, 30; Conneely, 69.

[27] Bieler, introduction: *Hymn on Saint Patrick*, ACW 17:57–59.

[28] *Audite Omnes Amantes*, trans. John Carey, *King of Mysteries: Early Irish Religious Writings* (Dublin: Four Courts Press, 1998) 153.

[29] *King of Mysteries*, 154.

the revival of the Church in that country. Thirty years before, his spiritual brother, Columba, later known as Columcille, "sailed away from Ireland to Britain, choosing to be a pilgrim for Christ." Apart from a handful of visits to his native country, Columba lived on the island of Iona for thirty-four years: "Fasts and vigils he performed day and night with tireless labor and no rest, to such a degree that the burden of even one seemed beyond human endurance. At the same time he was loving to all people."[30] Columba's biographer, Adomnán, introduces him as one whom Bishop Mochta, in "a marvelous prophecy," had foretold would bring light to the world. Described as "a pilgrim from Britain, a holy disciple of the holy Bishop Patrick," Mochta expressed his own, and therefore Patrick's, close spiritual kinship with the future abbot: "The fields of our two monasteries, mine and his, will be separated by only a little hedge. A man very dear to God, and of great merit in his sight."[31]

Columba's monastic witness and concern for people represented a paradigm of what Gregory was hoping to achieve in the wider Church. Renunciation of earthly status, adoption of the spirit of simplicity, and sharing in the life of a religious community engendered in both men a sensitivity to the needs of others. In Rome, neglect by the imperial powers in distant Constantinople meant that Gregory had to care for refugees, the destitute, and victims of famine. He organized the preparation of daily meals for the sick and infirm, with much of the food grown on his former hereditary lands in Sicily, which were now part of the Church's patrimony.[32] The pope maintained careful oversight of the papal estates, ensuring that the workers were fairly treated. He denounced exorbitant prices, dues, and "unjust exactions," which "cripple the peasants," and stipulated that, when farmers died, the right of succession to property should be respected. He even expressed criticism of "immoderate" marriage fees, insisting that reasonable sums be set for all who lived on Church lands.[33]

Columba also dedicated himself to the service of God and the good of others. The humblest individuals were worthy of his attention. He dispatched blessed bread from Iona across the sea to the region around

---

[30] Adomnán, *Life of Saint Columba*, Second Preface; trans. Richard Sharpe (London: Penguin Books, 1995) 105–6.

[31] Adomnán, *Life of Saint Columba*, Second Preface; Sharpe, 104–5.

[32] Peter Llewellyn, *Rome in the Dark Ages* (London: Faber and Faber, 1971) 95–96.

[33] Gregory the Great, Ep 1.44; NPNF 12:88–90.

Dublin, where people and animals were enduring pestilence. He blessed Nesan's tiny herd, which then began to thrive. His intercession helped a woman in childbirth who was suffering violent pain.[34] An incident from the abbot's old age suggests his popularity in Ireland. Spending some time at the new foundation of Durrow, he visited Clonmacnoise. Alerted to his arrival, those working in the fields converged on the monastery from every direction. So great was the crush of admiring people as he reached the boundary wall that, to protect him, four monks "kept pace with him, holding about him a square frame of branches tied together."[35]

Columba had a profound regard for his brethren. Whether undertaking hazardous sea crossings, toiling late at harvest time, or suffering illness, they were always in his thoughts. Once, in the depth of winter, the abbot's prayers on Iona helped to ease the difficult conditions under which monks in faraway Durrow were being forced to work. Even when "worn out with age" and approaching death, Columba asked to be drawn in a wagon to visit those laboring on the west coast of Iona. One of his final actions was to bless the grain stored in the community barn. As he did so, he rejoiced that the brethren would have sufficient bread in the coming year.[36]

Both Gregory and Columba were effective peacemakers. When Rome was at the mercy of the Lombards and appeals for help to the imperial court in Constantinople went unheeded, the pope negotiated a peace treaty with Agilulf, the Lombard leader. He also engaged in prolonged and patient communication with the turbulent and volatile Merovingian dynasty in Gaul, enabling the Church in that country to survive the shocks of constant warfare.[37] Cultivation of similar understandings with a variety of leaders enabled him to re-evangelize regions where religious observance had suffered through barbarian attacks and settlement. He drew on skills acquired as a member of the Roman ruling class, but his influence with rapacious leaders also derived from a formidable moral authority, which he shared with ascetics in the mold of Basil, Anastasius, Martin, and Columba.

Like Gregory, Columba was of noble lineage. Kinship with the powerful Uí Néill dynasty probably led to his early denunciation by fel-

---

[34] Adomnán, *Life of Saint Columba*, 2.4, 2.20, 2.40; Sharpe, 157, 169, 194.

[35] Adomnán, *Life of Saint Columba*, 1.3; Sharpe, 115.

[36] Adomnán, *Life of Saint Columba*, 1.29; 3.23; Sharpe, 133, 225–26.

[37] Gregory the Great, *Pastoral Rule*, Prolegomena; NPNF 12: xix–xx, xxiv–xxv.

low churchmen, whose hostility was dissipated when Abbot Brendan of Birr convinced them that the charges against the abbot were "trivial and very pardonable." A sentence of excommunication, "wrongly" passed at a synod, was not pursued. It was after this experience that Columba sailed to Britain at the age of forty-one "with twelve disciples as his fellow soldiers."[38] His membership of the Cenél Conaill of Tirconell earned him a unique social status. However, it was his spiritual prestige that, in the year 575, enabled him to organize the "conference of the kings" at Druim Cett in Derry. This led to peace between his kinsman Áed, king of the northern Uí Néill and Áedán, king of Dál Riata, an area extending from modern Antrim to Argyll, a region of northwest Britain which had been colonized by the Irish. Columba also earned the respect of the pagan Picts in the extreme north of Britain.[39]

In his efforts to renew monastic life, Gregory urged monks to be faithful to their *Rule*, a sure guide in the work of energizing the spiritual life of the Church. By promoting monastic privilege, he protected them against immersion in secular affairs. While recognizing the right of bishops to consecrate abbots, engage in visitations, guard against abuses, and apply discipline when necessary, he advised against unnecessary intrusion into monastic life. Settling a dispute between the bishop of Rimini and the abbot of a nearby monastery, the pope cautioned against interference with monastic property, revenues, or writings. Nor was the bishop to intervene in the appointment of an abbot, who should be elected by his community. Gregory also forbade prelates to promote monks to diocesan posts without the permission of abbots and advised against the celebration of public masses in monasteries.[40]

The same principle was applied to communities of women. Writing to Respecta, abbess of Marseilles, and to the abbess Thalassia, Gregory reiterated his conviction that bishops should not involve themselves in internal monastic affairs and insisted that, on the death of the superior, a successor be chosen by the sisters themselves, and not imposed from without.[41] His reliance on the spiritual assistance gained through the prayer of the ascetics is evident in a letter he wrote three years after his accession. Donating clothing, beds, and mattresses to a hospital for the

---

[38] Adomnán, *Life of Saint Columba*, 3.3; Sharpe, 209.

[39] Adomnán, *Life of Saint Columba*, 1.49, 2.6, 2.35; Sharpe, 151, 159, 184.

[40] Gregory the Great, Epp 2.41, 2.42; NPNF 12:112, 113.

[41] Gregory the Great, Ep 7.12; NPNF 12: 215–16.

aged run by the saintly John Climacus of Sinai, Gregory begged the abbot's prayers for the perilous "voyage" on which he had embarked as bishop of Rome.[42]

The pope demonstrated his faith in ascetics by appointing them bishops or nominating them for arduous duties abroad. It was a practice he followed when planning the conversion of the English people. In the mid-nineties of the sixth century, Bertha, a Frankish Christian princess, married Aethelbert, king of Kent. Her chaplain, a Frankish bishop, accompanied her to England. In 597 the pope sent forty missionaries to Kent. All were monks from his old monastery, Saint Andrew's. They were led by the prior, Augustine. It was an inspired choice, for, less than thirty years before, Gildas placed his final hopes for the doomed British church in the commitment of monks, "whose life I praise and indeed prefer to all the rest of the world," and even expressed the desire to be "a participant in that life before I die."[43] Like the Briton, Gregory knew that, as men schooled in asceticism and obedience, the monks would reject all material inducements, endure every trial, and remain faithful to their commitment.

Gregory left nothing to chance, even planning the brethren's resting places on the journey. Symbolically, their first stop was at the renowned monastery of Lérins, in the south of Gaul. On the way to Paris, they paused at Tours, city of Martin. When the group reached Canterbury in 597 Augustine established a monastery dedicated to Saints Peter and Paul. The monks' arrival in the year of Columba's death ensured that the island of Britain, north and south, was now being served by dedicated ascetics. Pope Gregory's conviction on the benefits to the Church of the monastic spirit of self-sacrifice, simplicity, and prayer was shared a century later by Columba's biographer, Adomnán, for whom the communal life of the early monks of Iona represented the ideal. In his *Life* of the monastic founder, Adomnán acknowledges the abbot's kinship with Antony and Benedict and invests him with the moral authority of Martin, who was invoked, with other saints, during the celebration of the Eucharist at Iona.[44]

Columba was a healer of souls, and a stream of penitents converged on Iona from all parts. Fiachnae, just arrived from Ireland, threw himself

[42] Gregory the Great, Ep 11.1; NPNF 13:52.

[43] Gildas, *Ruin of Britain*, 65.2; Winterbottom, 52.

[44] Adomnán, *Life of Saint Columba*, 3.12; Sharpe, 214–15.

at the abbot's feet. "Weeping and grieving," he confessed his sins. Weeping himself, Columba told him, "Stand up, my son, and be comforted. Your sins are forgiven, because, as it is written, 'A broken and a contrite heart God will not despise.'"[45] The spiritual medicine prescribed by the abbot, always salutary, could also be rigorous. Libran traveled all the way from Connacht to expiate his sins through pilgrimage. For his transgressions, which included killing a man and breaking an oath of service, Columba imposed seven years' penance. Libran was also asked to seek reconciliation with his former master and make good his neglected filial service to his father.[46]

While Gregory was attempting to restore monastic culture in continental Europe, learning was flourishing in the monasteries of Ireland, enriching the Church's devotional and liturgical life, not least through skillful transcription of the Scriptures. Adomnán's Columba was constantly at work in the scriptorium. In the eyes of the monks, his books acquired an almost miraculous quality, surviving brushes with disaster, such as immersion in water. Even the spilling of his ink-horn's contents on the desk was worthy of his biographer's attention.[47] His name has always been associated with the *Cathach*, a copy of the psalter which contains early examples of the art of illumination for which the Irish were to become renowned. Since Columba was also credited with literary creativity, poems were later ascribed to him, with many suggesting his contribution to the Church's treasury of spiritual works.

> My hand is weary with writing; my great sharp point is not thick; my slender-beaked pen juts forth a beetle-hued draught of bright blue ink.
>
> A steady stream of wisdom springs from my well-colored neat fair hand; on the page it pours its draught of ink of the green-skinned holly.
>
> I send my little dripping pen unceasingly over an assemblage of books of great beauty, to enrich the possessions of men of art, and so my hand is weary with writing.[48]

---

[45] Adomnán, *Life of Saint Columba*, 1.30; Sharpe, 134.

[46] Adomnán, *Life of Saint Columba*, 2.39; Sharpe, 189–90.

[47] Adomnán, *Life of Saint Columba*, 2.9, 1, 2; Sharpe, 160–61, 130.

[48] *Early Irish Lyrics*, trans. and ed. Gerard Murphy (Dublin: Four Courts Press, 1998) 71.

Adomnán presents a picture of the abbot at work in his hut, copying the psalter for the last time. Reaching the thirty-fourth psalm, Columba ends at the verse, "But they that seek the Lord shall not want for anything that is good."[49] When he died on Iona in 597, three days and three nights of storms "prevented anyone from coming across the waters in a small boat from any direction."[50] Precisely a century later, Adomnán, accompanied by several monks, was anxious to return to the monastery after attending a synod in Ireland. Delayed on a small island by contrary winds, the party invoked their patron. As dawn broke, the storm ended and a favorable wind began to blow. Once again, as in life, the holy founder had provided fair sailing weather, enabling the monks to reach Iona in time to "wash our hands and feet before entering the church with the brethren to celebrate together the solemn mass at the hour of sext, for the feast of St Columba and St Baithéne."[51]

---

[49] See Ps 34:10.

[50] Adomnán, *Life of Saint Columba*, 3.23; Sharpe, 228.

[51] Adomnán, *Life of Saint Columba*, 2.45; Sharpe, 202.

# 13

# THE POPE, THE ABBOT, AND THE GAULS

Eight years before Columba's death, his namesake Columban left Ireland as a "pilgrim for Christ." It was a journey of faith which led to the ascetic's substantial contribution to the growth of European monasticism. Columban was over forty years old when Abbot Comgall reluctantly approved his decision to "obey the command that God gave Abraham." With twelve companions he "went to the seashore" near the monastery and boarded a boat bound for Gaul. An enterprise undertaken in the belief that one who aspired to goodness should be "molded to the example of his redeemer," it led him to the very places on the continent for which Pope Gregory felt greatest pastoral concern.[1]

Reared in Leinster, Columban had moved north when "a holy, devout woman" advised him to leave his native place if he wished to advance spiritually. He entered the monastery of Sinell, disciple of Finnian, at Cleenish on Lough Erne. Later, he was accepted at Bangor, teaching "by example" in the monastic school, "giving himself entirely to fasting and prayer, bearing the easy yoke of Christ and mortifying the flesh."[2] That Columban's teaching was in the patristic tradition is evident in his observation that the well-disposed man "is righteous by his acts, and a martyr through his suffering for the sake of righteousness."[3] When undertaking "exile for Christ," he must have recalled that the devout woman of his youth spoke of her unfulfilled ambition to "cross the sea" in God's name.[4]

---

[1] Jonas, *Life of Saint Columban*, 9–10, ed. Dana Carletin Munro (Felinfach: Llanerch Publishers, 1993) 17–19.

[2] Jonas, *Life*, 8–9; Munro, 14–16.

[3] Columban, *Letters*, 2.3, trans. G. S. M. Walker, *Sancti Columbani Opera* (Dublin: Dublin Institute for Advanced Studies, 1957) 15.

[4] Jonas, *Life*, 8; Munro, 14.

In 590 Columban arrived in Gaul, which was regarded by the Irish as the source of their ascetic tradition. The adopted country of John Cassian and Martin of Tours had experienced a decline in faith since the fall of the empire, for reception of baptism by the warlike Frankish elites who now ruled the country had been of little benefit to the fortunes of the Church. In recounting the terrors of the time, Gaulish historian Gregory of Tours presents a sorry litany of prelates and priests who were unfaithful to their commitment but pays tribute to those who continued to lead saintly lives.[5] Both Columban and Gregory the Great worked to bring the much-needed renewal.

Anxious to maintain communication with the religious leaders of the ravaged country, the pope cultivated its leaders. He won the trust of King Childebert II, who succeeded his uncle Guntram in 593 as ruler of Burgundy and Austrasia, which embraced parts of modern France, Germany, and Switzerland. He also corresponded with Childebert's powerful mother, Brunehild. Writing in 595 to Virgilius, bishop of Arles, whom he appointed vicar of the region, Gregory detailed the various irregularities which wrung from him "a cry of grief." Men have been admitted to the priesthood without preparation or training, with many so afflicted by the disease of avarice that, in parts of Gaul and Germany, no one entered holy orders unless a "consideration" was given. "If this is so," the pope exclaims, "I say it with tears, I declare it with groans, when the priestly order has fallen inwardly, neither will it be able to stand outwardly for long."

Acknowledging that simoniac practices often arose from the efforts of powerful men to buy influence in the Church, Gregory begged Virgilius to "admonish" King Childebert "to remove the stain of this sin entirely from his kingdom."[6] He wrote to the bishops, advising regular episcopal meetings and asking that prelates devote themselves to their sees, which should never be left for trivial reasons, lest "the prowling wolf invade and tear the sheep entrusted to them." In suggesting that, by working harmoniously under the authority of the vicar, Virgilius, they could resolve disagreements in a spirit of charity, the pope echoed Clement's advice to the Corinthians at the end of the first century, adding that there must be recourse to Rome in the event of failure to agree on matters of importance.[7]

[5] Gregory of Tours, *History of the Franks*, 2.3–5; Thorpe, 113–15.

[6] Gregory the Great, Ep 5.53; NPNF 12:182–83.

[7] Gregory the Great, Ep 5.54; NPNF 12:183–84.

In the year of Gregory's accession to the papacy, Columban and his brethren arrived in eastern Gaul. They were welcomed by King Guntram, who granted them land at Annegray, in the Vosges Mountains. It was a remote area, suited to contemplation and prayer and one in which they could "sow the seeds of salvation." The monks' austere and dedicated lives impressed the local people, with the sick "seeking aid for all their infirmities." Columban's biographer, Jonas, notes that the brethren, holding everything in common, and "leading lives of humility and renunciation," attracted to their ranks the sons and daughters of the still-barbarian nobility. Like the young men and women who had followed Patrick and Martin, Columban's Gaulish converts to the ascetic way "sought eternal rewards, despising the trappings of the world and the pomp of present wealth." Some were to become bishops or abbots, contributing to the restoration of faith and religious practice in their country.[8]

Much-favored by Childebert, who succeeded Guntram, Columban established two further monasteries within twenty years. At Luxeil, the fallen idols of the pagans and the ruins of the Roman baths were a reminder of the dark forces which still challenged the truths championed by the monks. Many people came in search of healing and "the remedy of penance." At Fontaines, his third foundation, Columban formulated the *Rule* which he and the brethren were to follow.[9] The communities which worked and prayed at Annegray, Luxeil, and Fontaines were emulating those of Bangor and its sister monasteries in Ireland:

> Excellent rule of Bangor,
> Correct and divine,
> Holy, exact and constant,
> Exalted, just and admirable.
>
> Blessed the family of Bangor
> Founded on unerring faith,
> Graced with the hope of salvation
> Perfect in charity.[10]

---

[8] Jonas, *Life*, 10, 14, 17; Munro, 19, 27, 32.

[9] Jonas, *Life*, 17–18; Munro, 32–33.

[10] *Antiphonary of Bangor Vol. 2*, 95, ed. F. E. Warren, Bradshaw Society (London: Harrison and Sons, 1895) 28; O'Laverty, 44.

Meanwhile, a series of letters from Gregory to the Gaulish spiritual and secular leaders suggested that in Gaul at large there was still much work to be done.[11] The abuses included unwillingness to condemn injustice, reluctance to guard the rights of monks, and clerical failures to observe the vow of chastity.[12] Saddened that "fierce cupidity" still held many hearts captive, Gregory demanded that self-seeking be condemned and "avarice cast out of the house of the Lord." What place in the Church can be safe from this vice, he asked, if it is opened up to bad priests: "How can he keep the sheepfold inviolate who invites the wolf to enter?"[13] Employing a blend of reproach, diplomacy, and tact in pursuit of reform, Gregory displayed the patience and understanding which typified his considered approach to complex problems.

Columban proved to be less emollient. With the asceticism of the Irish winning the awed admiration of the Frankish aristocracy and people, he rapidly gained an independence of action that proved irksome to local bishops. He condemned the irregularities identified by Gregory and resisted episcopal authority in the matter of dating Easter, rejecting the calendar of Victorius of Aquitaine, composed in 457, "after the age of great Martin and great Jerome and Pope Damasus." Pope Leo had unsuccessfully attempted to achieve a *computus* which could be observed by both east and west and under his successor the cycle of Victorius of Aquitaine was adopted. Irish monasteries, with their reverence for tradition, preferred Anatolius of Laodicea, whose *computus*, which appeared in 277, had been "commended" by Jerome. Asking that the bishops should agree to differ, Columban reminded them of his sacrifice in coming to Gaul: "It is for the sake of Christ the Savior, our common Lord and God, that I have entered these lands a pilgrim."[14]

In 603 the abbot refused to attend a synod convened to resolve the disagreement. Claiming that his presence might inflame feelings, he penned an epistolary sermon which reveals a remarkable disdain for the art of persuasion. Admonishing the churchmen vigorously, Columban recommended that the proposed assembly be devoted to the elimination of episcopal shortcomings. Advising the holding of more regular synods, he insisted that pastors should guide their people by "becoming

---

[11] Gregory the Great, Ep 9.109–17; NPNF 13:28–33.
[12] Gregory the Great, Ep 9.111, 114; NPNF 13:30–32.
[13] Gregory the Great, Ep 11.55; NPNF 13:70.
[14] Columban, Ep 2.6–7; Walker, 17–19.

humble and poor for Christ's sake." For the "uncanonical lives" being led by some, he prescribed the spirit of martyrdom. "Faith without works is dead in itself," the bishops were bluntly told.[15] It is advice characteristic of an ascetic who observed the austere *Rule of Bangor*, whose lofty principles are implicit in the *Audite Omnes Amantes*, sung by the monks of that monastery. Dedicated to Saint Patrick, the hymn defines the exemplary qualities embodied in the great missionary, and demanded of any religious leader:

> A faithful minister of God, and a splendid messenger,
> he gave to the good the example and form of an apostle.[16]

It is improbable that such injudicious advice from a foreigner moved many episcopal hearts. In tone and expression, the Irishman's letter is worthy of Jerome, who also wielded an incisive pen. Columban's frequent references to the fiery ascetic's writings suggest that they were the model for his own forceful style. It is even possible to detect personality traits common to the abbot of Luxeil and the old war horse of Bethlehem. Columban's barely concealed pugnacity is reminiscent of Jerome's frequent encounters with others, which include the "sudden whirlwind" that scattered that first group of friends in Aquileia, the rupture with Rufinus, the clash with Augustine, the forced exit from Rome and subsequent bitter debate with Bishop John of Jerusalem.[17] Neither Jerome nor his Irish admirer is unaware of having mastery of the written word. Since both men revel in contention, they reveal a taste for colorful rhetoric, overstatement, and wordplay. They even share the tendency to digress that is so well expressed by Jerome in his letter to Laeta: "I have nearly wandered into a new subject, and while I have kept my wheel going, my hands have been molding a flagon when it has been my object to form a ewer."[18]

The lack of concern for decorum characteristic of Jerome and Columban may derive, in part, from their commitment to the most austere vision of the monastic vocation. It certainly accounts for the peremptory tone of the Irishman's famous letter to Pope Gregory, in which condemnation of the Gaulish practice of admitting unworthy men to the

---

[15] Columban, Epp 2.7, 2.5, 2.3; Walker, 19–21, 25, 15.
[16] *Audite Omnes Amantes, Antiphonary*, 13.6; Warren, 14; *King of Mysteries*, 153.
[17] Jerome, Ep 3.3; NPNF 6:5.
[18] Jerome, Ep 107.3; NPNF 6:190; Columban, Ep 5.15; Walker, 53.

episcopacy is buttressed by blunt allegations that there are some prelates who, as deacons, had enjoyed marital relations with their wives. The last-named shortcoming was forbidden under current Church law and regarded by religious teachers in Ireland as adultery. Claiming to have heard of priests being raised to the episcopacy "after buying orders for money," Columban asks the pope, "Are we really to communicate with them?"[19] It is possible that these allegations provided the raw material for Gregory's letter to the bishops, though the pope's vicar, Virgilius, may have forwarded his own catalogue of abuses to Rome.

Columban was similarly robust in acquainting Gregory with his views on the matter of Easter, with the pope expected to decide for the Irish practice. Bishop Gregory of Tours, historian of the Franks, noted that, in 590, the very year of Columban's arrival in Gaul, two cycles were being observed in the Gaulish church. The bishop's own see was one of a group which followed Victorius, while others were celebrating the feast seven days before.[20] Columban deployed weighty astronomical and mathematical calculations to advance his claims.[21] After Gregory's death, he proposed an accommodation with the Gaulish bishops and asked one of the pope's successors to concede that the two ways be contained "in the peace of church unity." In the process, Columban displayed his knowledge of Church history by citing the agreement, in AD 154, of Polycarp of Smyrna and Pope Anicetus to accept differing dates for Easter, "without offence to the faith."[22]

In his letter to Pope Gregory, the abbot balances his "impudence" and tendency to "challenge, question and ask" with high praise for the pope's *Pastoral Rule*. The book is hailed as "pregnant in doctrine, replete with sacred lore . . . sweeter than honey to the needy." Gregory himself is Columban's "holy lord and father in Christ," who "does lawfully occupy the chair of Peter, the apostle and bearer of the keys."[23] He himself would visit Rome, says the abbot, "did not bodily weakness and the care of my fellow pilgrims keep me tied at home." Were he to do so, it would be in the spirit of Jerome, for he would be seeking in Rome, not the ancient

---

[19] Columban, Ep 1.6; Walker, 9.
[20] Gregory of Tours, *History of the Franks*, 5.17, 10.23; Thorpe, 274, 581–82; Columban, *Opera*, Walker, xvi.
[21] Columban, Ep 1.3–5; Walker, 3–9.
[22] Columban, Epp 2.6, 3.2; Walker, 17, 25.
[23] Columban, Epp 1.9, 1, 5; Walker, 7–8, 9, 11.

city, but the person of the successor of Peter, "saving the reverence due to the ashes of the saints."[24] Columban later addressed an equally audacious missive to Boniface IV, the third pope to succeed Gregory, but tempered it by greeting him "in the unity of the mutual faith that is between us," reiterating his desire for "the consolation of a visit to each occupant of the apostolic chair," and recalling Boniface's great predecessor as "Pope Gregory of blessed memory."[25]

While differing in background and temperament, Gregory the Great and Columban shared a profound belief in the Gospel message. In one of his first letters as pope, Gregory expresses reverence for the Gospels and the four Church councils, "since, on them, as on a four-square stone, rises the structure of the holy faith."[26] He depicts his own writings as a "paltry stream," from which no one used to imbibing "the swiftly flowing rivers, deep and clear, of Ambrose and Augustine" would wish to drink. He recommends that those who wish to take their fill of delicious spiritual food "read the works of the blessed Augustine and seek not our chaff in comparison with his fine wheat."[27]

Though a skilled exponent of traditional apostolic and patristic teaching, with the capacity to kindle in ordinary Christians a deep appreciation of the faith, Gregory did not subject religious belief to intellectual scrutiny in the manner of Augustine. An ascetic schooled in the monastic tradition of prayer and contemplation, he felt that the mysteries should be approached simply through the reverence which comes from faith.[28] Gregory's reluctance to apply reason to the truths of faith derived, in part, from his experiences of deep doctrinal differences in the east. While in Constantinople, he wrote his commentary on Job, the prophet noted for his unquestioning acceptance that God and his designs cannot be comprehended by unaided human understanding: " 'Who is this that hides counsel without knowledge?' Therefore I have uttered what I did not understand, things too wonderful for me, which I did not know."[29]

---

[24] Columban, Ep 1.8; Walker, 11; Jerome, Ep 15.1; NPNF 6:18; see Col 1:8.

[25] Columban, Ep 3.2; Walker, 23.

[26] Gregory the Great, Ep 1.25; NPNF 12:81–82.

[27] Gregory the Great, *Homily on Ezekiel*, prologue; F. Homes Dudden, *Gregory the Great*, vol. 2 (London: Longmans, Green, 1905) 293–94.

[28] Dudden, *Gregory the Great*, vol. 2, 296–98.

[29] Job 42:3.

Columban concurred with Gregory, convinced that God is understood by the "pious faith of a pure heart and not by the gabble of an impious mouth."[30] It is a faith that should be buttressed by a well-lived life, and not, in the abbot's words, by a "proliferation of idle words," uttered by people who do not know, "according to the apostle, what they speak or what they affirm."[31] Columban's sermons are colored by the teachings of Gregory and the other fathers. The first opens with the symbolum, in which the abbot expresses his faith in the Trinity and asserts, like Patrick, that, since faith involves truths that are "unspeakable, undiscoverable, unsearchable," spiritual wisdom is attained "when the invisible is believed in a manner that passes understanding."[32]

While pope and abbot were at one in faith, they differed in their approach to mission. The outspoken Columban had been educated exclusively within an austere monastic milieu. Gregory, with a Roman education, secular administrative experience, and six years in Constantinople as representative of Pope Pelagius, possessed diplomatic skills that were foreign to the Irishman. Consequently, in 595, when King Childebert died, the pope continued to correspond with his redoubtable mother Brunehild, now regent because of the youth of the king's two sons. He also wrote to the young successors, hoping to encourage them in humane and Christian modes of behavior. His communication with the bishops went on as before. As his mission to the English passed through Gaul, he organized the delivery of eight papal letters to leaders of Church and state. These were models of diplomacy and testified to the pope's determination to sustain and promote the faith in that country. The recipients included six bishops, an abbot, Queen Brunehild and Childebert's sons, Theudebert II and Theuderic II, now kings of Burgundy and Austrasia, respectively.[33]

In his final letters to Brunehild and her grandson Theuderic, Gregory was still contemplating a general synod for the Frankish church. Writing for the last time to the queen, whose reputation left much to be desired, he praised her generosity in building a church dedicated to Saint Martin and a monastery "for handmaidens of God." Theuderic too was

---

[30] Columban, *Sermons*, 1.4, trans. G. S. M. Walker, *Sancti Columbani Opera* (Dublin: Dublin Institute for Advanced Studies, 1957) 65.

[31] Columban, S 1.4–5; Walker, 65; see 1 Tim 1:7.

[32] Columban, S 1.2–3; Walker, 61–63; Patrick, *Conf*, 4; Bieler, 22.

[33] Gregory the Great, Ep 11.58, 59, 60, 62; NPNF 13:71–74.

lauded for so "transcending" his youth in prudence that the happiness of his subjects was assured.[34] Eschewing the diplomatic path pursued by the pope, Columban bluntly lectured the bishops and Theuderic on their responsibilities. The youthful ruler rejected the abbot's repeated demands to put away his concubines and marry. Total rupture came when Brunehild, a "second Jezebel" in the eyes of Columban's biographer, asked the abbot to bless the king's sons. Determined not to support, even indirectly, the old queen's promotion of her grandson's irregular lifestyle, he refused.[35]

Columban's fate was sealed. In 610, twenty years after entering Gaul and six years after the death of Gregory, the aged abbot was banished from the country. Under military escort, he and the surviving Irish monks were transported westward from Luxeil by land and river. They moved rapidly by way of Auxerre, city of Saint Germanus, through Nevers on the River Loire, for the journey downriver to Nantes. On reaching the coast they were to be placed on a ship bound for Ireland. After passing Orleans, Columban asked permission to stop at Martin's city of Tours, now a place of pilgrimage. The unwilling soldiers were forced to capitulate, "and landing, Columban went to the tomb of Saint Martin and spent the night in prayer."[36] As he entered the church, built just forty years before, he would have seen the final words of the inscription carved there:

> Every cure shows forth miracles worthy of the apostles. He who comes in weeping, goes out rejoicing. All clouds are dispelled. Martin is the remedy which calms remorse. Ask for his assistance: it is not in vain that you knock at this door. His generous goodness extends over the whole world.[37]

A last letter to his "sons and disciples," written during that enforced departure, suggests the sense of purpose which had guided Columban since leaving Bangor. Checking his tears, "for it is no part of a brave soldier to lament in battle," he warns those left behind not to ignore the enemy's strength, for in deserting a post demanding goodness, patience,

---

[34] Gregory the Great, Ep 13.6–7; NPNF 13:93–94.

[35] Jonas, *Life of Saint Columban*, 31–33; Munro, 53–59.

[36] Jonas, *Life of Saint Columban*, 37–40; 42; Munro, 65–70; 73.

[37] J. N. Hillgarth, ed., *Christianity and Paganism*, 350–70 (Philadelphia: University of Pennsylvania Press, 1986) 31–32.

fidelity, wisdom, and steadfastness, they would fail to join battle and so "remove the crown."[38] It is an expression of fortitude typical of the monastery of Bangor and an echo of a hymn sung by Columban monks in honor of the martyrs:

> most steadfast warriors of Christ the king,
> leaders of the army of the omnipotent God,
> victors singing to God in heaven.[39]

Reaching the coast of Brittany, the party boarded an Irish trading vessel. As the boat carrying Columban approached the open sea, a huge wave drove it back to the beach, where it lay for three days. Blaming the abbot for the setback, the superstitious captain refused to carry the ascetics, who, with their possessions, were returned to the shore. Seeing in the incident a providential reversal of his sentence, Columban, turning eastward, continued his epic journey by way of Paris, to Metz and Trier, then to Coblenz and the River Rhine.[40] The passage through Gaul enabled him to meet, for the last time, some of the monks whom he had left behind and to win new recruits to the ascetic life from among the ranks of the Frankish aristocracy.

Columban's vigorous *Rhine Boat Song*, inspired by the memory of being rowed up the great river, calls for courage, strength, and endurance, both physical and spiritual:

> Stand fixed in your intent, and spurn the foeman's wiles,
> Duly protect yourselves with armor of the virtues.
> Let your mind, my men, recalling Christ, sound Ho![41]

The party rested at Mainz, where they received shelter, nourishment, and encouragement from the bishop. Finally reaching Lake Constance, the monks made their way to the eastern shore and settled at Bregenz, where they lived and worked till 612.

---

[38] Columban, Ep 4.6; Walker, 31.35.
[39] *Antiphonary*, 11.1; Warren, 12.
[40] Jonas, *Life of Saint Columban*, 47; Munro, 80.
[41] Columban, *Poems*; Walker, 190–93.

# 14

# SCHISM IN ITALY

Columban and his brethren arrived in Bregenz in 610, six years after the death of Gregory the Great. During fourteen years of pastoral activity the pope had enhanced Rome's relations with eastern sees, enlivened the faith in Africa and Europe, advanced church renewal in Gaul and Italy, and initiated the evangelization of England. His Italian ministry was hampered by the actions of the Arian Lombards, who, after settling in the north of the country, were attempting to subdue the entire peninsula. Gregory's efforts in the north were further complicated by a schism which had persisted there since 553.

The schism had been precipitated by Emperor Justinian's attempt to placate the Monophysites, an influential presence at his court in Constantinople. Their belief that the humanity of Jesus is absorbed into his divinity was an extreme response to the Nestorians, who were accused of teaching the total separation of the human and divine in Christ.[1] The Council of Chalcedon concluded in 451 that, united in the person of Jesus, born of Mary, there are two natures, human and divine. A century later, the authoritarian Justinian, whose ambitions included recovery of the former imperial territories in Africa and Italy, planned a new Church council which would devise a formula acceptable to orthodox believers and Monophysites alike.

The emperor envisaged an assembly which would not only condemn "three chapters" deemed heretical by the Monophysites but uphold the essential teaching of Chalcedon. The three chapters embraced the writings of a trio of bishops who had been present at the council. Theodore of Mopsuestia died in 428 with his teachings unquestioned. Theoderet

---

[1] Leo, Ep 28; NPNF 12:38–43.

of Cyrrhus and Ibas of Edessa, both former Nestorian sympathizers, had participated at Chalcedon after subscribing to the orthodox teaching. Pressured by Justinian, some eastern bishops assented to his plan, while others hesitated. Justinian turned to Pope Vigilius, an ambitious churchman who had achieved his position by cultivating influential people. The pope prevaricated and then refused his approval.

Arrested in 545 and brought to Constantinople in 547, Vigilius was subjected to prolonged intimidation and abuse. Under conflicting pressures from orthodox believers in the west and court circles in the east, he twisted and turned. Finally, when the three chapters were condemned at Constantinople in 553, he gave his assent. Two years later, a broken man, he died in Sicily, on the return journey to Rome. Though it was accepted by most bishops that the council's conclusions did not affect orthodox teaching on the nature and person of Jesus, some perceived in the denunciation of the three chapters an attack on Chalcedon. In the north Italian provinces of Aquileia and Milan a schism was born.

In 569 the area of strongest support for the schism became the heartland of the barbarian Lombard invaders, whose Arianism further complicated the divisions. While still a deacon, Gregory had been appointed by Pope Pelagius to negotiate with the dissidents but failed to convince them that Chalcedon had not been invalidated. On becoming pope, he communicated with Theudelinda, wife of the Arian Lombard king, Agilulf. Though a Catholic, she was sympathetic to the schismatics, and Gregory registered his distress at her trust in "unskilled and foolish men, who not only do not know what they talk about, but can hardly understand what they have heard."[2]

With the path to a resolution obstructed by the interplay of nationalities and religious affiliations, the pope patiently sought to win bishops from the schism by assurances that Rome stood firmly by the first four Church councils' teachings on the Trinity and the nature and person of Jesus. He told the Istrian prelates that, since the proceedings at the Constantinople synod "referred only to certain individuals . . . nothing pertaining to faith was subverted, not in the least degree changed."[3] A single sentence in a letter to the orthodox bishop of Milan encapsulates Gregory's position. The bishop was advised to assure the dissidents that

---

[2] Gregory the Great, Ep 4.4; NPNF 12:145–46.
[3] Gregory the Great, Ep 2.51; NPNF 12:117.

Constantinople dealt, not with the faith, but with people, and that he "neither takes away anything from the faith of the synod of Chalcedon nor receives those who do, and that you condemn those whom it condemned, and absolve whomsoever it absolved."[4]

In 612, eight years after the death of Gregory, three years before his own and following the celebrated parting from his disciple Gall, Columban crossed the Alps into Lombard Italy. The most recent Frankish dynasty to have favored him had succumbed to another orgy of mutual slaughter. Greeted by Agilulf and Theudelinda, who donated land for a monastery at Bobbio, not far from Milan, the Irishman traveled no more. His biographer claims that, within this schismatic Christian area governed by barbarian heretics, the abbot opposed the errors of the Arian Lombard ruling class, even composing "an excellent and learned work against them."[5]

No copy of this work remains. What survives is Columban's dramatic epistolary intervention in the debate on the schism. He reveals that he has learned of the division "almost on my arrival at the frontiers of this province." Encouraged by Agilulf, "whose request reduced me to amazement and manifold anxiety," he immediately wrote to Pope Boniface IV, convinced that a rapid resolution of this impasse between Christians would render the Arian king and his fellow Lombards ripe for conversion. Boniface had been elected pope four years after Gregory's death. A fervent disciple of his great predecessor and an advocate of asceticism, he converted his house into a monastery and transformed the pagan pantheon into a Christian church dedicated to the Virgin Mary and all the martyrs. In the year of Columban's arrival in Italy, Boniface held a synod to regulate life and discipline in the monasteries.[6]

As forthright as those written in Gaul, Columban's letter to Boniface may have been inspired by Jerome's epistle to Pope Damasus on the feuding Christians in the east. Referring to those who believe that heretics have been favored at Justinian's council and that Rome is failing to answer them, the abbot professes to seek only "the edification of the Church." Calling on the pope to speak if he is to "maintain the apostolic faith," he acknowledges that his own words may be hurtful, but "better the wounds of a friend than the treacherous kisses of a foe." Acerbic as

[4] Gregory the Great, Ep 4.39; NPNF 12:159–60.
[5] Jonas, *Life of Saint Columban*, 59; Munro, 98.
[6] J. N. D. Kelly, *Oxford Dictionary of the Popes* (Oxford: University Press, 1986) 69.

Jerome, he even adapts that abbot's pun about the lack of vigilance of Vigilantius, an old foe in theological debate, and applies it to the unhappy Vigilius, source of the present problem.[7]

Columban tells Boniface, current incumbent of the chair of Peter, that his letter represents a tactic aimed at goading him, holder of the primacy as bishop of Rome, into a public declaration of orthodox teaching which will dispel confusion: "I have dared to arouse you against those who revile you and call you partisans of heretics and describe you as schismatics, so that my boasting, in which I trusted when I spoke for you in answer to them, should not be in vain, and so that they, not us, might be dismayed." On the pope's behalf, Columban has assured the northern critics "that the Roman Church defends no heretic against the Catholic faith." Professing incredulity that Rome has not moved publicly to dispel misunderstanding and division, he fears for the unity and orthodoxy of the "apostolic faith."[8] Indeed, it is a matter of grief "if the Catholic faith is not maintained in the apostolic see," for Boniface, as pope, is duty-bound to restore unity.[9]

Grieving that this continuing silence brings only "disgrace to Saint Peter's chair," Columban assures Boniface that his own blunt words come from "a friend, a disciple, and close follower of yours, not a stranger." It is his right to be critical, since he is one of the Irish, "inhabitants of the world's edge, a people who have kept the faith, followers of Peter and Paul and of all the disciples who wrote the sacred canon by the Holy Ghost." He reminds the pope that the Irish "accept nothing outside the evangelical and apostolic teaching" and that, among them, "the Catholic faith, as it was delivered by you first, who are the successors of the holy apostles, is maintained unbroken."[10] This reference to Celestine's mission represents no empty boast, for in the Bangor hymn "*Audite omnes*," Patrick is praised as one

> Constant in the fear of God, and immovable in faith,
> Upon whom, as upon Peter, the Church is built;
> Whose apostleship has come from God
> And against whom the gates of hell do not prevail.[11]

[7] Columban, Ep 5.4–5; Walker, 41–43; Jerome, Ep 109.1; NPNF 6:212; *Against Vigilantius*, 6.212; NPNF 6:417–23.

[8] Columban, Ep 5.3; Walker, 39.

[9] Columban, Ep 5.9–11; Walker, 47–49.

[10] Columban, Ep 5.3; Walker, 39.

[11] *King of Mysteries*, 152.

Adopting the posture of Old Testament prophet sounding a warning note, Columban paints a somber picture of discord and confusion, with lurid images of the Church slipping under the waves and of sheep trembling before wolves. Invoking traditional Pauline battle imagery, and addressing Boniface as a captain and shepherd who must act to "dispel confusion," he declares that, since God's army is "sleeping rather than fighting in the field," the pope must declare war, rouse the generals, make a call to arms, sound the trumpets, "and enter the conflict with your own person in the van."[12] Boniface is again assured that the abbot, like Jerome, is bound to the "chair of Peter," head of the churches of the world, source of the faith of the Irish. He is reminded that, if Rome, which holds the keys of Peter, does not speak, it is the right and duty of faithful followers like Columban to articulate the true teaching.[13]

The abbot could not have known that, during the years of his own sojourn in Gaul, Queen Theudelinda had received from Pope Gregory a convincing statement of Rome's acceptance of Nicaea: "For we venerate the four holy synods, the Nicene, Constantinople, the first of Ephesus, and Chalcedon, declaring that whosoever thinks otherwise than those four synods alienates himself from the faith. We also condemn whomsoever they condemn and absolve whomsoever they absolve." Gregory pronounced an anathema on anyone who "presumes to add to or take away from the faith of the same synods and especially Chalcedon."[14] Columban hoped that his heightened rhetoric would provoke the pope into ending the scandal of division and creating "a single choir," singing in harmony and peace. However, while his fiery polemic is worthy of Jerome, his letter's concluding words express a Gregorian desire for reconciliation, for "peace after the wars." There is a final request that the "holy father and the brethren in Rome" pray for him and his fellow pilgrims. It is important that they do so "beside the holy places and the ashes of the saints, and especially beside Peter and Paul."[15]

One wonders whether Columban's impassioned plea reached Rome, for he refers to previous failures in communication, when "once and again Satan hindered the bearers of our letters written to Pope Gregory

---

[12] Columban, Ep 5.3; 5.7; Walker, 39; 43–44.
[13] Columban, Ep 5.12; Walker, 51.
[14] Gregory the Great, Ep 4.38; NPNF 12:159.
[15] Columban, Ep 5.17; Walker, 57.

of blessed memory."[16] With his concern for tradition and orthodoxy, he would have been gratified had he known that the longed-for reconciliation would come within a century of his death, representing a triumph for the strategy of patient communication initiated by Gregory.

[16] Columban, Ep 3.2; Walker, 23.

# 15

# THE WISDOM OF THE ASCETICS
## BENEDICT, COLUMBAN, CASSIAN

Augustine asserted that reason enables the individual believer to attain temporal truth and to advance in the knowledge of God, but that contemplation of the divine results from the deeper wisdom, born of faith, through which "I shall know even as I am now known."[1] An episode from John Cassian's *Conferences* illuminates the bishop's insight. Abbot Moses once heard the desert elders, in Antony's presence, discussing the virtue most helpful to an ascetic. After hearing a variety of suggestions, which included fasts, vigils, and acts of charity, Antony concluded that, while all are needful, discretion alone enables a monk to persevere.[2] Like Paul, he saw in this spiritual judgment the noblest gift of the spirit, "no earthly or paltry matter, but a very great bestowal of divine grace." Conveying the ability to discern good and evil, it is acquired through prayer and attention to the teaching and example of elders.[3]

Through the wisdom born of faith, fathers and ascetics were able to embrace the Christian paradox which perplexed the rational Athenians addressed by Paul.[4] By the world's standards, they were fools for following a leader who stated, "Foxes have holes, and birds of the air have nests; but the Son of Man has nowhere to lay his head." The apostles had been guilty of the same "folly" when embarking on their first major mission to similar words: "Take nothing for your journey, no staff, nor bag, nor

---

[1] Augustine, *On the Trinity*, 12.14.22; FCh 45:363.
[2] Cassian, *Conf*, 1.1; ACW 57:83–84.
[3] Cassian, *Conf*, 1.2; ACW 57:84–85; see 1 Cor 12:8–11.
[4] See Acts 17:21, 32.

145

bread, nor money—not even an extra tunic."[5] In an empire where luxury and self-indulgence coexisted with poverty and hunger, the lives of the fathers and ascetics reflected those of the earliest Christians, who owned everything in common.[6] They trusted that their example of renunciation would confirm the belief of fellow Christians in God's generosity and elicit a response of praise, thanksgiving, and simplicity of life.

The wisdom born of faith led ascetics like Columban and Gregory the Great to conclude that monastic life, with its emphasis on worship and renunciation, was the surest way to happiness. This is convincingly expressed in John Cassian's *Conferences*, where Abbot Moses' reflection on the story of Martha and Mary illustrates the author's belief that human beings are certain of attaining the highest good, not through active engagement in the world, however praiseworthy, but by exclusive devotion to God.[7] Though Martha's action was a sacred service, Mary drew closer to God through contemplation of his word.

Columban believed that the wisdom extolled by Cassian enabled the monk to see through the temporal to the eternal, through the "toil and weariness of the journey" to the glorious reality. It involved a winnowing process through which the dedicated person, finding "nothing solid to rest in among those things which the world possesses, turns, in wisdom, to the one thing which is eternal." The wise monk will "keep his discernment pure, that he may employ it for living well, and not look on what is, but on what shall be." This will ensure that no outward thing will merit his complete love. Since only what is "inspired and quickened by the eternal, wonderful, ineffable, invisible and incomprehensible" will suffice, he must avoid deceptions and deceits and "attempt to be what he was created." As this is a task impossible to unaided human effort, the monk should "call upon God's grace to help his striving." By conquering himself, he will spurn the ephemeral things of this world for those that are everlasting.[8]

Gregory, too, was familiar with Cassian's teaching that discretion, or discernment, would enable him to find God in the joys and hardships of life. He felt that the ability to judge rightly, which was the fruit of medita-

---

[5] Matt 8:20; Luke 9:1–6.

[6] See Acts 2:42–44; 4:32.

[7] Cassian, *Conf*, 1.8, trans. Edgar C. S. Gibson, NPNF 11 (Grand Rapids, MI: Eerdmans, 1998) 298.

[8] Columban, S 3.1–2; Walker, 73–75.

tion, familiarity with the Scriptures, and the works of the fathers, should be part of the armory of every bishop. Discernment had supported him during his six-year sojourn at the imperial court in Constantinople, where he was representing Pope Pelagius II. Fearful for his spiritual well-being in that worldly setting, Gregory had brought several brethren from Saint Andrew's Monastery in Rome. He felt that, with the monks' prayerful and studious company providing a peaceful haven amid the turbulence of the great city, he would be bound, "as by the cable of an anchor, to the placid shore of prayer."[9] Gregory was also guided by discretion when elected pope. Forced to choose between a life of action and one of contemplation, seen by him as a choice between Martha or Mary, Rachel or Leah, he succeeded in reconciling the two ways by following the semimonastic life as Augustine had done.[10]

Born of his spiritual wisdom, Gregory's *Pastoral Care* enabled generations of medieval churchmen to become effective spiritual leaders. In this book, the pope asks the prospective pastoral guide to examine his motives and reflect on how he should conduct his life while teaching others, for "no one ventures to teach any art unless he has learned it after deep thought." The thoughtful pastor will consider his own weakness, "lest humility be wanting when office is assumed, the way of life be at variance with the accepted office, teaching divest life of rectitude, and presumption overrate teaching."[11]

Gregory's advice is characterized by its balance. All teaching or preaching, even when directed toward many, must take account of "individuals and their respective needs."[12] In their efforts to bear with patience whatever is vexatious, husband and wives should be encouraged to assist each other to salvation by mutual encouragement. Generous individuals who support others are to be advised against a sense of superiority by accepting that they are merely dispensers of what the Lord has given. Those who love peace must realize that, if they achieve it at the cost of failing to reprove evil conduct, it is not true peace.[13]

Gregory dispenses similar wise counsel through his letters. The abbot of the monastery of Lérins is reminded that, in guarding his monks

[9] Gregory the Great, *Prolegomena*, Select Epistles; NPNF 12: xvi.
[10] Gregory the Great, Ep 5; NPNF 12:75–76.
[11] Gregory the Great, *Pastoral Care*, 1. Introduction; ACW 11:20.
[12] Gregory the Great, *Pastoral Care*, 3. Prologue; ACW 11:89.
[13] Gregory the Great, *Pastoral Care*, 3.27, 3.20, 3.22; ACW 11:188, 152–53, 165–68.

against spiritual failure, he should "love persons and visit faults." Otherwise, correction would pass into cruelty, "and you will destroy those whom you wish to amend." Harsh invective could cause the hearts of sinners "to fall into dejection and despair."[14] Gregory's moderation is evident in his balanced response to Augustine of Canterbury's anxiety about introducing liturgical practices to his English converts. The missionary is advised to select customs from Gaul, Rome, or elsewhere and "teach the church of the English, which is still young in the faith, whatever you have been able to learn with profit . . . for we ought not to love things for places, but places for things."[15]

That his removal from a life of exclusive contemplation of God enhanced the pope's appreciation of asceticism is evident in his book of saints, the *Dialogues*, where he writes of a monk who had died just forty years before: "There was a man of saintly life; blessed Benedict was his name, and he was blessed also with God's grace."[16] A student in Rome during the first years of the sixth century, Benedict rejected the prevailing self-indulgence of the city and retreated to the wilds of Subiaco, where he lived as a hermit, then as leader of a religious community. Thirty years after leaving Rome, he traveled to Monte Cassino. Finding a temple dedicated to Apollo, he overturned the pagan altar and felled the sacred trees. He transformed the temple into a chapel, appropriately dedicated to Saint Martin of Tours.

Gregory revered Benedict, whose *Rule* he praised for its "good judgment." Anyone wishing to know the abbot's character and way of life, he says, can find him in all the teaching of the *Rule*, "because his life could not have differed from his teaching."[17] The unaffected language in which the pope relates the monastic founder's achievements reflects that employed by the abbot himself. Benedict's modesty is manifest in his invitation to those wishing to join him in the ascetic life. They are asked, "with Christ's help, [to] keep this little rule that we have written for beginners."[18] The monastery is presented as "a school for the Lord's

---

[14] Gregory the Great, Ep 11.12; NPNF 13:52–53.

[15] Bede, *Ecclesiastical History*, 1.27.II, trans. Leo Sherley-Price (London: Penguin Books, 1990) 79.

[16] Gregory the Great, *Dialogues*, 2.1; FCh 39:55.

[17] Gregory the Great, *Dialogues*, 2.8, 2.36; FCh 39:74, 107.

[18] *RB 1980: The Rule of St. Benedict*, 73.8, ed. Timothy Fry et al. (Collegeville, MN: Liturgical Press, 1981) 297.

service," where there will be "nothing harsh, nothing burdensome." However, adds Benedict, "the good of all concerned . . . may prompt us to a little strictness in order to amend faults and to safeguard love."[19] For those who wish to progress further, there are the pages of Scripture and "the teachings of the holy fathers." As "tools for the cultivation of virtues" in such "good and observant monks," the abbot recommends the *Conferences* and *Institutes* of Cassian, the *Lives of the Fathers*, and the *Rule of Saint Basil*.

Monks and abbot alike find the will of God in Benedict's humane *Rule*, with its concern for the strengths and weaknesses of individuals. The *Rule's* lucid demands embody a judicious balance of worship, work, study, and rest. The aspirant chooses to live under a spiritual leader who has vowed to set mercy above judgment, to hate faults but love the brothers, one who will use prudence and avoid extremes, "otherwise, by rubbing too hard to remove the rust, he may break the vessel."[20] Above all, Benedict insists that, while the abbot should make no distinction in persons, he must take account of the needs of individuals, "coaxing, reproving and encouraging them as appropriate." In this way, he will ensure that his flock, far from dwindling, will actually grow.[21]

Columban also wrote a rule. Like Benedict, he envisaged the abbot standing in the place of Christ. It is a theme developed in one of his sermons, where the spiritual leader is not only a guide who encourages and reproves but a father who must teach goodness by deeds and words. He should have no regard for earthly things but inspire his community to seek the kingdom of God. In another sermon, the Irishman echoes Cassian by presenting the demanding life of the monk as training for eternity. Nothing of worth in this world, whether the tradesman's craft, the musician's genius, or the doctor's skill, is gained without the toil of training: "What is learned without sorrow and toil?" How much more should a monk be willing to endure to gain his eternal objective, which will bring the "delight of unending joy"?[22] Columban trusts that

> no one and nothing separate us from the love of Christ, no trial, no difficulty, no persecution, no hunger, no nakedness,

---

[19] RB Prol. 45–47; Fry, 165.
[20] RB 73.1–6; Fry, 295–97; RB 64.7–13; Fry, 281–83.
[21] RB 2.30–32; Fry, 177.
[22] Columban, S 4.1; Walker, 79–81; Cassian, *Conf*, 1.2; ACW 57:41–42.

no danger, no death by sword, fire, cross, murder, nothing sad, nothing sweet, nothing hard, nothing fair, may none of the world's vanities separate us from Christ.[23]

Benedict identifies obedience as the keystone of community life; when given to spiritual superiors, it is given to God. All is done to "conform to the saying of the Lord: *I have come not to do my own will, but the will of him who sent me* (John 6:38)."[24] Columban's *Rule* too states that the absolute obedience shown to the spiritual master is shown to God. It brings the monk close to Christ, who, for the sake of man, obeyed the father unto death.[25] Both abbots had imbibed Cassian's teaching that monks should respond to the wishes of their spiritual superior "as if commanded by God."[26] Cassian had learned this from Abbot John of Egypt, who, having lived as a hermit for many years, finally chose to join a community. Questioned about his decision, John explained that, by subjecting himself to the judgment of others, he would absorb the essential virtues of obedience and humility. Since the "true humility" of obedience is the supreme virtue for a monk, his greatest temptation is pride, called by Cassian "the beginning of all sins and faults."[27]

Benedict names twelve steps of humility. Love, obedience, and fear of the Lord, sources of worship and prayer, rest on the creature's recognition of the nature of his relationship with the Creator. That service of God is no passive matter, but a willing sacrifice, freely undertaken, leads Cassian to employ Pauline imagery of the monk as a soldier of Christ who, at every moment, is ready for battle.[28] Columban, for his part, when forced to part from his brethren in Gaul, and seeing them threatened by the evils of the world, urges them "to take up that armor of God to which the apostle points, and make a path to heaven, hurling these arrows, as it were, of earnest prayers."[29] The imagery is just, for, in the battle against the evil which threatens to separate a person from God, prayer and worship represent the Christian's pacific arms.

---

[23] Columban, S 4.3; Walker, 83–84; see Rom 8:35–39.

[24] RB 5.13; Fry, 189.

[25] Columban, *Rule*, 1.1; Walker, 123–25.

[26] Cassian, *Institutes*, 4.10, trans. Boniface Ramsey, ACW 58 (New York: Newman Press, 2000) 83.

[27] Cassian, *Institutes*, 12.1; NPNF 11:280; *Conf*, 19.2; NPNF 11:490.

[28] RB 7; Fry, 189; Cassian, *Institutes*, 1.1; ACW 58:20–26.

[29] Columban, Ep 4.2; Walker, 27.

Monastic life revolves around the liturgy, called by Benedict "the work of God." At its heart is the biblical book of Psalms. Cassian devotes books 2 and 3 of his *Institutes* to the duty of intoning the hymns and canticles of the psalter at fixed hours. He traces the practice back to the desert monks and beyond, even to the Scriptures themselves.[30] Columban carefully presents Irish monastic practice, detailing the number of psalms to be sung, day and night, in the various seasons. Benedict notes that, in this worship due to the Creator, around which all else revolves, God is present in an especial way: "Let us consider, then, how we ought to behave in the presence of God and his angels, and let us stand to sing the psalms in such a way that our minds are in harmony with our voices." Benedict asks that this "work of God" be carried out "with humility, seriousness and reverence, and at the abbot's bidding."[31]

The inner harmony toward which the *Rule of Saint Benedict* leads chimes with the principle of discretion. In establishing the pattern of work, prayer, and study to be followed in his monastery, Benedict is invariably concerned for the needs of those who are weaker, so "care of the sick must rank above and before all else."[32] He moves the focus of monastic life from the personality of the charismatic leader to the *Rule* itself, through which individual monks harmonize their lives with the will of God. By faithfully observing its reasonable demands under the guidance of a wise abbot, a monk can make his spiritual journey with quiet confidence. The balance and humanity of Benedict's relatively detailed *Rule* of seventy-three chapters have been noted. In many ways it mirrors Basil's *Rule*, whose nucleus is contained in a letter to Gregory of Nazianzen and whose forty-eight precepts seek to create a simple and harmonious way of life for a dedicated community.[33]

Columban's *Rule*, relatively brief, is infused with the passion and urgency to be expected of a document issuing from an inspirational leader. Though invoking discretion's place in achieving the mean, the tone of earnest exhortation encourages a sense of constant striving not found in the more measured words of Benedict. The final clause embodies a quotation from Jerome's long letter to Rusticus on monastic life, where the latter is advised not to rely on his own unaided discretion but to live

---

[30] Cassian, *Institutes*, 2–3; ACW 58:35–76.
[31] RB 19.6; Fry, 217; RB 47.4; Fry, 249.
[32] RB 36.1; Fry, 235.
[33] Basil, Ep 22; FCh 13:55–60.

as a member of a religious community. There, under his abbot, he will learn to "come weary to his bed and sleep while walking, and be forced to rise while his sleep is not yet finished. Let him keep silence when he has suffered wrong, let him fear the superior of his community as a lord, love him as a father and believe whatever he commands is healthful for himself." This is the monasticism of Martin and the desert fathers, which came to Ireland from Gaul at the time of Celestine's mission. It demanded an austerity that made few concessions to human weakness.[34]

It is evident from Columban's parting letter to his monks that the Irish monastic commitment involved a bond with an austere, charismatic, and beloved leader. The abbot wishes to write a tearful letter, "but for the reason that I know your heart . . . I have used another style, preferring to check than to encourage tears."[35] The loyalty won from his monks has enabled him to elicit heroic sacrifices from them, but the deeply personal nature of the commitment has brought its trials. Columban implores the brethren to avoid divisions and "preserve unity of spirit in the bond of peace." There is emotional advice to the new abbot and an admission that Columban himself has been broken by the strife, through which "I have almost been driven mad." He reminds his successor, Attala, that sufferings will always follow those who tell the truth, who prefer the foolishness of God to the wisdom of man, who persevere, like Job, in the face of suffering.[36]

Columban's writings, particularly the sermons, reveal his faith in an all-powerful, benign, and generous God, who stirred in the ascetics a generous and cheerful acceptance of the demands of their monastic rule. It must account for the regularity with which the Irish monks intoned the *Te Deum*, most solemnly sonorous of the hymns included in the *Antiphonary of Bangor*. Not just a majestic paean of praise but a prayer of faith and invocation, it expresses gratitude that the second person of the Trinity "did not shrink from entering the Virgin's womb" to open the kingdom of heaven to mankind.[37] It is a hymn which enables the monastic family to join with the entire Church in praise and thanksgiving: "The choir of apostles, of glorious fame, the band of prophets, worthy of our praise, the array of martyrs, in their robes of white, all give praise

---

[34] Columban, *Rule*, 10; Walker, 141; Jerome, Ep 125.15; NPNF 6:249.

[35] Columban, Ep 4.6; Walker, 31.

[36] Columban, Ep 4.3–6; Walker, 29–31.

[37] *Antiphonary*, 7.20; Warren, 10.

to you. The holy Church in all parts of the earth acknowledges you, the father of boundless majesty, your adorable, true and only Son and also the Holy Spirit, the Paraclete."[38]

The *Rule of Saint Benedict* ultimately replaced the older, more demanding monastic codes in the Frankish kingdoms, which extended beyond Germany and Gaul into Italy. The Franks admired and favored the fierce commitment of the Irish ascetics. Touched by their example, many men and women followed Columban and his monks into religious life. In the years after the abbot's departure from Gaul, Luxeil and its related monasteries were joined by other foundations. Bobbio in Italy became renowned for the productivity of its scriptorium and enjoyed the special favor of Rome. For several centuries, Columban's *Rule* continued to be followed on the continent, often in conjunction with that of Benedict. Not till the turn of the first millennium did the Benedictine way gain universal acceptance. Since then, the statutes of most monastic foundations have been based on Saint Benedict's *Rule*.

When viewed from the world's perspective, the asceticism of men like Gregory, Columban, Cassian, and Benedict may be seen as a form of folly. Paul experienced the cold breath of the rational, skeptical world when presenting the Christian message before the Council of the Areopagus in Athens, where "all the Athenians and the foreigners living there would spend their time in nothing but telling or hearing something new." Hearing the apostle speak on the resurrection, some burst out laughing, while "others said, 'We will hear you again about this.'"[39] Through the wisdom born of faith, the fathers and ascetics illuminated the paradoxes of Christianity in which the weak become strong, the poor become rich, and the humble inherit the earth.

It was this spiritual insight which led Basil to reject a life of "vanity" and devote himself to the spiritual welfare of his people. It inspired Ambrose and Paulinus to abandon successful secular careers for service of God and neighbor. It enabled the relatively unschooled Martin and Patrick to serve God more effectively than many of "those wise and learned in law and skilled in speaking."[40] Through the spiritual judgment born of faith, fathers like Leo taught that since Jesus chose his spiritual leaders, not "from among philosophers or orators, but from the lowly

---

[38] *Antiphonary*, 7.7–13; Warren, 10.
[39] Acts 17:21–23, 32.
[40] Basil, Ep 223.2; FCh 28:127; Patrick, *Conf*, 13; Conneely, 65; see 1 Cor 4:10.

and from fishermen," it is not the "wisdom of words" that is needed to preach the "foolishness" of the cross, but "the power of God."[41] The same wisdom led Augustine, who had for so long fruitlessly pursued truth through reason alone, to the conclusion that "unless you believe, you will not understand."[42]

[41] Leo, Ep 164.2; NPNF 12:106; 1 Cor 1:17–25; Patrick, *Conf*, 11–13; Conneely, 65.
[42] Augustine, *Faith and the Creed*, 1.1; FCh 18:301–2; Augustine, Ep 120; FCh 18:301–2; see Gal 3:11.

# 16

# SUFFERING, SIN, AND FORGIVENESS

For five centuries the fathers supported fellow Christians by word and example. They reassured those faltering on their pilgrimage, reminding them of the compassionate God who assumed human nature, suffered, and died for them.

In a time of constant war and deprivation, with many tempted to abandon hope, Gregory the Great pondered the mystery of human suffering. Seeing in the troubles of the time a preparation for eternity, he concluded that, since they were permitted by God, there must be spiritual benefit for those who endure them with faith:

> What therefore remains except to give thanks with tears amidst the scourges we suffer for our sins? For the very one who created us is also made our Father through the spirit of adoption that he has given. Sometimes he nourishes his sons with bread, at others he corrects them with the scourge, since through sorrows, wounds and gifts he trains them for their eternal inheritance.[1]

Gregory first broached this theme during his time in Constantinople, where he began his *Magna Moralia*, a series of reflections on the book of Job. Perceiving in Job's plight an anticipation of the sufferings of Christ and the Church, he confessed that he himself was enduring chronic illness. Later, as pope, in the dedicatory letter which accompanied a volume of the work to his friend Leander, he referred to his immense responsibilities, speaking of being "tortured by frequent pains in

---

[1] Gregory the Great, Hiez 2.10.24, trans. Carole Straw, *Gregory the Great: Perfection in Imperfection* (London: University of California Press, 1988) 184.

the flesh . . . faint with lack of good digestion, breathing with difficulty under mild yet constant fevers."[2] Accepting that suffering and death were the products of a sinful world, he saw in his own ailments opportunities of identifying with Christ. Giving "thanks with tears" for his ordeals, he recognized that his Creator was also a Father, who sent his Son to share the plight of his earthly children and redeem them from sin.

Gregory's greatest trials as pope came from his stewardship of the Church, which he had to steer through every kind of turbulence. With the ship suffering damage from the "bilgewater of vices," he was inclined to blame his own negligence. However, he followed Jesus, who had shown the way by fleeing from the "exalted glory offered him" to the humiliation of the cross, so that "his members might flee from the favors of the world."[3]

Columban shared Gregory's perception of the inevitability of suffering for believers. From brethren encountering "toil and weariness" on the journey of faith, he asked a willingness "to lay down whatever we love, apart from Christ, for Christ's sake."[4] To reach the goal they "must discipline themselves savingly." Faced with the "tribulation and persecution" of banishment from Gaul, the abbot prays that those left behind may be "of one heart and one mind." He reinforces his desire with the words of Jesus himself, "He who does not gather with me, scatters."[5] As soldiers of Christ, Columban and his monks must bravely bear the cross, which is inseparable from being a disciple of Christ: "Blessed then is the man who becomes a sharer in this passion and this shame." With Saint Paul, he concludes that, though the present seems to be a matter of sorrow, it can finally bring joy.[6]

Columban warns that some of the wounds suffered on the journey of life come from the action of the human will, which, if not fettered, seeks what is denied and desires what can never appease it. Asking his listeners to "pay the least service to our short-lived will," he follows Augustine in acknowledging that, when the will concurs with God's

---

[2] Gregory the Great, *Dedicatory Letter: Commentary on Job*, Early Medieval Theology, vol. 9, trans. George E. McCracken and Allen Cabaniss, Library of Christian Classics (London: SCM Press, 1957) 189.

[3] Gregory the Great, Ep 43; NPNF 12:87–88; *Pastoral Care*, 1.3; ACW 11:26.

[4] Columban, S 10.2–3; Walker, 102–3.

[5] Columban, Ep 4.9; Walker, 37; see Luke 11:23.

[6] Columban, S 10.2; Walker, 103; Columban, Ep 4:6; Walker, 31; see Heb 12:11.

grace, the kingdom of heaven can be won from "the field of strife." The brethren should cast aside pride and put their trust in God, "for human goodness is not strong enough to reach the goal it wishes . . . unless the mercy of God also supports the will." If they "eat, drink and share with the poor," they will be "present to the eyes of the Lord" and prepare to pass from the "roadway of this age to our eternal homeland with God."[7] Concluding his sermons, Columban turns to the Song of Songs, begging Jesus, "our all, our life, our light, our salvation, our food, our drink, our God," to wound the souls of the brethren with his love. Inflicted by Christ, "the physician of righteousness and health," these wounds are life-enhancing.[8]

Gregory similarly consoles his friend Andrew, just recovered from grave illness, with the Augustinian reflection that what he has endured has not been without meaning. To be fruitful, the branch must be pruned and grain must be beaten with the flail, just as "the bunches of grapes, pounded with the heels, liquefy into wine."[9] All healing, says Gregory, comes from Christ, the great physician. As Christ's representative, the priest is reminded that "he is a poor and unskillful physician, who aims at healing others but is ignorant of his own ailment."[10]

Gregory is speaking of moral healing. Two centuries earlier, Augustine reflected on his aimless wanderings and concluded that he failed to see the truth because his eyes had been swollen and "puffed up with pride." Thanking the Lord for applying the "goads" which helped to heal his wounds, he rejoiced that God now stands "plain before my spiritual sight." Augustine's contemporary, Cassian, was also concerned with the spiritual injuries suffered by Christians. In sin he saw a "turning of the mind's glance" away from the Creator toward what is created, a preference for the things of this world to those of God, an illness which, without divine grace, can lead to spiritual death.[11] Concerned with the plight of sinners, the fathers taught that, through repentance, prayer, and good works, penitents were released from their burden of guilt. The greatest transgressions were confessed to the bishop, whose power to forgive and retain comes from the risen Christ to his apostles: "Receive

---

[7] Columban, SS 7.2, 8.2, 9.2, 10.3; Walker, 93, 97, 101, 105.
[8] Columban, S 13.3; Walker, 141; see Song 5:6–8.
[9] Gregory the Great, Ep 9.33; NPNF 13:11–12.
[10] Gregory the Great, *Pastoral Care*, 3.24; ACW 11:174.
[11] Augustine, *Conf*, 7.8–9; Ryan, 168; Cassian, *Conf*, 23.8; ACW 57:799.

the Holy Spirit. If you forgive the sins of any, they are forgiven them; if you retain the sins of any, they are retained."[12]

Against the Novationists, who claimed that there were certain transgressions which could not be remitted, Ambrose wrote *Concerning Repentance*, in which he noted that the penitent was absolved through confession, a spirit of amendment, and hearing the words, "Your sin is forgiven." Aware that Jesus treated sinners with mercy and compassion, he counseled gentleness when dealing with penitents.[13] Almost a century later, Leo the Great told priests and bishops that, in dealing with repentant sinners, they should place no limits on God's mercy, since the very feeling of penitence "springs from the inspiration of God." Agreeing with Ambrose that liberation from grave sins committed after baptism cannot be gained "except through the prayer of priests," Leo saw in the rite of forgiveness a doorway through which those "purged by salutary reparation" could pass to the other sacraments.[14]

In earlier times, with baptism recognized as the primary means of remitting sin, writers had differed on how often post-baptismal transgressions could be forgiven. Tertullian envisaged a second repentance, "but now once for all, but never more."[15] The Church did not accept this view. However, while Ambrose's biographer claims that when sinners confessed the bishop often wept with them, access to forgiveness remained demanding, even forbidding.[16] Grave violations of the moral code brought rigorous forms of self-denial and a lengthy period of separation from the sacraments, followed by public reinstatement in church. Jerome celebrates one such act of reconciliation. Fabiola, a Roman aristocrat, deserted her violent husband to live with another man. Repenting her adultery, she "put on sackcloth and made public confession of her error." Restored to communion, she devoted herself to prayer, sold her property to help the poor, and founded a hospital, where she helped to nurse the sick.[17]

---

[12] John 20:22–23.

[13] Ambrose, *Concerning Repentance*, 1.1–3; 2:10, trans. H. De Romestin, NPNF, vol. 10 (Grand Rapids, MI: Eerdmans, 1997) 329–31, 356.

[14] Leo, Ep 108:3–5; NPNF 12:80.

[15] Tertullian, *On Repentance*, 7; *A New Eusebius*, trans. J. Stevenson (London: SPCK, 1999) 174.

[16] Paulinus, *Life of Saint Ambrose*, 39; WF 178.

[17] Jerome, Ep 77.4–6; NPNF 6:159–60.

The failure to frame a less demanding penitential rite accounts, in part, for deferral of baptism, a practice widespread in the fourth and fifth centuries. It resulted in the catechumenate being perceived as a form of nominal Christianity, with its members remaining unbaptized but living according to Christian values. There was even an initiation ceremony for catechumens, who often waited till well into adulthood before having all sin forgiven through baptism. Ambrose argued strongly against putting off repentance "by deferring baptism to old age." In the *Confessions*, Augustine, who strongly favored infant baptism and argued against deferral, notes that he himself became a catechumen "as soon as I issued from my mother's womb" by being "signed with the sign of his cross and seasoned with his salt." He then suffered a serious boyhood illness. Monica, a fervent Christian, was on the point of having him "initiated into the sacraments of salvation and be washed in them" when the danger passed and baptism was again deferred.[18]

Ambrose was thirty-four years old and still a catechumen when he was elected bishop of Milan. His brother Satyricus was even older when baptized just before his premature death in 375. Jerome received the sacrament in his teens, Paulinus of Nola at thirty. The eastern fathers Basil, Gregory of Nazianzen, and John Chrysostom were baptized in early adulthood. It was a practice which began to decline as a more humane means of reconciling sinners evolved. Once again, the desert fathers provided an answer.

From Abbot Serapion, John Cassian learned of the eight principal vices and the corresponding virtues with which they could be replaced through the judicious guidance of a spiritual mentor.[19] Cassian applied this remedy of opposites to minor breaches of the rule by his own monks, with the tendency to gluttony treated by fasting, covetousness by renunciation, and pride by humility. The abbot's innovation represented, not a new penitential service, but a simple exercise in monastic discipline. Cassian's writings spread knowledge of the process through which the individual monk, assisted by a spiritual guide, could conquer weaknesses and continue his journey toward God. In the monasteries of the west there was recognition of the psychological and spiritual validity of his

---

[18] Augustine, *Conf*, 1.11.17–18; Ryan, 53–54.

[19] Cassian, *Institutes*, 5.1–3; trans. Edgar C. S. Gibson, NPNF 11 (Grand Rapids, MI: Eerdmans, 1998) 233–34.

teaching on the confession of faults to monastic seniors: "Take heart, my boy. Your confession freed you from this captivity."[20]

The Irish applied the method with particular enthusiasm. A century after John Cassian's death, the *Penitential of Finnian* presented the "remedies of Penance for the several kinds of spiritual ills to be cured." For these remedies Finnian, abbot of Clonard, claimed the authority both of Scripture and of very learned churchmen.[21] In submitting to them, the individual monk was led along the road to spiritual health by his *anamchara*, or soul friend, an experienced director. Providing similar "medicine for the salvation of souls" a century later, another Irish abbot, Cummean, also invoked "the remedy of opposites" to heal the eight principal vices, presenting it as "the medicine for the salvation of souls."[22] Both abbots extended the benefits of their *Penitentials* to lay members of the Church.

Columban composed a *Penitential*, claiming that it originated with "the holy fathers."[23] Applicable to both monks and the faithful, it could be applied by "spiritual doctors." Just as a physician has differing treatments for eye diseases, wounds, boils, fractures, and burns, doctors of souls will "treat with diverse kinds of cures" the spiritual wounds of penitents, "their sicknesses, offences, griefs, distresses, and pains," returning victims of sin to spiritual health. "Prescriptions," or penances, were related to a variety of sins ranging from pride, drunkenness, or slander to murder and adultery.[24] Emphasizing the need for a goal if vices are to be uprooted and replaced by virtues, Columban quotes Cassian's observation that tilling of the virtues is an art which the monk, like the farmer, must perfect. All the sacrifices of the monastic life are void unless the mind and heart rejects pride and other sins: "Then, lest perhaps we should labor without fruit, let us take pains to be freed from our vices by God's help, that thereafter we can be adorned with virtues."[25]

[20] Cassian, *Conf*, 2.11; Ramsey, 57:92.

[21] Finnian, *Penitential*, epilogue, *The Irish Penitentials*, trans. Ludwig Bieler (Dublin: Dublin Institute for Advanced Studies, 1963) 95.

[22] Cummean, *Penitential*, prologue, *Irish Penitentials*, Bieler, 94–95.

[23] Columban, *Penitential*, A1; Walker, 169.

[24] Columban, *Penitential*, A12, B; Walker, 171–73; Gregory the Great, *Pastoral Care*, 3.36; ACW 11: 226–27. Thomas O'Loughlin, *Adamnan at Birr* (Dublin: Four Courts Press, 2001) 3.

[25] Columban, S 2.2; Walker, 69; Cassian, *Conf*, 1.2; NPNF 11:295.

Pope Gregory's understanding of Cassian's remedy is revealed in his *Pastoral Care*, where he acknowledges the necessity of contrition and satisfaction if God the physician is to heal the soul.[26] However, it was the Irish who first applied the monastic system of forgiveness to the needs of Christians at large. Having confessed privately, the penitent was required to engage in prayer, fasting, and good works, and even to abstain from the sacraments for a time, but did not have to endure a public reconciliation before fellow Christians.

It could be claimed that the new, relatively private, process lacked the communal dimension that characterized the other sacraments. However, this feature must account, in part, for the large numbers who flocked to Columban's first monastery in Gaul, seeking "the remedy of penance for their spiritual ailments."[27] Even the Gaulish bishops and clergy, with whom the abbot had such an uneasy relationship, came to him for spiritual refreshment. To modern sensibilities, the penalties prescribed were harsh, but the penitentials led to an advance in pastoral care. By the end of the first millennium, an apparently intractable problem had been resolved by adoption of a remedy appropriate to the age.

The rite of repentance did not occur in isolation but was seen as an episode in the Christian's journey, on which he was supported by confirmation, Eucharist, and the other sacraments, through which the believer was bound to Christ and to fellow pilgrims. This theme of support for the Christian's arduous pilgrimage to the heavenly city runs through Columban's thirteen sermons. In the final homily he reaches the goal, symbolized in the Fountain of Life, which is none other than "the Lord himself, our Lord Jesus Christ." The abbot tells his monks that, in following their calling, they can make their way through the world's snares if they "eat the same our Lord Jesus Christ as bread and drink him as the Fountain, who calls himself the living bread, who gives life to this world."[28]

Through these words of the Gospel of John, Columban invokes the surrounding passage on the Eucharist, which is related to "the bread from heaven" given to the travelers in the desert. Here Jesus, proclaiming himself the "living bread" of life which, when eaten, banishes hunger and thirst, adds, "Whoever eats of this bread will live forever; and the

[26] Gregory the Great, *Pastoral Care*, 3.29; ACW 11:200; 203.
[27] Jonas, *Life of Saint Columban*, 14, 17; Munro, 27, 32.
[28] Columban, S 13.1; Walker, 117; see John 6:32ff.

bread that I will give for the life of the world is my flesh."[29] John's words would have reminded Columban of the *Sancti Venite*, a communion prayer found in the *Bangor Antiphonary*.

> Approach you who are holy, receive the body of Christ;
> Drinking the holy blood by which you are redeemed.
> Saved by Christ's body and blood, by it nourished,
> Let us sing praises to God.

Here the monks acknowledge that, through the sacrament of the altar, they are "rescued from the jaws of hell" by Christ, who "saved the whole world by his cross and blood." They celebrate Christ as victim, sacrificed for all, the heavenly bread given to the hungry, a living fountain for the thirsty. All who believe and approach with pure hearts will achieve eternal salvation.[30] Toward the end of the *Dialogues*, Gregory too applauds the power of the sacrifice of the altar, in which the faithful can receive the body and blood of the Savior. Through communion, he says, "the lowliest is united with the most sublime, earth is joined to heaven, the visible and the invisible somehow merge into one."[31]

---

[29] John 6:51.

[30] *Antiphonary*, 8.1–2, 4–8; Warren, 10; James O'Laverty, *History of Down and Connor*, vol. 2 (Dublin: M. H. Gill and Son, 1880) 117.

[31] Gregory the Great, *Dialogues*, 4.60; FCh 39:273.

# 17

# DISPELLING THE DARKNESS

I n preaching the good news of salvation, the fathers spoke of the innate goodness of creation which, tainted by sin, was redeemed through the incarnation. Surveying a somber landscape blighted by war and famine, Gregory the Great found hope in the power of faith, prizing its ability to restore suffering humanity and illuminate the darkness enveloping a generation crushed by insecurity and fear. His mentor, Augustine, had expressed similar confidence in contrasting the vision of the saving grace of God sanctifying a sinful world with the Manichaean vision of a material creation governed by dark satanic forces.

Given the tenor of the time, Gregory was drawn to the prophetic books, whose symbolism he applied to present troubles. Aware that, in suffering similar trials, prophets like Ezekiel and Zechariah had assured believers of God's faithfulness, he delivered and published his twenty-two *Homilies on Ezekiel*. It was an appropriate choice for the author of the *Pastoral Care*, as the prophet not only condemns shepherds who feed themselves rather than caring for their flock but records God's pledge as a "true shepherd": "I will seek the lost, and I will bring back the strayed, and I will bind up the injured, and I will strengthen the weak."[1]

Ezekiel had written darkly on the fall of Jerusalem in terms of God's judgment on an unfaithful people but prophesied a glorious return from the humiliations of Babylon and the birth of a new spirit. Jerome, composing his commentary on Ezekiel in 410 during the sack of Rome, and painfully aware of parallels with the prophet's Jerusalem, saw "the whole world perish in one city."[2] Almost two centuries later, with Rome once

---

[1] Ezek 34:16.
[2] Jerome, *Commentary on Ezekiel*, preface, bk 1; NPNF 6:500.

more at the mercy of barbarians, Gregory reflects on Ezekiel's words and exclaims: "What Rome herself, once deemed mistress of the world, has now become, we see; wasted away with afflictions grievous and many."[3] Overcome by the sufferings of the people, he again echoes Jerome in claiming that he can preach no more: "I am compelled to refrain my tongue from speaking, for my soul is weary of my life . . . and my harp turned into mourning."[4]

Though the prevailing turmoil did not deflect Gregory from attending daily to the material needs of his long-suffering people, he asked them not to give themselves wholly to earthly affairs but to turn to Christ, who is "the way, the truth and the life." In a world which is transient, he encouraged them to amend their lives and to conquer their besetting sins: "Give not your heart, then, my brethren, to what cannot last."[5] Awareness that the plight of human beings in his time resembled Job's evoked the pope's reflection on the brevity and pathos of the life of man, which blossoms, then withers like a flower. Another image he deployed warns that the Christian way does not represent a facile escape from reality but entails a hazardous journey over testing terrain, across plains, through rocky passes, so that, without fail, "now prosperity, now adversity, befall us in this life."[6]

Gregory's words were directed to all the faithful. Columban addressed his monks, who trusted that, through faithfully observing their vows, they would become inheritors of the true life, "by the gift of our Lord Jesus Christ." He too spoke of the "treachery of life . . . so fleeting, shifting, dangerous, short and uncertain, which shall be dissolved like a shadow, a mirage, a cloud, or something null and void." The present life, "mortal, brief, tottering, unsure, inconstant, transient, fickle, changeable," seeks to allure, beguile, and deceive the dedicated ascetic but should cause him to "hasten from the shadow of a pictured life to the true life's truth."[7] The brethren are asked to regard the life of this world as "the roadway of mortals, not their life," an impermanent way to be

---

[3] Gregory, *Homily on Ezekiel*, 6.22; Dudden, *Saint Gregory the Great*, vol. 2, 19.

[4] Jerome, *Commentary on Ezekiel*, 1, preface; NPNF 6:499–500; Dudden, *Saint Gregory the Great*, vol. 2, 18–21.

[5] Dudden, *Saint Gregory the Great*, vol. 1, 256.

[6] Straw, *Gregory the Great*, 107–8; see Job 14:1–4; Gregory the Great, Ep 9.218; NPNF 12:140; 196.

[7] Columban, S 5.2; 6.2; Walker, 85; 89.

questioned, not believed, traversed, not occupied by believers. Though enduring toil and weariness on the journey, they will at last reach their objective, where there will be "life eternal, rest, perpetual peace, a blessed eternity, a joy unending."[8]

In his letter to Gregory, Columban requested a copy of his *Homilies on Ezekiel*, reportedly "compiled with wonderful skill." Informing the pope that he had already read six books of Jerome's commentary on the prophet, he begged him to "expound all the obscurity of Zechariah" and forward a copy of his writings on the Song of Songs. Familiar with Ezekiel's concluding image of the rebuilding of the temple in Jerusalem, signifying the heavenly city which is the destination of every Christian, the monk asked Gregory for his "final expositions of the book."[9]

Had Columban received the commentary, he would have found that the troubled times brought it to an end before Gregory could reflect on the spring or fountain which, issuing from under the temple threshold and flowing east, gradually deepens as it nears the sea. Ezekiel tells how life teems both in the river and on its banks, observing, "Wherever the river goes, every living creature that swarms will live."[10] Below can be seen the marshes and lagoons which remain salt. The picture is clear: Christ lives in his Church, which heals a wounded world through the pure waters of faith, winning men and women from the salt marshes and lagoons of darkness and unbelief.

In pondering this image Columban may have recalled a similar stream. Named Slan or Health, it flows east, down a hillside close to Saul, through verdant countryside, into one of the lagoons exposed by the ebbing tides of Strangford Lough. Writing just eighty years after the abbot's death, Muirchú recalls that Patrick, on his return to Ireland, sailed northward from Inber Dee, finally entering the lough, where "he and his company disembarked at Inber Slane."[11] At nearby Saul, where he was to die, he began his health-giving mission to the Irish. Columban, a pilgrim who wished to do "reverence to the ashes of the saints" in Rome, had lived for twenty years at Bangor, not far from the burial place of that earlier "pilgrim for Christ" who had helped to bring the faith to Ireland.[12]

---

[8] Columban, S 5.1–2; 9.1; Walker, 85–87; 97.
[9] Columban, Ep 1.9; Walker, 11.
[10] Ezek 47:9.
[11] Muirchú, *Life of Saint Patrick*; De Paor, 180.
[12] Columban, Ep 1.8; Walker, 11.

Study of the prophetic writings sustained Gregory and Columban in the violent, chaotic world of their time. In the prophets they found the images of barrenness and refreshment, darkness and light which enabled them to express their trust in the sustaining power of God's grace. Surveying the spiritual deserts caused by war and famine, Gregory calls on priests to respond to the command of Scripture: "Let thy fountains be conveyed abroad, and in the streets divide the waters." Preachers must first drink deeply from Christ, the source, and then direct these refreshing riches to others.[13] Writing to the pope, Columban expresses the desire "to journey to you, to drink that spiritual channel of the living fountain and the living stream of wisdom which flows from heaven and springs up unto eternal life."[14] To the abbot, Christ is "that Fountain ever and again to be desired, though ever and again to be imbibed." He is also the "physician of righteousness and health," the source of life for those who drink from the fount of living water, springing up to life eternal.[15]

Prophets, apostles, fathers, and ascetics were at one in choosing light as another potent symbol of the divine presence in the world. In John's gospel, Jesus proclaims himself the "light of the world" and assures those who believe that they will never have to walk in the dark again. In the prologue to that Gospel the Word become flesh is hailed as a "light [that] shines in the darkness," which "the darkness did not overcome." Believers are reminded that some, preferring the darkness, would turn their backs on such a brilliant illumination of truth and goodness.[16] In Genesis, God is extolled as Creator of light.[17] Isaiah announces the coming of a messiah to a people who are experiencing "only distress and darkness":

> The people who walked in darkness
>     have seen a great light;
> those who lived in a land of deep darkness—
>     on them light has shined.[18]

In the second century, Church father Clement of Alexandria welcomed Christ as the Sun of justice who illuminates a world long lost in darkness:

---

[13] Gregory the Great, *Pastoral Care*, 3.24; ACW 11:175–76, quoting Prov 5:15–17.
[14] Columban, Ep 1.8; Walker, 11.
[15] Columban, S 13.3; Walker, 119, 121.
[16] John 8:12; 9:5; 12:46; 1:5; 3:19.
[17] See Gen 1:3–5.
[18] Isa 8:22; 9:2.

Hail, O Light! For in us, buried in darkness, shut up in the shadow of death, light had shone forth from heaven, purer than the sun, sweeter than life here below. That light is eternal life; and whatever partakes of it lives. But night fears the light, and hiding itself in terror, gives place to the day of the Lord. Sleepless light is now over all, and the west has given credence to the east. For this was the meaning of the new creation.[19]

For Augustine, Christ is "the true Sun of justice," giving everlasting day to his kingdom, revealing the truth and obliterating the darkness of evil: "He is our salvation, of whom the psalmist says elsewhere, 'May God have mercy on us, and bless us; may he cause the light of his countenance to shine upon us . . . that we may know your way upon the earth.'"[20] In the triumph of light Pope Gregory finds an image of this liberation of human beings born into "the darkness of this earthly exile." Their plight is that of a child delivered in a dungeon and growing up in the dark:

Suppose the mother describes to him the sun, the moon, the stars, the mountains and the fields, birds flying in the air and horses running in the fields. Born and raised in the dungeon, knowing only the perpetual darkness around him, he would doubt whether the things he heard his mother describe actually existed, since he had no experience of them. So it is with men born into the darkness of this earthly exile. They hear about lofty and invisible things, but hesitate to believe in them because they know only the lowly visible things of earth into which they were born.[21]

Gregory concludes this reflection on the two cities with the good news that, through the incarnation, death, and resurrection of Jesus, the darkness has been dispelled and all are free to live in the light.

Calling on his monks to watch and pray while they await the coming of Christ, Columban trusts that their lamps may be kindled by the light of the knowledge and love of God, which provides perpetual guidance through the world's darkness and is sought by all who wish to share in the divine happiness. Gregory sees those who truly seek God rejecting the

---

[19] Johannes Quasten, *Patrology*, vol. 2 (Antwerp: Spectrum Publishers, 1953) 23.
[20] Augustine, *Sermons*, 190, 3; 191, 1; FCh 38:23-24; 26; Ps 66:2.
[21] Gregory the Great, *Dialogues*, 4.1; FCh 39:190.

paltry light of this world for "the splendor of interior clarity," the true light, where light is not one thing and life another, but where the light itself is life, where the light "so encircles us outwardly that we are filled inwardly, and so fills us inwardly that, being limitless, it encircles us outwardly."[22]

The worship of the ascetics was suffused with images of light. Intoned daily in the monasteries, the psalms and canticles acclaimed the redemptive work of "the light of the world." The theme pervades the pages of the *Antiphonary of Bangor*, which encompasses the pattern of monastic worship around the time of Gregory and Columban. Matins anticipated the imminence of the light of day. Dawn's coming was celebrated at Lauds. As darkness fell and the lamps were kindled for Vespers, God's mercy was invoked. It was then that the *Ignis creator igneus* was sung. Invoking the lighting of the paschal candle, the hymn reminds the community that all worship is centered on the paschal mystery, through which God, creator of light and source of salvation, guides his people from the darkness of slavery to the light of freedom. *Ignis creator igneus* also rejoices that on Easter eve the warmth of the Holy Spirit burns away sin, just as the dark beeswax of the candle is consumed by the flame.[23]

*Praecamur Patrem* celebrates the redemptive light of Christ overcoming the darkness of sin and death, while the hymn in praise of Saint Patrick, *Audite omnes*, speaks of his bright deeds that "shine forth among men." To the monks of Columban's old monastery Patrick was

> a light of the world, the great burning light of the Gospel
> raised aloft on a candlestick, illuminating the whole age.[24]

Finally, the "Canticle of Zachary" enabled the brethren to praise their generous God for fulfilling the promise of redemption:

> For in the tender compassion of our God
> the rising sun from on high will come to us,
> to shine on those who live in darkness, under the cloud
>     of death,
> and to guide our feet into the way of peace.[25]

---

[22] Gregory the Great, Moralia 24.12.35; Straw, *Gregory the Great*, 227; see John 1:4.

[23] *Antiphonary*, 9; Warren, 9.

[24] *Antiphonary*, 3; Warren, 5; *Antiphonary*, 13.11; Warren, 15; trans. *King of Mysteries*, 155.

[25] *Antiphonary*, 4.78–79; Warren, 8; see Luke 1:78–79.

Gregory employs similar imagery to illumine man's relation with God, disrupted by sin but restored through the divine mercy. If, in this world, the light of truth shines on Christians and they experience the radiance of the heavenly kingdom, "it is indeed day, but not yet perfect day." Believers can play a part in spreading the light of faith, for "unless torches themselves burn, they will not kindle others."[26] If the spiritual guide allows the light of the spirit to be obscured by the dust of earthly cares, those he leads are like an army that has lost its way. Through his failure, "gold becomes dimmed, the finest color is changed, the stones of the sanctuary are scattered in the top of every street."[27] A potent source of light is sacred Scripture, which is "set up as a kind of lantern for us in the night of this life." But, warns Gregory, "when the words are not rightly understood, the result is darkness, not light."[28]

Gregory speaks for all the faithful. Columban's words are for his monks. On their behalf, he begs Christ "to kindle our lamps that they may shine continually in your temple and receive perpetual life from you, the Light Perpetual, so that our darkness may be enlightened and the world's darkness may be driven from us."[29] It is a fitting metaphor, for God, the source of light, created man in his own image and likeness. A darker image can be painted by those "who are fierce, wrathful or proud," or who choose falsehood instead of truth, unrighteousness instead of justice. The ascetics must be on guard, because the true image can be dispelled even by an angry word. It is restored through repentance. The key is love: "We know that we have passed from death to life, because we love the brethren." In seeking such love, the abbot begs the Lord "to inspire us richly," for only if man submits to the divine will can God paint his image in him.[30]

Like the poets who composed the Psalms, the fathers and ascetics did not espouse a facile faith which ignored the evils they encountered. However, believing in a creative and redemptive God, they rejected the Manichaeans' view of a world irretrievably enmeshed in darkness and celebrated God's creation which, though compromised by the fall, has been redeemed through the incarnation. In the antiphonal cadences

[26] Gregory the Great, Ep 9.120–21; NPNF 13:33–34.
[27] Gregory the Great, *Pastoral Care*, 2.7; ACW 11:70–71; quoting Lam 4:1.
[28] Gregory the Great, *Pastoral Care*, 3.24; ACW 11:172.
[29] Columban, S 12.3; Walker, 115.
[30] Columban, S 11.2–3; Walker, 109; see 1 John 3:14–15.

of the psalms Ambrose heard an echo of the rhythms of the glorious creation, so it is fitting that he wrote a commentary on Psalm 104, sung in praise of the God who placed mankind in a world that is essentially good and bountiful. Augustine too reflected on this psalm, whose first and final verses capture the essence of the praise which each human creature should offer the Creator.

> Bless the Lord, O my soul.
> O Lord my God, you are very great.
> You are clothed with honor and majesty,
> wrapped in light as with a garment.
>
> I will sing to the Lord as long as I live;
> I will sing praise to my God while I have being.
> May my meditation be pleasing to him,
> for I rejoice in the Lord.[31]

Moved by this praise of God's bounty, Augustine celebrates the single element of creation which will endure forever. Made in God's image, sharing the divine life, lost to sin and restored through the incarnation and redemption, each human being, by resisting pride, can outshine all purely natural wonders and beauties of creation. In the psalm's most potent words, directly addressed to God, the bishop finds confirmation of those gifts which, through God's beneficence, may be enjoyed by humanity: "You take away their spirit and they shall fall; send forth your spirit and they shall be created: and you shall renew the face of the earth."[32]

Several fathers wrote commentaries on the hexameron, the six days of creation, thanking God for the richness and variety of his achievement. Gregory Nazianzen marveled at Basil's composition, confessing that, on reading it, "I am brought into the presence of the Creator, understand the words of creation and admire the Creator more than before."[33] A similar effect is achieved by Ambrose's *Hexameron* and the related songs of praise which the bishop modeled on the psalms. In

---

[31] Ps 104:1–2, 33–34.

[32] Augustine, *Expositions on the Psalms*, 104.30–32; 40–43; NPNF 8:516–17.

[33] Gregory of Nazianzen, *Panegyric on Basil:Oration*, 43.67, trans. Charles Gordon Browne and James Edward Swallow, NPNF, vol. 7 (Grand Rapids, MI: Eerdmans, 1996) 417.

one of these Augustine found light and consolation on the death of his mother. Sung at daybreak, it evokes a calm confidence in the care of the Creator for his human family:

> Creator God, O Lord of all,
> who rule the skies, you clothe the day
> in radiant color; bid the night
> in quietness serve the gracious sway
> of sleep, that weary limbs, restored
> to labor's use, may rise again,
> and jaded minds abate their fret,
> and mourners find release from pain.[34]

In the communal intonation of the psalms Ambrose perceived a universal dimension, as the human family joined the entire creation in affirmation of the divine munificence. It is a quality that characterizes a canticle which has always been a staple of patristic and monastic prayer. The *Benedicite* is the song of the three young men in the book of Daniel who faced the extreme test by refusing to bow to Nebuchadnezzar's golden statue, itself an image of the perverse elevation of a part of creation at the expense of the Creator. Surviving the fiery furnace through faith, the three sing in praise of God's protective power. Capturing the spirit of the apostles and martyrs, their song unites all believers in praise of the Creator:

> Bless the Lord, all you works of the Lord;
>> sing praise to him and highly exalt him forever.
> Bless the Lord, you heavens;
>> sing praise to him and highly exalt him forever. . . .
> All who worship the Lord, bless the God of gods,
>> sing praise to him and give thanks to him,
>> for his mercy endures forever.[35]

---

[34] Augustine, *Conf,* 9.12.32; Boulding, 233.
[35] Dan 3:57–58, 90; see *Antiphonary,* 6; Warren, 8–9.

# 18

# AIDAN, BEDE, AND BONIFACE

G regory the Great died on 12 March 604, but followers of the
fathers continued to promote the Gospel message of salvation
and renewal. One devotee was Isidore, who was elected bishop
of Seville in succession to his brother Leander, friend of Gregory. He saw
the need to preserve the written treasury of the Church's teaching and
the culture that supported it. Included in his encyclopedic synthesis of
classical and Christian learning were scriptural writings, together with
works on church governance, doctrine and morality, liturgy and monastic life. The fathers, particularly Augustine and Gregory the Great,
found a place in Isidore's compendium, which was influential throughout
the middle ages.

At the beginning of the eighth century, Isidore's counterpart in the
east, John Damascene, entered the monastery of Mar Sabas, near Jerusalem. His *Fountain of Wisdom*, a compilation of Christian writings in
which the Scriptures and patristic teachings are generously represented,
opens with an Augustinian acknowledgment of the relation between
reason and faith.[1] It proceeds with consideration of the unity and trinity
of God, creation, the fall, and the urgent need for redemption. The nature
and person of Jesus, his death and resurrection, receive comprehensive
treatment. John's profound appreciation of apostolic teaching is evident
in his presentation of the Church's sacramental life and its power to unite
God and humanity, earth and heaven.[2]

---

[1] John of Damascus, *The Fount of Knowledge*, Philosophical Chapters 3; *Saint John
of Damascus: Writings*, trans. F. H. Chase, FCh, vol. 37 (Washington, DC: CUAP,
1970) 11.

[2] John of Damascus, *The Orthodox Faith*, 4.13; FCh 37:354–61.

John Damascene is regarded by many as the last of the Church fathers, yet even during his lifetime a devout Northumbrian monk was ensuring that the patristic tradition would endure. Bede, who became one of the best-loved spiritual writers in medieval times, was, for the greater part of his life, a member of the monastic community at Jarrow. "While I have observed the regular discipline and sung the choir offices daily in church," he wrote, "my chief delight has always been in study, teaching and writing." On visits to Rome, Benedict Biscop, the founding abbot of Wearmouth and Jarrow, obtained many books for the monastic library, among them works of Jerome, Ambrose, Augustine, and Gregory. From these, Bede compiled short extracts, "commenting on their meaning and interpretation . . . both for my own benefit and that of my brethren."[3]

Bede, whose commentaries, homilies, and lives of the saints were widely read, was an acknowledged authority on the intricacies of the *computus* and favored the calendar of Dionysius Exiguus, devised in Rome in the 520s. Inspired by the works and example of Gregory, to whom he devoted the first book of his *Ecclesiastical History of the English People*, he opened the second book with a heartfelt tribute to the great pope: "It is fitting that he should receive fuller mention in this history, since it was through his zeal that our English nation was brought from the bondage of Satan to the faith of Christ, and we may rightly term him our own apostle."

Displaying acute insight into Gregory's character and his teaching, Bede hails him as "a mighty champion of Catholic truth." Praising the *Moralia*, and that "notable book, the *Pastoral Care*," he acknowledges the excellence of the sermons on the Gospel and the homilies on Ezekiel. There is sympathy for a pope who sacrificed his life of monastic peace for the sake of the Church, and a conviction that "he lost none of his monastic perfection through his pastoral cares." With further words of praise for this father "of imperishable genius," Bede quotes Gregory's epitaph, which he arranged to have transcribed and brought from Rome. One stanza reads:

> The life of this high pontiff, here at rest,
> With good deeds past all reckoning was blest.

---

[3] Bede, *History*, Autobiographical Note 5.25; Sherley-Price, 329.

He fed the hungry and he clothed the chill
And by his teaching shielded souls from ill.[4]

In the *History*, completed in 731, Bede not only expresses gratitude for Gregory's evangelization of the pagan English who had supplanted the Roman Britons but celebrates the felicitous encounter between the English and the Irish, which led to the conversion of the people of his own region. He tells how the christianization of Northumbria was begun in 625 by Paulinus, one of Gregory's monks, who traveled north as chaplain to Ethelburga, new bride of the pagan King Edwin. Paulinus converted the king and many of his people. When Edwin was killed in battle in 633, his widow and her children, accompanied by Paulinus, returned to Kent. The Northumbrians reverted to paganism. Emerging from exile in Argyll, Oswald, a son of Edwin's predecessor, assumed power in 635. An admirer of the brethren of Iona, by whom he had been educated and baptized, the king asked the community to send him a monk who would bring the English people "the blessings of the Christian faith and the sacraments."[5]

Aidan came, was consecrated bishop, and established his see at Lindisfarne, not far from Bambrough, the royal seat. To Bede it was an event as natural as Lindisfarne's setting: "As the tide ebbs and flows, this place is surrounded by the sea twice a day like an island, and twice a day the sand dries and joins it to the mainland." Aidan is described as "a man of outstanding gentleness, holiness and moderation," who wisely decided that the brethren should follow the practice of the apostles by beginning their mission with the milk of simpler teaching, gradually nourishing the converts "with the word of God until they are capable of greater perfection and able to follow the loftier precepts of Christ." Bede presents the bishop, "not yet fluent" in English, preaching in Irish, with the king acting as his interpreter. Oswald had "obtained perfect command of the Irish tongue during his long exile."[6]

The Irish ascetics are admired by Bede because, as men dedicated to prayer, self-discipline, and continence, they "lived as they taught." Faithful to their *Rule*, they read the Scriptures and prayed together, wherever

---

[4] Bede, *History*, 2.1; Sherley-Price, 98–103.
[5] Bede, *History*, 3.3; Sherley-Price, 146.
[6] Bede, *History*, 3.3; Sherley-Price, 146–47.

they were or whatever their other responsibilities.[7] Aidan meditated on the Psalms daily, withdrawing to pray with his brethren even when the king was present. Leading a simple life, eating and drinking sparingly, he observed a fast on Wednesdays and Fridays. Traveling on foot unless compelled by necessity to ride, he neither sought nor cared for worldly possessions. What he received from the wealthy he donated to the poor or "used to ransom those who had been unjustly sold as slaves." Given a fine horse by King Oswin, the bishop characteristically presented it, with all its royal trappings, to a poor man who asked for alms. Chided by the king, he replied, "What are you saying, your majesty? Is this foal of a mare more valuable to you than this child of God?" Bede approvingly comments that many men and women were inspired to follow Aidan into religious life.[8]

Reflecting on the wider contribution of Iona, Bede praises its founder, Columba, who, before leaving his native land for Britain, had "established a noble monastery in Ireland known in the Irish language as *Dearmach*, anglicized Derry, the field of oaks, because of the oak forest in which it stands." Three chapters of the *History* are allotted to Adomnán, who became ninth abbot of Iona in 679. Interest in this abbot's moral influence is apparent in Bede's reference to his negotiations on behalf of sixty Irishmen captured by Ecgfrith of Northumbria.[9] In 685 the prisoners were released by Ecgfrith's successor, Aldfrith, who had spent many years studying in Ireland and was fluent in its language. Just before gaining the throne, the king had been living in the vicinity of Iona.[10]

Since the patrimony of Iona included foundations as far apart as Derry and Durrow, Adomnán's influence extended deep into Ireland. It was an authority that was not confined to spiritual matters. In 575 Columba had brought warring kings together at Druim Cett, where they agreed to a peace. Precisely a century after Columba's death, Adomnán achieved a similar success in 697, when his *Cain*, or *Law of the Innocents*, was promulgated at the Synod of Birr in Offaly.[11] Ratified by more than ninety leaders of church and state, the law afforded protection to "clerics,

---

[7] Bede, *History*, 3.5; Sherley-Price, 150–51.
[8] Bede, *History*, 3.14; Sherley-Price, 166.
[9] Bede, *History*, 3.4, 4.26, 5.14; Sherley-Price, 148, 254, 293.
[10] Adomnán, *Life of Saint Columba*, 46–47; Sharpe, 350.
[11] Adomnán, *Life of Saint Columba*, 1.49, 2.6, 2.35; Sharpe, 151, 159, 184.

females and innocent youths" in times of military activity, with offenses against women given greatest prominence.[12]

The creative and artistic revival taking place in the Irish church during this time represented another episode in the presentation of the truths of creation, incarnation, and redemption. While Adomnán was engaged on his *Life of Columba*, Muirchú and Tirechan were writing their biographies of Saint Patrick. Adomnán also published *On the Holy Places*, an account of shipwrecked Gaulish pilgrim Arculf's pilgrimage to Palestine, in which veneration of the cross and celebration of the Easter liturgy are given prominence. The renaissance had begun in the mid-seventh century with the earliest examples of illumination of sacred books in Irish monasteries. The first, a copy of the Psalter known as the *Cathach* of Saint Columba, glorified God through fine script and skilled decoration. It was followed by the *Book of Durrow*, the first Irish Gospel book to include "carpet pages" of colorful abstract designs.[13] The book appeared just as the stone pillars with their incised crosses, familiar features of the Irish countryside, were evolving into the monumental crosses of later times. One of the most noteworthy of these, at Carndonagh in Inishowen, presents a rudimentary, but compelling, depiction of the crucifixion.

Bede values the witness of the Irish ascetics but, with his knowledge of the church calendar, disapproves of the "doubtful rules" they followed in determining the date of Easter. Even Aidan fails to escape censure. Though acclaiming the abbot's cultivation of peace, love, purity, and humility, his diligence in study and prayer, and care for the sick and the poor, Bede concludes, "I have dealt at length with the character and life of Aidan, but I cannot approve his inadequate knowledge of the proper observance of Easter." However, in recording the Irishman's nonconformity on the Easter question, the rigorous monk approvingly notes that "he believed, worshipped, and taught exactly as we do."[14] Bede provides an interesting account of the Northumbrian church's eventual rejection of the Irish *computus*. Having married a noblewoman from Kent, where the church observed a different paschal cycle, King Oswy discovered that while he was celebrating Easter, the queen and her attendants were still

---

[12] O'Loughlin, *Adamnán at Birr*, 50–53.

[13] R. G. Calkins, *Illuminated Books of the Middle Ages* (London: Thames and Hudson, 1983) 33–63.

[14] Bede, *History*, 3.4, 3.17; Sherley-Price, 149, 170.

fasting and observing Palm Sunday. To deal with the anomaly, a synod was held in 664 at Abbess Hilda's monastery in Whitby.

When the arguments of Abbot Wilfrid of Ripon against the Irish practice prevailed, Colman, bishop of Lindisfarne, felt so deeply that, with a number of like-minded monks, both English and Irish, he returned to Iona. He then crossed to Ireland, where he established a monastery on Inishbofin, off the Mayo coast.[15] Notwithstanding the rebellious monks' intransigence, Bede praises their Christian witness, frugality, and austerity. He presents their way of life as an example to English churchmen. All donations of money received by them were "immediately given to the poor." When one of the priests visited a village, the residents were quick to gather in one cottage to hear "the word of life, for Colman's priests came solely to preach, baptize, visit the sick and, in short, care for the souls of the people." Even when the king visited these dedicated men, he normally stayed to pray. If he occasionally remained to have a meal, he ate the same plain fare as the brethren.[16]

Long before Whitby, the Victorian calendar was gradually being adopted in Ireland. In 628 Pope Honorius I had written to the Irish bishops and abbots, asking them not to imagine that they, "isolated at the uttermost ends of the earth, had a wisdom exceeding that of all churches, ancient and modern throughout the world."[17] Four years later, a monastic scholar called Cummian wrote to Segéne, abbot of Iona, urging acceptance of the Victorian cycle, informing him that, after an inconclusive synod held not far from Durrow, the matter was referred to Rome, "the chief of cities." Irish delegates spent three years there, discovering that the proposed cycle was being observed by people of all nationalities.[18] What could be more disparaging of mother Church, asks Cummian, than to claim, "Rome is in error, Jerusalem is in error, Alexandria is in error, Antioch is in error, the whole world is in error; the Irish and the Britons alone have true wisdom."[19]

Shortly before his death in 704, Adomnán persuaded most of the remaining doubters in Ireland to accept change but failed to win over

---

[15] Bede, *History*, 3.25–26; Sherley-Price, 186–94.

[16] Bede, *History*, 3.26; Sherley-Price, 193–94.

[17] Bede, *History*, 2.19; Sherley-Price, 138–39.

[18] James F. Kenney, *Sources for the Early History of Ireland: Ecclesiastical* (New York: Columbia University Press, 1926) 220–21.

[19] Kenney, 220, n. 179.

the monks of his own monastery. When Egbert came from Ireland as abbot in 716, he was welcomed at Iona "with honor and great joy" and, through his "constant devout exhortations," was able to "wean" the community from its traditional paschal practice. An Englishman who had spent much of his monastic life among the Irish, Egbert is praised in the *History* as "a most persuasive teacher who faithfully practiced all that he taught."[20]

Bede acknowledges Ireland's contribution to the education and training of the numerous scholars who, like Egbert, crossed the sea to study under its spiritual teachers: "The Irish welcomed them all kindly and, without asking for any payment, provided them with daily food, books and instruction."[21] An English abbot and bishop of the time, Aldhelm, also attests to the prestige of Ireland's monastic teachers. In a florid letter to Heathfrith, a former student, he notes the mass of "ravenous scholars and sagacious students," all English, emerging from Ireland "drenched and overflowing with floods" of learning after "sucking the teat of wisdom" there.[22]

A dramatic product of this mutual spiritual enrichment was the creation of the *Lindisfarne Gospels*, completed early in the eighth century and dedicated to "God and Saint Cuthbert and all the saints whose relics are on the island." Cuthbert had been prior of the Irish abbey of Melrose before being transferred to Lindisfarne in the turbulent wake of Whitby. Later, he became a bishop celebrated for his missionary zeal and concern for the poor. He lived as a simple ascetic and died on lonely Farne Island in 685.[23] It is fitting that an Englishman who was a product of Irish asceticism should inspire a work of devotional art which so supremely encompasses the cultural traditions of the two neighboring countries.

Bede notes that Wilfrid was the first English churchman to win converts among the Germanic peoples when, passing through pagan Frisia on his way to Rome in 678, he gained the friendship of a local ruler.[24] He also explores the impulse to evangelize the German pagans which developed among the English monks living in Ireland. A quarter

---

[20] Bede, *History*, 5.22; Sherley-Price, 294; 321.

[21] Bede, *History*, 3.27; Sherley-Price, 195.

[22] Aldhelm, Ep 5; *Aldhelm: The Prose Works*, trans. Michael Lapidge and Michael Herren (Cambridge: D. S. Brewer, Rowman and Littlefield, 1979) 161–63.

[23] Calkins, 63.

[24] Bede, *History*, 5.19; Sherley-Price, 303.

of a century before becoming abbot of Iona, Egbert heard of the Frisians, Danes, and Saxons who had no knowledge of God and determined to convert these cousins of his own people. Asked in a vision to forget his resolve and persevere in the monastic life, he persuaded his friend and fellow countryman, Wictbert, to take his place on the mission.

After experiencing failure, Wictbert returned to Ireland, "his beloved land of exile."[25] In the year 690 Egbert sent Willibrord, another English monk, who had been in Ireland for twelve years. Leaving with eleven companions, Willibrord worked among the Frisians. Six years after his arrival, he was consecrated bishop of Utrecht by the pope. Bede observed that, as he wrote, the bishop was still active, though he had been ministering abroad for thirty-six years.[26] Bede died in 737, Willibrord four years later.

The missionary endeavors of these ascetics led directly to the achievements of Wynfrith, subsequently known as Boniface, who had been a monk of Wessex in the south of England. He had no links with Ireland. At the age of forty Wynfrith left Nursling for the Germanic lands. His purpose was to convert the pagan Saxons. First he visited Rome, where the significantly named Pope Gregory II, a fervent advocate of asceticism, appointed him to the regions of Hesse and Thuringia, which bordered on Saxony. After briefly joining Willibrord, Wynfrith immersed himself in the epic work which was to absorb all his energies till his violent death in 754. In 722 he was consecrated bishop and given his new name by the pope, whose successor, the third Gregory, also a devotee of the ascetic ideal, appointed him archbishop and legate ten years later. Boniface now had the task of promoting Christianity in most of the territories east of the Rhine.

Many of this great English missionary's actions recall those of previous ascetics. In requesting guidance from Rome on matters of faith and morals, he followed the example of Augustine of England. His destruction of the sacred oak of Geismar in 727 is reminiscent of the felling of the pine by Martin over three centuries before. He emulated Martin and Columban when, in 746, with several other Anglo-Saxon missionary bishops, he denounced the dissolute behavior of Ethelbald of Mercia, contrasting his actions unfavorably with those of the pagan Saxons and

[25] Bede, *History*, 5.10; Sherley-Price, 280.
[26] Bede, *History*, 5.9, 5.11; Sherley-Price, 278, 280.

Serbs. Within a year the king had changed his ways. With his ascetic brethren, the missionary brought many people to belief because he exemplified faith, endurance, and the spirit of self-sacrifice. His exchanges with Pope Zacharias suggest the trust and understanding they shared.[27]

Boniface's letters to friends in England reveal a man who, despite hardship, disappointment, and loneliness, retained his humanity. The English church did not fail him. Devoted friends sent books, food, clothing, and comforting letters. He never wavered in his purpose, or in his commitment to the patristic tradition. In 735, facing pastoral problems and vainly searching the papal archives for Gregory's letters of advice to Augustine, he sought the help of Archbishop Nothelm of Canterbury. When the letters were finally found in Rome, Boniface offered copies to Archbishop Egbert of York, requesting, in return, the biblical commentaries of Bede, whom "divine grace has endowed with spiritual intelligence and permitted to shine forth."[28]

Writing to Archbishop Cuthbert of Canterbury in 747, he declared his fellowship with fathers like Clement of Rome, Cyprian and Athanasius, who had guided the Church, "teaching, defending, laboring and suffering even to the shedding of blood." To Buege, an abbess praying for the success of his mission, Boniface wrote in the spirit of the apostles, fathers, and ascetics, begging her to "hold fast" in the hope of a heavenly fatherland. Buege was asked to rejoice and be glad always and "scorn earthly trials with your whole soul, for all soldiers of Christ, of both sexes, have despised the storms and troubles and infirmities of this world and counted them as nought."[29]

Boniface's work was deeply appreciated by Pope Zacharias, who, like his two predecessors, was an admirer of Gregory the Great, whose *Dialogues* he translated into Greek. It was in the spirit of Gregory that the pope encouraged Boniface to convene reform synods in the Frankish regions of Austrasia and Neustria, where the Church's structure, discipline, and liturgy had been reduced to disarray by decades of warfare. By working within episcopal structures while promoting monasticism, the ascetic archbishop was emulating the fathers.[30] He founded Benedictine

---

[27] Boniface, Ep 73, 69–71, *Letters of Saint Boniface*, trans. Ephriam Emerton (New York: Columbia University Press, 1940) 124–30; 156–64.

[28] Boniface, Ep 33; 75; Emerton, 62–63; 132–33.

[29] Boniface, Ep 62; 94; Emerton, 138; 170–71.

[30] Boniface, Ep 78; Emerton, 136–41.

houses for both men and women, inviting other English ascetics to set up monasteries in the German lands. In 744 he cooperated with his disciple Sturm in the foundation of Fulda. A decade later, in search of a deeper understanding of the Benedictine tradition, Sturm spent some time at Monte Cassino.

When Boniface was killed by pagans on the shores of Frisia in 754 his body was taken first to Utrecht, and then up the Rhine to his see of Mainz. As was the case with so many admired ascetics, there was a short disagreement about the location of his last resting place. In accordance with his wishes he was buried at the monastery of Fulda. On all his missionary journeys Boniface took a chest containing his "treasure," or library, which included copies of the Bible, works of the fathers, and commentaries on the Bible. Among his possessions when he died, and now on display at Fulda, were three books: a Gospel harmony, a collection of patristic texts, and a Gospel book "written, in part, by an Irish monk named Cadmug."[31]

---

[31] J. M. Wallace-Hadrill, *The Frankish Church* (Oxford: Clarendon Press, 1983) 158–59.

# 19

# THE CAROLINGIANS
# AND THE TWO CITIES

The rigorous life and eventual fate of Boniface suggest the magnitude of the task facing those who worked to further faith and renewal in the eighth century. Just twenty years after the Englishman's death, his attempted reform of the Frankish church was succeeded by Charlemagne's ambitious efforts to restore religion, learning, and social structures across his vast domain. The king spared no expense in working for the advance of education and religion, but his primary purpose remained the security and extension of his burgeoning empire. It is a measure of the realization of this less worthy ambition that, at the end of a reign of forty-seven years, Charlemagne controlled most of the lands west of the Elbe and Danube and north of the Pyrenees.

The scholars selected to further the king's grand religious and social objectives were products of the monastic and cathedral schools of Italy, England, Ireland, Spain, and the Frankish regions. As a first step in educating clergy and others they devised a program of learning which embraced Latin grammar, orthography, dialectics, and rhetoric. Since reinvigoration of church life required restoration of biblical studies and liturgical practice, monastic libraries and scriptoria were absorbed in retrieval and transcription of ancient manuscripts. Skilled scribes ensured provision of accurate copies of the Bible, Psalter, missals, canon law, and the writings of the fathers, particularly those of Augustine. Priests were trained in the correct modes of celebrating the liturgy, with emphasis on the Eucharist. Study of the Psalter was prescribed for monasteries. A visit to Monte Cassino in 787 provided Charles with a copy of the *Rule of Saint Benedict.* Five years later, abbots and monks were summoned to a council in Aachen, where the *Rule* was "expounded by learned men."[1]

In 782 Alcuin was appointed master of the palace school and leader of the reform. He had directed the school of York for fifteen years. His familiarity with the writings of the fathers is manifest in his poem *On the Saints of the Church of York*, in which the works represented in the "wondrous treasury" of the cathedral library are enumerated, among them

> The thought of Jerome and Hilary,
> Of Bishop Ambrose, Athanasius,
> Augustine too, and old Orosius,
> And all the teachings of great Gregory
> Pope Leo, Basil and Fulgentius,
> And Cassiodoros, John and Chrysostom;
> Aldhelm and Master Bede, and everything
> That Victorinus wrote, and Boetius.[2]

Treated generously by Charlemagne, the scholars eulogized him as another David or Constantine, who pacified and ruled his kingdom in accordance with the divine will. Einhard, the royal biographer, paid tribute to the king's regard for learning: "He gave the greatest attention to the liberal arts, and showed the greatest respect and bestowed high honors upon those who taught them."[3] In 799 Alcuin alluded to Charles's "well-known interest that a new Athens is being created in Francia." He claimed that it was far finer than that inhabited by Plato because, "being ennobled by the teaching of our Lord Christ, it surpasses all mere academic education, for while Plato's teaching was based solely on the seven arts, the teaching of the palace school is enriched by the seven gifts of the Holy Spirit."[4]

Theodulf, a Goth from Spain who became one of the king's most trusted advisers, composed a poetic panegyric containing a charming picture of the monarch at his dining table, surrounded by family and a

---

[1] *Documents of Medieval History* 2, ed. H. R. Loyn and John Percival (London: Edward Arnold, 1975) 138–40, 144–45.

[2] Alcuin, *On the Saints of the Church of York, Alcuin of York: His Life and Letters,* trans. Stephen Allott (York: William Sessions, 1974) 165.

[3] Einhard, *Life of Charlemagne,* 25, trans. Evelyn Scherabon and Edwin H. Zeydel (Coral Gables, FL: University of Miami Press, 1972) 93.

[4] Alcuin, Ep 77; Allott, 93.

talented band of helpers, who converse, discuss, and debate, answering to names adopted from biblical and classical sources. Alcuin is Flaccus the poet. Einhard is Bezaleel the biblical artificer. Charles, predictably, is David, biblical model for all rulers. Decades later, in an introduction to Einhard's *Life of Charlemagne*, Walafrid Strabo, tutor of the great king's grandson Charles the Bald and author of a noted biography of Saint Gall, rejoiced that Charles had transformed the cultureless realm, "which God had entrusted to him," from a place of darkness to one with "new enthusiasm for human knowledge."[5]

Consolidating the generally accepted image of Charlemagne, Strabo's enconium cannot mask the reality of the king's fearsome record. Falling far short of Christian principles, some of Charles's campaigns, particularly those against the Saxons, flew in the face of Augustine's insistence that mercy should temper justice and that Christian rulers, remembering that they are mere men, should rule without pride, and be "slow to punish, ready to pardon."[6] Nor did any of the scholars emulate Ambrose and Martin in challenging the king's military excesses. Alcuin expressed unhappiness on occasions, but in terms that would not offend his royal master. Again, though he and his colleagues wrote copiously in the spirit of the fathers, their lives did not reflect patristic austerity. Subject to the rivalries and intrigues of court life, none among them followed the example given by Gregory while serving as ambassador at Constantinople. Consequently, though Charlemagne's great design ensured the survival of culture and religion, his legacy included a negative component which, in time, became increasingly burdensome to the Church.

Meanwhile, a less ambitious renewal, confined to monastic communities, was taking place in Europe's most western reaches. The numerous hermits recorded in annals after the mid-eighth century provide evidence of the decline of institutional religious life in Ireland, with the ascetics' actions implying a determination to withdraw from secularized religious houses and reject worldly values. The reform was centered on several monasteries, among them Finglas, Tallaght, Roscrea, and Terryglass. At the heart of this return to the values of Finnian, Comgall, and Columba were the Céli Dé, servants of God, led by Mael-Ruain, abbot of the mon-

---

[5] *Einhard and Nokter the Stammerer: Two Lives of Charlemagne*, trans. Lewis Thorpe (Middlesex: Penguin Books, 1980) 50–51.

[6] Augustine, *City of God*, 5.24.24; Bettenson, 220.

astery at Tallaght, who died in 792. The Céli Dé rule embraced prayer, self-denial, study of Scripture, and celebration of the liturgy, especially the duty of intoning psalms and canticles, described as "the labor that excels all labors," a phrase reminiscent of Benedict's "work of God."[7]

Late in the eighth century, Óengus, a monk of the Céli Dé, composed, in his own language, a *Félire* or *Martyrology* whose many saints exemplify the principles of the reform. In the prologue, he proclaims its essentially spiritual nature:

> Though great are the world's kings, whose strongholds you see,
> A hundred times nobler are Jesu's lowly soldiers.[8]

They are verses which may be contrasted, in sense and tone, with those addressed to Charlemagne by Theodulf:

> The entire world resounds to your praise;
> If the Meuse, Rhine, Saone, Tiber and Po
> Could be measured, then praise of you is measurable too.[9]

This excerpt, from Theodulf's *To King Charles*, a panegyric to an earthly leader which is rich in hyperbole, highlights the divided loyalties of the Carolingian reformers. The sole ruler acclaimed by Óengus and his brethren is "the bright Sun who illuminates heaven with much holiness, the ruler of angels and Lord of men."[10]

Charlemagne's immense program of reform was published in detailed ordinances or capitularies, organized by talented teachers or clerics, and monitored by representatives of the king, *missi dominici*, who included some of the kingdom's leading men. Among them were bishops, abbots, and counts.[11] The Céli Dé renewal, promoted through example and confined to certain monasteries, was directed at the spiritual order alone. Óengus's *Félire* rejoices that, though Nero's grave is unknown, multitudes come to "Peter's little tomb" in Rome; that while the splendor of Pilate's

---

[7] William Reeves, *Culdees of the British Islands* (Felinfach: Llanerch Publications, 1994) 96.

[8] Óengus, *Martyrology*, prologue, 149; H.B.S., 23.

[9] Peter Godman, *Poetry of the Carolingian Renaissance* (London: Duckworth, 1985) 151.

[10] Óengus, *Martyrology*, prologue, 5–8; H.B.S., 17.

[11] *The Reign of Charlemagne*, 9–13; 16ff.; 73 ff. *Documents of Medieval History* 2, ed. H. R. Loyn and John Percival (London: Edward Arnold, 1975) 7–63.

haughty queen has vanished, Mary the virgin is still magnified by "Adam's race" and a host of angels. "Valiant" pagan high king Lóiguire's pride has been vanquished, but Patrick's name, "splendid, famous, is exalted." Monasticism is also triumphing, for "Ailenn's proud fortress has perished, and great is victorious Brigid." With only the stones of Emain-Macha, abode of ancient kings, remaining, the monastery of Glendalough thrives.[12]

Óengus was a contemporary of Mael-Ruain. His heroes are not leaders who won victory in battle, but a royal company who were "impaled before hosts, crushed in assemblies and slain before kings."[13] There is a universal sweep to the *Félire*, which celebrates the fathers and ascetics. Stephen, the first martyr, is present, as are Benedict and Antony, the desert hermit. "Heroic" Martin, whose feast day is 11 November, is "the mountain of gold of the western world." His spiritual father Hilary, bishop and abbot, is hailed as author of *Hymnum dicat*, a sacred song celebrating the life of Christ whose popularity in medieval Ireland saw it placed at the beginning of the *Antiphonary of Bangor*. Martin's somewhat vain biographer, Sulpicius, is also found among the spiritual heroes acclaimed by the Irish.[14] Augustine is the "famous one out of Africa" and the "pure" Ambrose has the happiness of sharing "one of Mary's feasts."[15]

While Alcuin's formal invocation of the fathers in his poem on the saints of York leaves that dynamic band lying inert upon the page, the ascetics of the *Félire* spring vividly to life through Óengus's rich imagery. That Gregory enjoys pride of place as champion of monasticism and the first monk to become pope mirrors Irish affection and admiration for the ascetic "abbot of Rome" who, as "winner of a hundred victories for Christ's sake, crucified his body."[16] Holy people named by the fathers mingle with Irish saints drawn from the country's "host of books." Óengus presents his creation as "a city of protection," a "strong rampart" against men and devils, and

> a vehement prayer to God, a vast strength against the Devil,
> a psalm which declares great might, and a truly accurate
> martyrology.[17]

---

[12] Óengus, *Martyrology*, prologue, 113–29, 169–96; H.B.S., 22, 24–25.

[13] Óengus, *Martyrology*, prologue, 33–36; H.B.S., 18.

[14] Óengus, *Martyrology*, 13 January; H.B.S., 35.

[15] Óengus, *Martyrology*, 28 August; H.B.S., 179; 1 April; H.B.S., 104.

[16] Óengus, *Martyrology*, 12 March; H.B.S., 82.

[17] Óengus, *Martyrology*, epilogue, 137–56; H.B.S., 270–71.

It was in the context of this Irish reform that, around the year 800, Ferdomnach the scribe completed the task of transcribing the treasured documents compiled by the "heirs of Saint Patrick" and assembled them in the *Book of Armagh*. They include a copy of the New Testament, the *Life of Martin* by Sulpicius Severus, claimed to be "the most faithful heir of the original composition," and an abbreviated version of Patrick's *Confession*.[18] Ferdomnach's task was completed during the abbacy of Torbach of Armagh.

The literary and artistic fruits of the Céli Dé reform may not have been as numerous as those of their Carolingian counterparts but were not inferior in quality. On the continent, no expense was spared in creating works like *Charlemagne's Gospelbook*, written in golden uncials and sumptuously illuminated with pictures of the evangelists and images of Christ in glory. With their Roman and Byzantine influences, this book and the *Ada Gospels* are among the highest achievements of European monastic illustrators. Around the same time, Irish illumination of Gospel books attained its apotheosis in the *Book of Kells*, in which words, color, and iconography unite to celebrate the incarnation and redemption.[19]

High crosses erected at Kells and Moone during the period of reform depict the redemption in stone, portraying incidents from the Old Testament which prefigure Christ's sacrifice. These include the fall of Adam and Eve, the sacrifice of Isaac, the killing of Abel, and the infant Christ's flight into Egypt. At Moone there are depictions of Daniel with the lion and the three children in the fiery furnace. All speak of the sustaining protection of God's power, a theme found in Óengus's plea, toward the conclusion of the *Martyrology*, that the Lord should save him from every ill:

> Free me, O Jesus
> into your many graced heaven . . .
> as you saved Daniel from the den of lions . . .
> as you freed the children
> from the fiery furnace . . .

Óengus concludes with the hope that, facing the final peril, he will be safely conveyed to heaven by the holy individuals commemorated

---

[18] *Book of Armagh*, ed. John Gwynn (Dublin: Hodges Figgis, 1913) cclxvii–cclxxv.
[19] Calkins, 82.

in the *Félire*.[20] Popular in Ireland and beyond during the early middle ages, the prayer offered by Óengus employs images which still speak to Christians. More than a millennium after its creation, the hand of God on the underside of the north arm of Muiredach's cross at Monasterboice proclaims, to the person below, the same protective power confidently invoked by that earlier generation, and affirmed in "lorica" like the *Breastplate of Saint Patrick*.

Though the witness of the Céli Dé was not forgotten, the small numbers of dedicated individuals involved failed to arrest the Irish decline as lay involvement in monasteries and churches continued. It was a phenomenon that affected the wider Church, for, while Charlemagne's reforms benefited religion in a variety of ways, the dioceses were increasingly burdened by secular engagement in episcopal and abbatial appointments. The pattern of attempted renewal and spiritual decline continued under the king's son, Louis the Pious. Like his father, Louis was responsible for further secularization of church affairs but also supported the work of Benedict of Aniane, a reforming abbot whose first foundation was in Aquitaine, where John Cassian's monastery had flourished four centuries before. In 816 and 817, at synods in Aachen, bishops and abbots were asked to regularize cathedral canonries and monastic communities. The primitive *Rule of Saint Benedict* was prescribed for monasteries, while priestly renewal centered on Scripture and the fathers. Benedict of Aniane died in 821 and was invoked by subsequent reformers.

Educators and churchmen continued to function during the power struggles that preceded and followed the death of Louis the Pious. Hrabanus Mhor and Walafrid Strabo, both distinguished products of monasticism, were biblical commentators in the tradition of the fathers. The former, who had been a favored pupil of Alcuin, was appointed archbishop of Mainz, while Strabo became abbot of Richenau, on Lake Constance.[21] With other church leaders, they were increasingly immersed in public affairs as Charlemagne's descendants vied for power and the empire fragmented into three kingdoms. Later in the ninth century, the western kingdom was ruled by Charles the Bald, the grandson who most resembled Charlemagne in his concern for learning. Within

---

[20] Óengus, *Martyrology*, epilogue, 441–66, 449–64; H.B.S., 284–88.
[21] Godman, 179.

this region Hincmar, archbishop of Reims, dominated religious and secular affairs for almost forty years, till his death in 882.

During this turbulent time, as society suffered immense strain under internal pressures and attacks by the Vikings, scholarship continued to flourish. The leading scholastic light at the court of Charles the Bald was John Scottus Eriugena. A product of the monastic schools of Ireland, John asserted that, while Homer and Virgil composed verse about great men, he would celebrate "the power of the Father and his true wisdom."[22] He was equally capable of praising his earthly master, Charles. A knowledge of Greek enhanced John's work as philosopher and theologian. His major treatise, *On the Division of Nature*, was a philosophical exploration of God's creative work and his plan for humanity. Presenting nature through the senses and reason, John scrutinized it under four categories: that which is not created but creates, that which is created and creates, that which is created but does not create, and that which is not created and does not create. He demonstrated that every aspect of creation comes from God and will return to him, the final cause of all. That return is achieved through the Logos, whose incarnation, death, and resurrection won humankind from the "non-being" of sin. Though a self-declared proponent of orthodoxy, John was forced to deny persistent allegations of pantheism in his writings.[23]

Together with Boethius, John Scottus was the only notable philosopher from the death of Augustine in 430 till Anselm began to write in the mid-eleventh century. Perhaps it was with John in mind that Heiric of Auxerre, in the preface to his *Life of Saint Germanus*, referred to the numerous Irish philosophers serving the Frankish kings. Even Greece, he observed, could be rightly envious of a country where "the more learned a man is, the more likely is he to sentence himself to exile that he may serve the wishes of our most wise Solomon."[24] Strabo, whose monastery on the island of Reichenau was at the western reaches of Lake Constance, was aware that Columban's old monastic site was at Bregenz

---

[22] Godman, 301.

[23] Frederick Copleston, *Medieval Philosophy*, History of Philosophy, vol. 2 (London: Continuum, 2003) 116–35; John Marenbon, *Carolingian Thought*, in Rosamond McKitterick, ed., *Carolingian Culture: Emulation and Innovation* (Cambridge: University Press, 1994) 171–92.

[24] James F. Kenney, *Sources for the Early History of Ireland: Ecclesiastical* (New York: Columbia University Press, 1926) 593.

on the lake's eastern margin. In his *Life of Saint Gall* he celebrated Ireland of the scholars, "from which so great a glory has shone upon us."[25] He also published a life of Blathmac, killed by the Vikings in the church at Iona for refusing to reveal where Columba's reliquary was concealed.

In those times, monks and laymen from Ireland, many fleeing the depredations of the Vikings, were arriving in such numbers that bishops at consecutive Councils of Meaux were forced to ask Charles the Bald for help in restoring the hospices for Irish pilgrims.[26] One of these wanderers was Sedulius Scottus who, like John Scottus the philosopher, employs poetry to suggest that his presence in the land of the Franks represents an act of piety:

> I read and write, teach and study scripture;
> Day and night I pray to my creator enthroned on high.[27]

However, Sedulius also unashamedly celebrates the convivial evenings he enjoys with his fellow scholars when the day's work is done. It is then that they brighten their dull lives and poor living conditions with witty badinage, fuelled by generous drafts of the local vintage. Sedulius even bemoans the fact that his patron lives in a splendid house while his own is dark and sooty. In another poem, he recalls a time when, with his greatest need a patron under whom he could teach in comfort and peace, records that, around the year 848, he and his friends received shelter from Hartgar, bishop of Liege, when snow lay on the ground, the leafless trees stood like reeds, and the travelers themselves were exposed to the harsh winds. In grateful verse, he thanks the bishop, who,

> With kindness and generosity has succored and saved
> Three scholars exhausted by noisy southerly gusts.
> He has clothed and enriched the three of us handsomely,
> And, a delightful shepherd, has made us his own sheep.[28]

With the approach of the tenth century, the Church's dependence on powerful magnates became acute as the Carolingian empire was impelled toward extinction by endemic violence and ever more daring attacks by Vikings in the north and Saracens in the south. Scholars and

---

[25] *Walahfrid Strabo*'s Life of Saint Gall, prologue, ed. Maud Joynt (London: Society for Promoting Christian Knowledge, 1927) 61.

[26] Kenney, 600.

[27] Godman, 283.

[28] Godman, 287.

churchmen sought security by drawing even closer to civil powers. The final collapse of Charlemagne's great edifice in the course of the tenth century caused hightened insecurity and a proliferation of small duchies, which spawned increasing levels of patronage. Benefactions from powerful men led to further lay interference in episcopal and abbatial appointments. Proprietary lords maintained control of donated land or property by ensuring that family members became heads of sees or monasteries. The favored abbot or bishop was invested in a ceremony involving reception of a staff of office, or an episcopal ring from a secular leader, with the appointee swearing an oath of loyalty to his lord.

Charlemagne had similarly mingled the secular and the sacred by exercising his "right" to reward loyal servants with ecclesiastical and monastic positions. When Alcuin retired from the palace school in 794 Charles appointed him to the abbacy of Saint Martin's at Tours, the most prestigious in the kingdom. The king rewarded Theodolf the Goth with the bishopric of Orleans, while Paulinus, an Italian, became patriarch of Aquileia. Royal favorite Angilbert received the lay abbacy of Saint Requier. Charlemagne, Louis the Pious, Charles the Bald, and other leaders appointed lay abbots to administer monasteries.[29] During the later tenth century, the see of Rome itself suffered as it became the preserve of contesting noble families who, with notable lack of scruple, vied to have relatives appointed pope. It was a situation that called out for reform.

It was a call felt in Ireland, where traditional attitudes to possession of land had long seen religious leaders chosen from proprietary families. With the appointment of dedicated clerics like Columba and Adomnán, the Church had not suffered, but the waning of the great age of asceticism in the final centuries of the first millennium brought ever-greater proprietary insistence on rights to monastic lands and increasing numbers of lay abbots who administered the monastic patrimony. Through time, Ireland's esteem for monastic life had created another anomaly. A tradition of appointing monks to episcopal roles, once a source of strength, had led to the consecration of abbot-bishops, then to the appointment of a third category of governance, abbots who had sole jurisdiction over sees. A bishop deprived of his administrative function

---

[29] Wallace-Hadrill, 291; Rosamond McKitterick, *The Frankish Kingdoms under the Carolingians 751–87* (London: Longman, 1983) 122, 188.

by the abbot administering the see continued to exercise his episcopal powers of ordination, confirmation, and instruction of the faithful.

These deviations from the norm of ecclesiastical life were facilitated by the Irish system of small rural kingdoms which lacked the towns in which continental sees had been based since the first century. As time passed, more widely flung monastic administrative regions or paruchiae tended to absorb original episcopal sees.[30] This is the Ireland left behind by wandering scholars like Sedulius Scottus and John Scottus Eriugena, whose learning testified to the continuing high quality of Irish monastic education. That some returned is seen in Colman's farewell to his younger namesake, whose concern for his native country has overcome all other considerations.

> Since you are in haste all of a sudden to visit those sweet lands,
> And desert and flee the life which we have shared,
> Hurrying swiftly to depart, unmoved by any prayers,
> Nor can the persuasion of a flatterer's voice hold you back,
> I yield to your love of our homeland.
> Who can gainsay a lover?[31]

On his return, young Colman would have found the fervor of many individual ascetics undiminished by the problems plaguing Irish church life. The devotional poetry of early tenth-century Ireland expresses yearning for renewal. In "Be thou my vision," a monk begs God to be all to him, his speech and understanding, his shield and sword, his honor and delight, his shelter and fortress. Aware that he can do nothing without God's grace, he places himself entirely in the divine hands, pleading,

> Be thou every good to my body and soul;
> be thou my kingdom in heaven and earth.
> Be thou alone my heart's special love;
> let there be none other save the high-king of heaven.[32]

A late tenth-century poet seeks Christ's forgiveness by invoking his incarnation, death, and resurrection. There is an appeal to the prophets

---

[30] For an overview of this problem, see Colman Etchingham, *Church Organisation in Ireland AD 650 to 1000* (Maynooth: Laigin Publications, 1999) 12–46.
[31] Godman, 281.
[32] *Early Irish Lyrics*, 18; Murphy, 43–45.

and "sinless apostles, the holy virgins, distinguished lay women" and "wondrous maiden Mary." With every avenue of supplication explored, the poem represents a litany in the Irish tradition.[33] Another ascetic, plagued by straying thoughts during intonation of the psalms, wanders "on a path that is not right . . . through assemblies, through companies of foolish women, through woods and through cities." Swifter than the wind and "without a ferry," his thoughts traverse every sea, or "leap in one bound from earth to heaven." Repentant, the offender begs divine assistance:

> Rule this heart of mine, o zealous God of creation,
> that you may be my love, that I may do your will.[34]

Some ascetics aspired to the total renunciation desired by Manchán in his wish for

> a hidden little hut in the wilderness that it might be my dwelling,
> all-grey shallow water beside it, a clear pool to wash away sins
> through the grace of the Holy Spirit.[35]

Many monastic poets of the time celebrated the Creator of their invariably rural world. All felt the urgent need to "adore the Lord, maker of wondrous works, great bright heaven with its angels, the white-waved sea on earth."[36] Consciousness of God's presence in all his creation excludes any hint of pantheism as the hermit Marbán celebrates the glories of his surroundings. The ash and the hazel, the wells and waterfalls, the myriad animals, insects, and birds, the berries and fruits are "given me by my gentle Christ."[37] Even a brief metric exercise for the instruction of students, possibly written in Bangor, serves as a reminder of the beauty of God's creation:

> The little bird which has whistled from the end of a bright
>    yellow bill:
> It utters a note above Loch Laig, a blackbird from a yellow-
>    heaped branch.[38]

---

[33] *Early Irish Lyrics*, 16; Murphy, 37–39.
[34] *Early Irish Lyrics*, 17; Murphy, 39–43.
[35] *Early Irish Lyrics*, 12; Murphy, 29–31.
[36] *Early Irish Lyrics*, 4; Murphy, 5.
[37] *Early Irish Lyrics*, 8; Murphy, 11–19.
[38] *Early Irish Lyrics*, 5; Murphy, 7; Lough Laig: Belfast Lough.

Perceiving the divine hand in every element of life and nature, these ascetics rejoiced that, despite the fall, man's ability to celebrate God's gifts was undiminished. Centuries before, when circumstances were equally dark, Augustine, in the *City of God*, expressed his wonder at the Creator's generosity to man. He celebrated the human capacity to enjoy the God-given variety of natural phenomena, the beauty of the sky and the sea in sunshine or storm, the light of heavenly bodies, the shade of trees, the perfume of flowers, the variety of birds and animals, of which the tiniest, like the bees and ants, are most astonishing. If these are the gifts of God to fallen man, Augustine exclaimed, what must be anticipated for the blessed in heaven.[39] As the second millennium approached, those who, like Augustine and the ascetic poets, maintained faith in God's providence continued to pray and hope.

---

[39] Augustine, *City of God*, 22.24; Bettenson, 1072–73.

# 20

# THE GREGORIAN REFORM

In 909, at a time of ever-encroaching darkness for Christians, the foundation of the monastery of Cluny, north of Lyons, proved to be the harbinger of a renewal which would envelop the Church within a century. The monastery was endowed by William, duke of Burgundy, and led by Berno, former abbot of Baume in Burgundy. Berno was a devotee of the reforming Benedict of Aniane. Hope for the future lay in the nature of the monastery's charter, which ensured freedom from engagement with secular authorities. As a further safeguard, Cluny was to be directly subject to Rome. The monks' ability to choose their superior led to the appointment of four outstanding abbots, who guided the community through much of the next century. Cluny's pattern of endowment and freedom from secular controls became an aspiration for reformers in the Church at large.

Odo, who succeeded Berno in 927, was a native of Tours. Devotion to Martin, whom he "loved above all the saints," led him to join the canons of his local cathedral. There he discovered the *Rule of Saint Benedict* and devoted himself to helping the poor, guiding the young, and caring for sinners.[1] He also wrote a summary of Pope Gregory's *Moralia*. As men in need of reform, his colleagues sensed a reproach in the young man's growing dedication and "began to inveigh against him, croaking like so many crows." Eventually leaving the irredeemable canons, Odo traveled far before finding what he sought in Berno's well-administered monastery at Baume. Given charge of the monastic school, he later became abbot.[2]

---

[1] John of Salerno, *Saint Odo of Cluny*, 1.13–15, ed. Gerard Sitwell (London: Sheed and Ward, 1958) 15–18.

[2] *Saint Odo*, 1.20, 1.38; Sitwell, 22, 40.

By the time he was elected to succeed Berno at Cluny, Odo had experienced various causes of the widespread religious decline. A particular problem lay in monastic communities which had scattered before the Vikings, with individual monks returning home "to seek again those things which it is pleasant for men to use, and which they had previously renounced." When the danger passed, those who returned experienced great difficulty in regaining the harmony and discipline that had been lost. Odo's biographer, John of Salerno, tells how the abbot brought peace to one such monastery, where the monks, "scattered far and wide through fear of the enemy," had returned "with divided minds." The quarreling ceased when the community "received him as a father."[3]

In a chaotic period dominated by dynastic rivalry and invasion, when many churchmen had lost their way, reformed communities offered hope. As abbot of Cluny, Odo traveled widely in support of religious houses which were eager for renewal. He even restored a monastery in Rome at a time when succession to the papacy was being contested by feuding families whose interests seldom coincided with the spirit of Christianity. Those popes who considered reform turned to Cluny.[4] Odo's spiritual authority is evident on his first meeting, in Rome, with Brother John, his biographer. "I was involved in worldly interests and unhappy," says John. "In his pity, Odo caught me in his net and led me to the monastery of Saint Peter at Pavia."[5] During his final years, the dedicated abbot brought renewal to ten monasteries in France and five in Italy.

The Cluniac reform in France was matched by growth of the monastic spirit in the Germanic lands to the north and east. Many Irish ascetics were associated with this renewal, which began at the abbey of Gorze, near Metz, and was adopted at other religious houses in Lorraine. It spread to Hesse, Swabia, and Bavaria.[6] Later, the monasteries of Italy played their part, with Romauld capturing the spirit of the desert fathers through a return to the eremitic life at Camaldoli, established in 1022. Peter Damian, ardent reformer in the mold of Jerome, follower and admirer of Romauld, paraphrased Gregory of Tours on Pope Gregory

---

[3] *Saint Odo*, 3.2, 3.8; Sitwell, 72, 79–81.

[4] *Saint Odo*, 1.4; 2.21–22; Sitwell, 64–66; Kelly, *Dictionary of the Popes*, 124, 125, 132.

[5] *Saint Odo*, 1.4; Sitwell, 7.

[6] C. E. Lawrence, *Medieval Monasticism* (London: Longman, 1990) 103.

in praising the hermits of Camaldoli: "Who would not be astounded at seeing men previously dressed in silken and golden robes, escorted by cohorts of servants, and accustomed to all the pleasures of affluence, now content with a single cloak, enclosed, barefoot, unkempt and so parched and wasted by abstinence?"[7] John Gualbert's monastery at Vallambrosa was one of many other religious houses characterized by strict observance of the *Rule of Saint Benedict*.

The eleventh-century popes who engaged in the renewal forged firm links with the monasteries. From 1049 till his death in 1054, Leo IX worked effectively to end secular engagement in episcopal appointments and general church administration. Denouncing simony and lauding clerical celibacy, he welcomed the support of reforming abbots, together with clerics like Peter Damian and the able Hildebrand. Though Nicholas II was pope for only three years, till his death in 1061 he furthered revival by ensuring that future bishops of Rome would be chosen only by senior clergy, without royal or civil intervention. Archdeacon Hildebrand, elected pope on 22 April 1073, pointedly chose to be named Gregory. He was the unanimous choice of the cardinals, in the presence of the bishops and abbots, clerks, and monks, all of whom assented to his appointment, which was also hailed by "acclamations of vast crowds of both sexes and of different orders."[8] He himself felt that the choice was "evidently made by a special act of divine grace," for there had not been such unanimity since the election of Gregory the Great.[9]

Conscious of leading the Church in troubled times, the pope spoke in the spirit of the first Gregory: "Against our will we took command of the ship when she was tossed upon a troubled sea by the violence of storms, the shock of the whirlwind and of waves as high as heaven. Yet she steers her dangerous course with good courage around rocks hidden or towering into the sky." He vowed fidelity to "the words of the Gospels and of the apostles, the decrees of authoritative councils and the principles of distinguished doctors." From 1075, in a series of synods, Gregory assured all that he was "laying down nothing new, nothing of our own devising," but following the fathers in pursuing "the renewal

---

[7] Lawrence, 155; Gregory of Tours, 10.1; Thorpe, 544.

[8] *Register of Pope Gregory VII*, 1.1, *Record of Gregory VII's* Election as Pope, trans. H. E. J. Cowdrey (Oxford: University Press, 2002) 1.

[9] *The Correspondence of Pope Gregory VII*, 1.1, trans. Ephraim Emerton, *Records of Civilization*, 14 (New York: Octagon Books, 1966) 2.

and the benefit of holy Church."[10] A series of letters and decretals to clerics and the faithful fostered improved standards in Christian living.

Urging the clergy to adopt "a communal life, after the example of the primitive Church," Gregory referred to the observation in the *Pastoral Care* that Christians readily respond to pastors motivated by the spirit of self-sacrifice.[11] Citing praise of celibacy by Gregory the Great and Leo, he claimed that the wisdom of the fathers in this matter was "taught them by the inspiration of the Holy Spirit."[12] There was also a request to Christians in general to turn their lives to God, while reflecting on "how transitory and weak is the life of mortals, and how deceiving and deceptive is the hope of things present."[13] Recalling that the cries of widows and orphans represent the call of charity, the greatest virtue, Gregory repeated Ambrose's assurance that the Christian's source of strength is the Eucharist. He invoked Gregory the Great on this sacrament's sacrificial ability to unite things below with things above, so that earth is joined to heaven, and "a single thing comes into being from things visible and things invisible." Through the words of Saint John Chrysostom, he highlighted the power of the Eucharist to nourish the soul as surely as a mother's milk strengthens her infant.[14]

A former monk who "saw this life as an exile, not a home," Gregory lived simply and austerely. Like his namesake, he turned to the monasteries for support.[15] Writing to the "clerks, monks and laymen" of Vallambrosa during the first year of his pontificate, he encouraged them to imitate his zeal for reform, promising that he would "continue to support you with ever greater charity."[16] He asked Desiderius, abbot of Monte Cassino, to come to him "as quickly as may be, for you are not unaware how greatly the Roman church needs you."[17] Desiderius was with Gregory when Gregory died, an exile in Sicily, in 1085. Preaching

---

[10] *Register of Pope Gregory VII*, 3.10; Cowdrey, 189; *Correspondence*, 1.64; Emerton, 31; Gregory VII, *Epistolae Vagantes*, 10, ed. and trans. H. E. J. Cowdrey (Oxford: Clarendon Press, 1972) 23.

[11] Lawrence, 150; *Correspondence*, 8.21; Emerton, 174.

[12] Gregory VII, *Epistolae Vagantes*, 9; Cowdrey, 21; *Correspondence*, 53.

[13] H. E. J. Cowdrey, *Pope Gregory VII: 1073–1085* (Oxford: Clarendon Press, 1998) 513; Gregory VII, *Register*, 4.28; Cowdrey, 243.

[14] Gregory VII, *Register*, 1.47; Cowdrey, 52–53; Gregory the Great, *Dialogues*, 4.60; FCh 39:273.

[15] Cowdrey, 663.

[16] Gregory VII, *Register*, 1.2; Cowdrey, 7.

[17] Gregory VII, *Register*, 1.1; Cowdrey, 2.

in the Lateran Basilica in 1080, Gregory praised Cluny, which "has come to such a height of excellence and religion under its religious and holy abbots that it surpasses all other monasteries."[18] Hugh, abbot of Cluny and committed supporter of the reform, was appointed Gregory's legate to France.

The pope emulated Gregory the Great in protecting monasteries from intrusive prelates. He reproved the bishop of Rheims for appointing an abbot who had not been ratified by the monks and for failure to ensure that monastic resources were used solely for the benefit of the community.[19] Brought to task by Gregory for oppressing the monks of Saint Michael's Monastery, the bishop of Turin was reminded that, "through the privileges of the holy fathers," a bishop can intervene in a well-run monastery only when asked to do so by the abbot.[20] Gregory's belief in the monastic virtue of renunciation lies at the heart of his repeated denunciations of clerical simony. On one occasion he alleged that, in consecrating the worldly Godfrey of Milan, the bishops of Lombardy were "hurling stones and arrows against the Lord." He berated Godfrey for purchasing the very see of Ambrose.[21]

Gregory VII's most controversial decisions rested on a conviction that, whatever he achieved, there would be no meaningful renewal while secular involvement in Church appointments persisted. He denounced lay investiture, in which a ruler or other political leader, and not a churchman, presented the pastoral staff of office and ring which signified an abbot's or bishop's union with the Church. At a Roman synod of 1078, it was ordained that "no cleric shall receive the investiture of an abbey or a church from the hand of an emperor or a king, or any lay person, man or woman."[22]

With confidence in the justice of his cause, but impatient of delay or obstruction, Gregory lacked the calm, patience, and persuasiveness of his much-admired namesake. He was not blameless during the troubles which ensued, since some of his claims for the powers of the papacy in secular affairs could never have been accepted by rulers. The approaching storm had been suggested in an early letter to the German emperor, with

---

[18] Gregory VII, *Epistolae Vagantes*, 39; Cowdrey, 97–98.
[19] Gregory VII, *Register*, 1.13; Cowdrey, 14.
[20] Gregory VII, *Correspondence*, 2.69; Emerton, 73–75; Cowdrey, 511.
[21] Gregory VII, *Correspondence*, 1.11; Emerton, 8–9.
[22] Gregory VII, *Correspondence*, 6.5; Emerton, 133.

whom he was soon in bitter conflict. The emperor's excommunication led to a succession of ever-more divisive incidents, culminating in the pope's departure from Rome for exile and death, in Sicily, in 1085.[23]

It was during this period that Normandy became an area of influence for religious reform. The duchy had been established in 911 when the French king, Charles the Simple, granted territory to Rollo, leader of Norse Viking raiders who were harrying the area. Within a surprisingly short time, the pagan warriors became Christians and established one of the most stable and centralized political entities in Europe. That they retained their predatory and martial instincts was evident in the dispatch with which Norman mercenaries wrested the south of Italy from its Byzantine rulers and Sicily from the Muslims. In Italy Normans were soon presenting themselves as protectors of the papacy. By the mid-eleventh century, when Duke William had established himself as paramount ruler of Normandy, Cluniac monasticism and general church reform were in evidence there.

Around that time, the monastic school of Bec, directed by the prior Lanfranc, became one of the most influential educational establishments in Europe. With Bec favored as a center of sacred and secular learning by scholars from every country, Lanfranc became a prominent figure. He was equally renowned as a proponent of orthodox teaching on the Eucharist against the theology of Berengarius. These factors, and his presence at several church synods, won him influence with Pope Alexander II, a fellow Lombard and Gregory VII's immediate predecessor. Lanfranc enjoyed the implicit trust of Duke William, who, in 1063, appointed him abbot of a new monastery at Caen. Seven years later, with the duke now ruler of England, Lanfranc was installed as archbishop of Canterbury, where, under an appreciative monarch who was authoritative and able, his administrative skills enjoyed full play.

An aspect of English religious life which was to pose a problem for papal reformers was that monastic and episcopal appointments were firmly in ducal hands. The new archbishop was orthodox in belief and committed to renewal of both clergy and hierarchy but supported his royal master's steely determination to maintain control of various aspects of English church life and procedure. Royal approbation was required for communication with the pope, episcopal visits to Rome, and entry

---

[23] Gregory VII, *Register*, 3.10, 4.1, 4.23, Appendix 3; Cowdrey, 188, 206, 236, 446.

of papal legates to England. Lanfranc also accepted William's supervision of Church synods. Most challenging to the spirit of reform was the archbishop's endorsement of the conqueror's power to install and invest bishops and abbots, almost all of them members of the new Norman aristocracy of England. A primary concern of Lanfranc's early years was Canterbury's insistence on primacy over the see of York, a claim realized at Winchester when, in 1072, with the approval of Pope Alexander, a council presided over by the king declared for Canterbury's jurisdiction over York, the whole island of Britain, "and over Ireland as well."[24]

Within four years, the archbishop was able to exercise his claims in Ireland, when the people of Dublin asked him to ordain their new bishop. It has been conjectured that Dunan, first bishop of the Norse town, was consecrated in England forty years before, when that country was ruled by the king Cnut, whose counterpart in Dublin was Sitric. Both Viking kings were Christians.[25] Since the ninth-century creation of Dublin and other Viking enclaves like Waterford, Wexford, and Limerick, their inhabitants had tended to live apart from the indigenous population. To Dublin's hinterland the Irish gave the name Fingal, region of the foreigners. They referred to the inhabitants of the town as "the foreigners of Dublin." Ordained bishop by Lanfranc in 1074, Dunan's successor, Patrick, returned with a letter for Guthric, Dublin's Viking ruler.[26]

Another letter was delivered to Guthric's overlord, Toirdelbach Ua Briain, king of Munster, who was asked to ensure that "bishops and all men of religion assemble together" to overcome simony, remove irregularities in marriage customs, and confront abuses in the administration of baptism and the consecration of bishops.[27] A year before, Lanfranc himself had received a communication from the recently elected Pope Gregory, who, anticipating a sympathetic response, quoted Saint Paul to express his pain that "the kings of the earth have stood up and taken counsel together against the Lord and against his anointed." The pope concluded by accepting Lanfranc's jurisdictional claims over the church

[24] *Letters of Lanfranc, Archbishop of Canterbury*, 4, ed. and trans. Helen Clover and Margaret Gibson (Oxford: Clarendon Press, 1979) 51.

[25] Aubrey Gwynn, *The Irish Church in the Eleventh and Twelfth Centuries*, ed. Gerard O'Brien, (Dublin: Four Courts Press, 1992) 69–70.

[26] Gwynn, 68–78; *Writings of Bishop Patrick*, trans. Aubrey Gwynn (Dublin: Dublin Institute of Advanced Studies, 1955) 1–2; Lanfranc, Ep 9; Clover and Gibson, 67–69.

[27] Lanfranc, Ep 10; Clover and Gibson, 71–73.

in England and granting him "apostolic authority" to ensure the elimination of irregularities in the Irish church.[28]

However, as the archbishop, loyal to William, ignored repeated invitations to visit Rome, Gregory awoke to his lack of concern for what he saw as an essential element of the reform, the non-engagement of secular authority in church administration. In 1082, nine years after receiving the first summons, Lanfranc was asked to present himself in Rome within four months or face ecclesiastical sanction. It was a visit, commented the pope bitterly, that "either from pride or from negligence you have put off, abusing our patience."[29] The invitation went unheeded. England was not the only country in which Gregory's hopes were being frustrated. In 1082 he addressed a letter to all the faithful, asking for their prayers and telling them not to be surprised if the world hates them, "for we ourselves provoke it against us by opposing its desires and condemning its works."[30]

Two years later Gregory wrote to King Toirdelbach Ua Briain, church leaders, "and all Christians who dwell in Ireland," invoking the primacy of the see of Peter and extending his apostolic blessing. He exhorted the king and his fellow countrymen to "perform righteousness, keep and love the Catholic peace of the Church, and loving it to bind it to you with the arms of charity." If they were in need of advice or assistance, they should have recourse to Rome, "and whatever you rightly ask you will with God's help obtain."[31] Sixteen years after Gregory's death, the first reform synod of the Irish church was held at Cashel.[32]

[28] Lanfranc, Ep 8; Clover and Gibson, 65–67.
[29] Gregory VII, *Register*, 9.20; Cowdrey, 419–20.
[30] Gregory VII, *Register*, 9.21; Cowdrey, 420.
[31] Gregory VII, *Epistolae Vagantes*, 57; Cowdrey, 139–41.
[32] Gwynn, *Irish Church*, 155–56.

# 21

# ANSELM
## IN THE STEPS OF THE FATHERS

The eleventh-century Gregorian renewal saw the emergence of a monk whose contribution to the devotional, theological, and pastoral life of the Church is still celebrated. Firmly committed to Church reform and opposed to intrusion by secular leaders, Anselm was recognized by his contemporaries for his goodness, wisdom, and humanity. He was born in Aosta, then in the kingdom of Burgundy, in 1033. On reaching maturity he traveled through France in pursuit of higher education, eventually arriving at Bec, where he became Lanfranc's most able student. When the prior was appointed to Caen, Anselm succeeded him and became master of the school. He was elected abbot of Bec in 1078. From that time, the monastery began to disengage from the secular world as Anselm devoted his attention to nurturing the spiritual lives of the brethren, with whom he forged bonds of friendship and trust.

Anselm's monks benefited from their abbot's wisdom and particularly appreciated the simple and appropriate manner in which he illustrated the most difficult teachings. On one occasion, reminding his listeners of the serious consequences that could follow nonobservance of the minutiae of the monastic rule, the abbot spoke of the fishpond, a familiar feature of the ascetics' world. Just as the water runs away and the fish die when the untended banks of a pond slowly but surely break down, so the whole religion of the monastic order entirely perishes if the fervor of its observance grows cold through neglect of small faults.[1]

---

[1] Eadmer, *Life of Saint Anselm*, 1.31, ed. and trans. R. W. Southern (Oxford: Clarendon Press, 1962) 50.

As the first scholar to enhance understanding of the mysteries of faith through systematic rational scrutiny, Anselm has been named "the father of scholasticism." He was no arid logician, for his writings were informed by his immersion in Scripture and the patristic teachings. Though anxious to demonstrate that Christian belief conforms to reason, he was at pains to assure his listeners and readers that he would "not state anything at all unless I saw that it could readily be defended by canonical writings or by the words of Saint Augustine."[2] He remained faithful to the spirit of the bishop of Hippo, whose watchword he made his own:

> I do not attempt, O Lord, to comprehend your sublimity, for my intellect is not at all equal to such a task, but I yearn to understand some measure of your truth, which my heart believes and loves. For I do not seek to understand in order to believe, but I believe in order to understand. For I believe even this: that I shall not understand unless I believe.[3]

The first fruit of Anselm's application of reason to faith, the *Monologion*, completed when he was abbot of Bec, is described by his biographer, Eadmer, as "an example of meditation on the meaning of faith." Putting aside all authority of Holy Scripture, the abbot "enquired into and discovered by reason alone what God is, and proved by invincible reason that God's nature is what the true faith holds it to be, and that it could not be other than it is." He proves God's existence through the degrees of perfection found in creatures, but also from causality. At the heart of the work is the Trinity, for whose relationship of one nature and three persons Anselm draws analogies from human experience.[4] While Augustine perceives in the memory, understanding, and will of man a reflection of the Trinity, Anselm sees a similar analogy in the human capacities of memory, understanding, and love.[5] In his *Incarnation of the Word*, he turns to geography for a typically colorful and accessible

---

[2] Anselm, Ep 77, *The Letters of Saint Anselm of Canterbury*, vol. 1, trans. Walter Frohlich, CS 96 (Kalamazoo, MI: Cistercian Publications, 1993) 206.

[3] Anselm, *Proslogion*, 1, *The Works of Saint Anselm*, vol. 1, trans. Jasper Hopkins and Herbert Richardson (London: SCM Press, 1974) 93; Augustine, *Expositions on the Psalms*, 8.6; NPNF 8:29.

[4] Eadmer, *Life of Saint Anselm*, 1.19; Southern, 29.

[5] Augustine, *On the Trinity*, 10.11.18; FCh 45:311; Anselm, *Monologion*, 46–49; Hopkins and Richardson, vol. 1, 60–62.

image of the Trinity. Though formed by a spring, then becoming a lake here, and running as a river there, he says, the Nile is always the Nile. Each part can be separately spring, lake, or river, yet each is the Nile. So too the persons of the Trinity are distinct but united in their nature.[6]

The *Monologion* and the *Proslogion,* which followed it, were written at the request of the monks of Bec. In the latter work, described as an essay on "faith in search of understanding," Anselm develops a single argument "to prove that God really exists, that he is the highest good, needing nothing, that it is he whom all things need for their being and well-being."[7] He asks the God who gives understanding to faith to grant that he should understand "that you exist as we believe; and that you are what we believe you to be." At this point Anselm unveils his ontological argument for the existence of God: "For we believe that you are that being than which nothing greater can be thought."[8] It is interesting to place this declaration beside Augustine's protestation in the *Confessions* that no soul "could ever conceive anything better than you, who are the supreme and best good."[9]

That the *Proslogion* is no mere essay in cold reason is seen in the author's Augustinian opening call to the reader to seclude himself from disturbing thoughts, turn aside from cares and wearisome tasks, attend to God, and rest for a while in him: "Speak now, my whole heart; speak now to God; I seek your countenance; your countenance, O Lord, I seek. So come now, Lord my God, teach my heart where and how to seek you, where and how to find you." Also reminiscent of Augustine are the words applied to man's lost state, which had cried out for the intervention of the second person of the Trinity in human life: "O the wretched fate of man when he lost that end for which he was made! O that hard and ominous fall! Alas, what he lost and what he found, what vanished and what remained! He lost the happiness for which he was created and found a wretchedness for which he was not created." Articulating the challenge facing Christians in a world where the incarnation is now a reality, Anselm again turns to Augustine: "You have created me and created me anew, and have bestowed on me whatever goods I have; but

[6] Anselm, *On the Incarnation of the Word,* 13, *The Works of Saint Anselm,* vol. 3, trans. Jasper Hopkins and Herbert Richardson (New York: Mellen Press, 1976) 33.

[7] Anselm, *Proslogion,* preface; Hopkins and Richardson, vol. 1, 89.

[8] Anselm, *Proslogion,* 2; Hopkins and Richardson, vol. 1, 93.

[9] Augustine, *Conf,* 7.4.6; Ryan, 161.

not yet do I know you. Indeed, I was made for seeing you, but not yet have I done that for which I was made."[10]

In 1093 Anselm succeeded Lanfranc as archbishop of Canterbury. Eadmer, his biographer, reveals how the new archbishop and his powerful predecessor were viewed by their contemporaries: "There was no one at that time who excelled Lanfranc in authority and breadth of learning, or Anselm in holiness and the knowledge of God."[11] Praising Anselm's monastic discipline, his prayer, fasting, and ability to give good counsel, Eadmer says that he was "cheerful and approachable to all, conforming himself, so far as he could without sin, to their various habits." When he spoke to people, their hearts, "being wonderfully moved to love him, were seized with a ravenous hunger to hear his words, for he adapted them to every class of men, so that his hearers declared that nothing could have been spoken which was more appropriate to their station." Even the "stiff and terrifying" King William seemed "an altogether different man" when Anselm was present.[12]

The conqueror's son, William Rufus, who was in power when Anselm was installed at Canterbury, sought to maintain and extend his father's jurisdictional control over ecclesiastical affairs and church administration but found the new archbishop less accommodating than his predecessor. Lacking Lanfranc's experience of law and gift for statecraft, Anselm stoically resisted royal encroachment on the Church's affairs, earning two lengthy periods of exile, one under William, the second under the king's successor. In January 1095, less than two years after his installation, he confided in Hugh, archbishop of Lyons and papal vicar in France, who was committed to the Gregorian reform. William Rufus had banned reform synods, was denying Anselm an opportunity of receiving the pallium in Rome, and threatening to sequester church lands. The archbishop was resisting royal insistence on substantial financial contributions from the Church.[13]

During his first exile, which began in November 1097 and ended with the king's death in 1100, Anselm informed Pope Urban that he had left England because, unable to correct such abuses through his episcopal authority, he had been forced to witness "the law of God, the

---

[10] Anselm, *Proslogion*, 1; Hopkins and Richardson, vol. 1, 91.

[11] Eadmer, *Life of Saint Anselm*, 1.30; Southern, 50.

[12] Eadmer, *Life of Saint Anselm*, 1.1; Southern, 50–54.

[13] Anselm, Ep 176; Frohlich, vol. 2, 86–89; Eadmer, *Life of Saint Anselm*, 20; Southern, 29.

canons and the apostolic authority being overrun by arbitrary usages."
Writing from France in 1099, he insisted that he could not return to a
king who did not wish "the pope to be acknowledged or appealed to in
England." William had forbidden him to correspond with the pope or
obey his decrees, "except by [royal] command."[14]

Just a few months after communicating with Hugh of Lyons, Anselm
was in contact with the Irish for the first time. The occasion was another
request to Canterbury from Viking Dublin for consecration of a bishop.
When he ordained Samuel for the see, Anselm wrote to the bishops of
Ireland, expressing a desire to reveal, "especially to you, the calamities
which I am suffering." Among his hardships was the negative response
of his clergy to attempts "to cut back evils by pastoral rule, to restrain
usurpers and to bring back to due order any disorders which fell within
my domain." Those from whom he had expected support had taken
"deep offence, and God's cause, which should have flourished through
me, goes to ruin in my presence."[15]

Anselm is alluding to his humiliation by nobles and bishops during
the three-day Council of Rockingham, called in 1095 by a king angered
by the archbishop's desire to go to Rome to receive the pallium. Invoking
Gregory the Great, the archbishop confesses that when he remembers
"the fruitful peace" of monastic life which he has lost, "the bitterest sorrow overcomes me." He ends with a request for prayers, but not before
reminding his readers that where there is disagreement on canonical
matters in the Irish church, it should be drawn to his attention, "so that
you may receive counsel and comfort from us."[16]

The Irish bishops became beneficiaries of Anselm's wisdom, humanity,
and encouragement. Following Samuel's consecration for Dublin in 1095,
there was an appeal to Canterbury from another Viking city, Waterford.
It was supported not only by the inhabitants and some of the bishops,
but by Muircherta, who was overlord there also. The candidate Malchus
was worthy, they claimed, for he was "steeped in apostolic and ecclesiastical learning, Catholic in his faith, prudent, of even temper, chaste in
life, sober, humble, merciful, and possessing many other virtues."[17] After
this consecration, Canterbury's link with the Viking cities was sustained.

[14] Anselm, Epp 206, 210; Frohlich, vol. 2, 146–47, 157.
[15] Anselm, Ep 198; Frohlich, vol. 2, 131–32.
[16] Anselm, Ep 198; Frohlich, vol. 2, 131–33.
[17] Anselm, Ep 201; Frohlich, vol. 2, 137.

In 1106 Anselm sent another letter to Muircherta, who was ruling from Limerick. Here, praise for the Irish church is accompanied by references to the "many things to be corrected." Bishops have been irregularly consecrated or appointed without being assigned to a see, marriages dissolved or altered without grounds, and laws on consanguinity were not being observed.[18] Anselm's own pastoral domain was also suffering. While exiled in France just over a year before writing to Muircherta, he had learned that, in England, the number of priests was dwindling, the practice of religion was waning, and clerics were not observing their vows. There was widespread rejection of the law against close kinship in marriage and bishops were following the royal will even when it conflicted with the law of God.[19]

During the period in which he was enduring so many indignities at the hands of an earthly king, Anselm was writing about an infinitely greater ruler. *Cur Deus Homo*, (*Why God Became Man*) is the work which best demonstrates his attachment to the faith and prayerful preoccupation with its essential nature. In demonstrating, through reason, that the incarnation and death of Jesus were necessary events in human history because man, through sin, had challenged God's supremacy, Anselm is responding to those who wish to "delight in the comprehension and contemplation in the doctrines which they believe" and to answer those who seek "a reason for the hope which is in us."[20] Examining the various ways in which God could have redeemed the world, Anselm concludes that none of these would have given man, with his damaged will and human status, the opportunity of making adequate satisfaction. Thus, the necessity of the Word becoming flesh, sharing man's plight, and dying "to restore life to the world" is established. In the incarnation can be seen the magnitude of God's mercy, which Anselm has already established in the *Proslogion*. Adam's sin, with its historical outcome, calls for the application of divine justice, but the mercy of God is so great, and so harmonized with his justice, that it cannot be conceived to be greater or more just.[21]

Anselm's reputation for holiness, his writings, and his resistance to unjust royal claims won him admirers throughout the Church. It is fitting

---

[18] Anselm, Ep 427; Frohlich, vol. 3, 203.

[19] Anselm, Ep 365; Frohlich, vol. 3, 112.

[20] Anselm, *Cur Deus Homo*, 1.1; Hopkins and Richardson, vol. 3, 49.

[21] Anselm, *Cur Deus Homo*, 2.20; Hopkins and Richardson, vol. 3, 135–36; *Proslogion*, 9; Hopkins and Richardson, vol. 1, 99.

that *Cur Deus Homo*, a meditation on the human need for redemption, was begun in England during his troubled time as archbishop. It was completed in 1098 when he was an exile in Italy.[22] Anselm's explorations of the mysteries of religion were always undertaken in support of faith and invariably centered on prayerful reverence for God. Like Augustine, he was no remote academic, for his thought was inspired by the Gospels, the teaching of the fathers, and the spiritual needs of the people. Transcending nationality and culture, he was at home in the monasteries and churches of Italy, France, and England. During his first exile, the pope paid tribute to his learning by inviting him to address the Council of Bari. There, in October 1098, before eastern and western spiritual leaders, he spoke eloquently on the teaching that the Holy Spirit proceeds from the Father and the Son, a complex issue that had disrupted relations between the Latin and Greek branches of the Church for two centuries.

Anselm shared the fathers' simplicity of life and their genius for spiritual friendship. "Never think that you have enough friends," he wrote to the monks on leaving Bec, "but whether rich or poor, let them all be bound to you by brotherly love. This will be to the advantage of your Church and promote the welfare of those you love."[23] To the monk Ralph who protests friendship, he responds in kind, praying that their lives "should be a single thanksgiving" to God. Such friendship brings the responsibility of undertaking duties cheerfully, so that, "whatever you are engaged in, carry it through." Indeed, the response must be willing even if one is "drawn from reading and prayer by serving." Ralph is reminded that, in the matter of duty, "while you are drawn back, someone else is drawn on; while you are bent down, someone else is raised up; while you are weighed down by a burden, someone else's burden is being lifted."[24]

It was Anselm's accessibility that, in 1099, encouraged Malchus of Waterford to request a copy of his book on the Holy Trinity, which, wrote the bishop, "I have recently heard, has been recommended by apostolic authority." Malchus, who assured Anselm that his exile from England was example of "how patience is to be learned in whatever troubles assail us," had already sought a copy of his sermon on the incarnation, "which you gave us during the meal on the feast of Saint Martin." This meal possibly took place at the time of

---

[22] Eadmer, *Life of Saint Anselm*, 2.39; Southern, 116.
[23] Anselm, Ep 165; Frohlich, vol. 2, 59.
[24] Anselm, Ep 13; Frohlich, vol. 1, 99.

the Irishman's consecration as bishop. Malchus appreciatively recalls that the archbishop had foregone his food "to feed us with a spiritual repast." Himself a former monk, the bishop of Waterford must have felt privileged to hear, on his ordination day, a sermon by one great abbot on the feast of another. The request for these works of a master of spiritual writing is a reflection of the sophistication and commitment of the Irish church leaders of the time.[25]

They could not have received counsel from a better source, for Anselm's indifference to worldly concerns and his sense of justice are evident in the advice that he gave Lanfranc during the latter's early days at Canterbury. Characteristically, the new archbishop had not only been appointing newcomers from Normandy to superior positions in monastic and ecclesiastical life but was forbidding devotion to native English saints. This engendered a bitterness which was overcome only when he followed Anselm's recommendation to respect local religious traditions and cults of saints. Anselm showed similar sensitivity on learning that Irish church leaders had chosen to disengage the Viking towns from their relationship with Canterbury. In the year of the archbishop's return from his second exile, Gilbert, or Gille as he was known in his own language, was consecrated bishop of Limerick by his fellow prelates. Limerick, which was now the site of Muirchertach's court, was the first Norse city not to request the involvement of Canterbury in such an ordination. It represented an affirmation of the independence of the Irish church.

In conveying the good news to Anselm, Gilbert expresses sympathy for the archbishop's travails. He trusts that the outcome will ensure that future appointments and consecrations of the abbots and bishops of England can be carried out without royal interference and "according to the law" of the Church. Anselm's reply is typically cordial, generous, and prescient. Congratulating Gille on being "raised to the episcopal dignity by the grace of God," he wishes him well and encourages care and earnestness in the correction of vices among the people, and in "planting and sowing good morals as far as you can."[26] Gille, whose words suggest the Irish church's consciousness of the implications of the investiture controversy, prays that the Lord will give Anselm "perseverance and the reward of such great labor." Gratitude for the archbishop's

---

[25] Anselm, Ep 207; Frohlich, vol. 2, 150.
[26] Anselm, Ep 429; Frohlich, vol. 2, 205.

wise contribution to the Irish church is signified in the gifts which accompany Gille's letter. They include "twenty-five pearls, some excellent and some mediocre, as a small token of my poverty and devotion." Gille also asks Anselm "to remember me in your prayers, in which, through divine mercy, I have the greatest confidence."[27]

The archbishop had spoken to the Irish on the necessity of planting the seeds of much-needed renewal in their country. Religious decline had been exacerbated by a succession of internecine wars and by the Viking attacks which, beginning in 795, were directed mainly against monastic foundations. Five years before Gille's consecration, the reform process began in earnest at the Synod of Cashel, which was presided over by Maol Muire Ua Dunáin, a senior bishop in the north of the country. Described by the annalist as an "assembly of the men of Ireland around Muirchertach Ua Briain," it led to the restoration of the hierarchical structure which would endure through the remainder of the millennium and beyond.[28] As an earnest of his goodwill, Muirchertach, who had succeeded his father as king of Munster in 1086, donated Cashel, his royal seat, to the church.

The decrees of Cashel reflect the Irish church's determination to confront moral decline, irregularities in marriage practices, and the familiar ecclesial problems of the time, particularly simony, lay investiture, and breaches of clerical celibacy. Cashel's greatest challenge lay in the disarray of contemporary church administration, for the prestige won for asceticism by the early saints had led to monastic domination of the ecclesiastical structure established by Palladius and Patrick. In his final letter to Muirchertach, written at the time of Gille's consecration as bishop of Limerick, Anselm asked the Irish to remedy the tradition of appointing bishops who had no definite see to administer. Even the "paruchia of Patrick," centered on Armagh, had a bishop who had spiritual powers, but no jurisdiction. A lay abbot attended to administration, particularly in relation to property and lands.

One important conclusion reached at Cashel, that "in Ireland a layman shall not be an erenagh," superior of a monastery, dealt with this problem.[29] A dramatic sign of Cashel's success came within five years, when Ceallach, "son of Aed, son of Maol Iosa," was appointed

[27] Anselm, Ep 428; Frohlich, vol. 3, 204.

[28] Gwynn, 156; John Fleming, *Gille of Limerick c. 1070–1145* (Dublin: Four Courts Press, 2001) 32.

[29] Gwynn, 155–68.

traditional comarbh of Patrick, abbot of Armagh. The most prestigious of the traditional lay abbacies, Armagh had been in the hands of Ceallach's family, the O'Sinaigh, for eight generations. Influenced by the reform movement, the new comarbh broke with family tradition by seeking ordination to the priesthood. Shortly after, on the death of the bishop of Armagh, Ceallach was consecrated as his successor. For the first time in generations, the primatial see of Patrick had a spiritual leader in whom administrative authority and spiritual power were united. The restoration of the ecclesiastical system established by Patrick in the fifth century had begun in earnest.

Five years after Ceallach's action and a decade after Cashel, the Synod of Rath Breasail, presided over by Gille of Limerick, who had been appointed papal legate, ratified the establishment of the nucleus of the diocesan structure. There were to be twenty-four sees, of which two, Armagh and Cashel, were nominated for metropolitan status. As the only Norse city still clinging to Canterbury, Dublin was not included. The anomaly was resolved in 1121, when Gregory, newly appointed bishop of Dublin, returned from consecration in England and the Irish hierarchy refused him recognition. On accepting the primacy of Ceallach of Armagh, he was permitted to exercise his jurisdiction as a member of the episcopal body. That Gille was qualified to lead the complex work of spiritual regeneration is seen in his *De Usu Ecclesiastico*, which illustrates the nature of the changes proposed for Church administration in Ireland.[30] He ensured that the reform would continue to be strongly led when, in 1129, he and the other bishops urged the able Malachy to accept the see of Armagh in succession to Ceallach. Ten years later, when Gille, "through age, could no longer manage things," it was Malachy who went to Rome and was confirmed as the new legate. On the way, he visited the monastery of Clairvaux, whose abbot found in him an ascetic after his own heart, a bishop eminently worthy of emulation. Bernard and Malachy established an enduring rapport.[31] A spiritual friendship founded on a patristic understanding of the life of the Church and the needs of her people, it ensured that the reform in Ireland would benefit from the assistance of one of the most famed followers of the fathers.

---

[30] Fleming, 143–63.

[31] Bernard of Clairvaux, *The Life and Death of Saint Malachy the Irishman*, 16.37, trans. Robert T. Meyer, CF 10 (Kalamazoo, MI: Cistercian Publications, 1978) 51.

# 22

# THE LAST OF THE FATHERS

Anselm was the foremost spiritual teacher of the eleventh century. His counterpart in the twelfth, Bernard of Clairvaux, has often been referred to as the last of the fathers. Both men merit a place in that company. So pronounced was the Burgundian abbot's spiritual and moral influence in his time that he was deferred to by kings, popes, and prelates, and revered by Christians at large. His biographer, William of Saint-Thierry, saw in him an instrument of God, making the Church of his day "shine with grace and holiness, such as was common in the days of the apostles."[1] A defining moment in Bernard's life came when he was traveling to join his brothers, who were helping to lay siege to a castle in support of the duke of Burgundy. Stopping to pray at a wayside chapel, the young man was confirmed in an earlier resolve to turn his life entirely to God. For a time, he and a small party of friends followed the ascetic way as Augustine and his companions had done at Tagaste. Bernard's biographer felt that they acted in the spirit of the earliest Christians, for "in the whole group there was only one heart and one soul in the Lord."[2]

In 1113, when he was twenty-two years old, Bernard, accompanied by several others, entered the monastery of Cîteaux, near Dijon, just as the community was "beginning to grow weary and disheartened at having no new members."[3] Cîteaux, from which the Cistercian order took its name, had been founded in 1098 by Robert of Molesme and some fellow monks, who were attempting to recapture the austere essence of monasticism. The order's formation represented the latest manifestation

[1] *The Life of Saint Bernard of Clairvaux by his Contemporaries*, preface, trans. Geoffrey Webb and Adrian Walker (London: A. R. Mowbray, 1960) 9.
[2] *Life of Saint Bernard*, 4, 6; Webb and Walker, 24, 32; see Acts 4:32.
[3] *Life of Saint Bernard*, 7; Webb and Walker, 34.

of dissatisfaction with current Benedictine practice, which, particularly in the monasteries of Cluny, had become associated with elaborate ritual, splendidly ornate churches, and relative neglect of the spirit of renunciation. Pledged to faithful observance of the *Rule of Saint Benedict*, the monks of Cîteaux valued simplicity of life and worship, directed to the glory of God. Shunning unnecessary contact with the world, they followed a balanced routine of prayer, work, and study of Scripture.

Bernard was twenty-four years old when chosen to establish the monastery at Clairvaux, but the way of life was so demanding that he suffered physical breakdown. Through the benign intervention of the local bishop, his monastic superiors withdrew him from responsibility for a year. Living in a hut just beyond the boundary of the monastery, he was visited by William of Saint-Thierry, who later described the dwelling as "the kind of shack built for lepers at the cross-roads." In the humble place William saw "tracks freshly made by men of our own day in the path that had first been trodden by our fathers, the Egyptian monks of long ago." During those trying early years the young abbot learned the importance of moderation in counseling others, especially those brethren who were "spiritually needy and weak."[4] He studied the fathers, says his earliest biographer, and, like them, "drank avidly of the one fountain, which is Holy Writ."[5]

Noted for his masterful development of patristic and ascetic teaching, Bernard was committed to meditation on God's word and communicating its riches to the monks of Clairvaux. His commentaries on Scripture, marked by a capacity to relate human experience to the life of the spirit, are celebrated for their blend of wisdom and limpid literary style. Composed during the last twenty years of his life, the sermons on the Song of Songs illuminate the poem by utilizing metaphor and simile favored by Ambrose and Augustine. In the imagery of the Song's celebration of the love of bride and bridegroom Bernard discerns the story of God's relationship with his Church and with the individual soul. It is a message of faith and hope, whose essence is love, which is its own merit and its own reward:

> Love is the great thing. As long as it returns to its beginning, goes back to its origin, turns again to its source, it will always

---

[4] *Life of Saint Bernard*, 10, 12–13; Webb and Walker, 49, 56, 58.
[5] *Life of Saint Bernard*, 8; Webb and Walker, 42–43.

draw afresh from it and flow freely. In love alone, of all the movements of the soul and the senses and affections, can the creature respond to its Creator, if not with an equal, at least with a like return of gift for gift.[6]

In Bernard's reflections on the Song of Songs Christians are seen to be enjoying a privilege which the prophets spoke of, longed for, but never fully experienced. God has embraced humanity in the person of his Son, "the Mediator between God and man, himself a man, Christ Jesus, who with the Father and Holy Spirit lives and reigns as God for ever and ever." "Stung by sorrow and shame" at man's response, the abbot notes the "lukewarmness and frigid unconcern of these miserable times," when man is "caught in the mire, enslaved by cares, distracted in business afflicted with griefs, a stranger in a hostile land."[7] Introducing his monks to the path which leads to union with God, Bernard directs their attention to "the book of experience," where souls are crippled and in darkness, unable to bear the light, and in need of medicine from the heavenly physician. The first step is to seek forgiveness, prostrate at the feet of Jesus. Rising from the dust, the penitent can "reach out for the hand that will lift us up and steady our trembling knees."[8]

Only then can the repentant sinner begin to contemplate intimacy with the God who has condescended to become incarnate for the sake of his creatures. Contrition and devotion, one stinging, the other soothing, lighten the burdens of life. Then there is loving-kindness, which is concerned with "the needs of the poor, the anxieties of the oppressed, the worries of those who are sad, the sins of wrong-doers, and the manifold misfortunes of all classes who suffer affliction, even if they are our enemies."[9]

Echoes of Ambrose, Augustine, Leo, and Gregory the Great are audible as Bernard tells his listeners that human beings had ignored God while worshipping aspects of creation. In his infinite mercy, God became incarnate, "pitched his tent in the sun," and suffered the outrage of death to bring salvation to humankind. He brought justice and mercy, which

[6] Bernard, *Sermons on the Song of Songs*, 83.2.4, trans. G. R. Evans, *Bernard of Clairvaux: Selected Works* (Mahwah, NJ: Paulist Press, 1987) 272.

[7] Bernard, *On the Song of Songs*, 83.1; *Selected Works*, 270; see Exod 2:22.

[8] Bernard, *On the Song of Songs*, 3.1-5; *Selected Works*, 221–23.

[9] Bernard, *On the Song of Songs*, 12.1, trans. Kilian Walsh, *On the Song of Songs 1*, CF 4 (Kalamazoo, MI: Cistercian Publications, 1979) 77.

induce fear and hope, giving the wisdom necessary for knowing God. The perfect love of the Father and the Son is a mystery, expressed in the words, "The Father and I are one." Remarkably, the human soul can share in that union through the action of the Holy Spirit.[10] In the ascetic tradition, Bernard insists that, as the preaching of the name of Jesus brings the light of faith "which irradiates our darkness," the understanding won from this experience differs fundamentally from the knowledge that can cause pride and bring ignorance of what is spiritual. It is a food that gives strength, enrichment, and spiritual refreshment, a medicine which dispels moral and spiritual illness.[11] In return for these gifts, Christians should follow Christ and be prepared to take up the cross.

Bernard empathizes with Christians who are enduring trials and testing and, toward the end of his reflections on the Song of Songs, gives an assurance which banishes any question of despair. Jesus has taught consistently that even if ensnared in vices, sunk in the mire, distracted by business, shrinking with fear, afflicted by griefs, astray in errors or troubled by anxieties, every individual, however condemned or despairing, can turn back and find forgiveness, mercy, and reconciliation with God. Bernard goes even further, reminding those sinners who seek God that "he has gone before and sought you before you sought him." The repentant sinner is told that he has turned to God again because grace has moved him to do so. Without that impetus, "our soul is no different from a wandering spirit which does not return if left to herself."[12] It is a teaching that draws on Gregory the Great and echoes Augustine, champion of the potency of God's grace, who says, "But lo! Here you are; you rescue us from our wretched meanderings and establish us on your way; you console us and bid us, 'Run, I will carry you, I will lead you and I will bring you home.'"[13]

At the heart of the abbot's message was the urgent need for conversion, change of life, a potent theme for the fathers. There is an Augustinian consciousness of sinners' separation from God and their need to respond to the divine call. In 1140, after hearing Bernard speak, twenty students of the Paris schools, among them Geoffrey, his future biographer, rejected worldly ambition and chose monasticism. They were assured that, by responding to the will of God, they would find their "true life," which

---

[10] Bernard, *On the Song of Songs*, 6; Walsh, vol. 1, 32–37; see John 10:30.
[11] Bernard, *On the Song of Songs*, 15.3–4; Walsh, vol. 1, 109–11.
[12] Bernard, *On the Song of Songs*, 83.1; 84.2–3; *Selected Works*, 270; 275.
[13] Augustine, *Conf*, 6.16.26; Boulding, 157; see Isa 46:4.

means turning from sin toward virtue, from worldly things to the things of God.[14] The urgency and compelling certainty with which Bernard told them that they were hearing the voice of the Lord can still be felt:

> There is no need to make an effort to hear this voice. The difficulty is to shut your ears to it. The voice speaks up; it makes itself heard; it does not cease to knock on everyone's door. "Forty years long," he says, "I was with this generation," and I said, "They err constantly in their hearts." He is still with us. He still speaks, even if no one listens. He still says, "They err in their hearts," Wisdom still cries in the streets, "Come to your senses, evildoers."[15]

On entering the monastery, young men like Geoffrey and his friends were told by the abbot that their new life was the way of true wisdom, a foretaste of "that Jerusalem which is above, which is our mother." Those who enter are freed from impediments, with no heavy burdens on their backs, so they can devote themselves solely to loving God. From Bernard they learned the source of true Christian living: "You wish to hear from me why and how God ought to be loved. I answer, 'The reason for loving God is himself. The way to love him is without measure.'" Man owes his existence and salvation to God "who gave himself for us."

From this love of the Creator flows all love, both for others and for oneself. "He loved us first," says Bernard, quoting John.[16] The monks are warned against anything that prevents them from acknowledging that God is the source of all they are, especially their wisdom, their virtue, and the dignity which is their free will. As the strength, fortress, refuge, and deliverer of human beings, God has shown his love, without limit, through the incarnation and redemption. To use these gifts as though they were one's own, says Bernard, echoing Augustine on the sin of the foolish virgins, and "to claim the glory which belongs to the generous giver," is presumption, arrogance, and pride, which is the greatest sin.[17]

---

[14] Bernard, *On Conversion*, 1–4, trans. G. R. Evans, *Bernard of Clairvaux: Selected Works* (Mahwah, NJ: Paulist Press, 1987) 66–70; see Matt 11:14; 1 Tim 6:19.

[15] Bernard, *On Conversion*, 2.35; *Selected Works*, 67–68; see Isa 33:15; 46:8; Rev 3:20; Prov 1:20–21; Ps 94:10.

[16] Bernard, *On Loving God*, 1.1, *Selected Works*, 174–79.

[17] Bernard, *On Loving God*, 2.4; *Selected Works*, 176–77.

Bernard's *On Loving God* reflects the teaching of Augustine in its depiction of the worldly man whose "perverted will" and wandering mind cause him to walk in circles, always "anxiously wanting what he does not have rather than enjoying what he has." Paradoxically, it is the wealthiest and most powerful who "labor day by day to add one field to another and to extend their boundaries." They inflict suffering on themselves by "knocking down what they build, altering rectangles to rounds" or "always restlessly sighing after what is missing." This very law of human desire, which causes man to hunger more for the things he does not have than for the things he has, says Bernard, would ultimately lead him to the one thing he really lacks, "the God of all." However, he warns those following such a path that life is too short to make the discovery by trial and error. They must use the mind, not the senses, look ahead, "choose the royal road and turn to neither right nor left."

A person's first step, given his weak and fragile state, is to love himself for his own sake, gradually learning to "help his brothers in their needs and share their pleasures."[18] As he meets with difficulty and tribulation, and finds that God treats him with generosity, he will come to return that love for his own benefit. This will lead him to love God for God's sake, the third degree of love. Ultimately, love of God leads to the joy of contemplation, where the divine becomes everything. To love God in this way is to become like him, says Bernard: "As a drop of water seems to disappear completely in a quantity of wine, taking the wine's flavor and color . . . is necessary for human affection to be dissolved in some ineffable way, and be poured into the will of God." This is a love rarely experienced on earth.[19] There is a warning that, while in this life there can be rejoicing in victory, "yet there is strain in battle and life is in danger." Final unity with God will come "in that land which is home, where there is no more sorrow or adversity."[20]

Bernard shared these insights with monastic brothers. He and they had found the "highway to heaven" in ascetic life, and he called on others to undertake the journey. However, since he saw his mission as the salvation of all, he reproved churchmen who were not providing similar spiritual nourishment for their people. He was particularly impatient with those who were more concerned with seeking their own advantage

---

[18] Bernard, *On Loving God*, 6.18–6.21; 8.23; *Selected Works*, 188–92.
[19] Bernard, *On Loving God*, 10.28–11.30; *Selected Works*, 196–97.
[20] Bernard, *On Loving God*, 15.39; *Selected Works*, 204–5.

than with preaching the Gospel message. Sharing the faith of the fathers and their commitment to asceticism, Bernard expressed his convictions with a passion that sometimes brought him into conflict with bishops and priests whom he felt had lost their way.

His work for reform attracted enemies and obloquy, but he was highly regarded by most clergy and by the faithful. Convinced that only through the exemplary work of committed priests and bishops could Christians travel "the road to Jerusalem," he was dedicated to the formation of spiritual guides. Toward the end of his life, he distilled his thinking on the subject in the simple biography of Malachy, for in the humble bishop he found the qualities required by those who exercise pastoral care in the monastery or in the wider Church. Bernard's experience of the Irishman, who was his guest at Clairvaux on two occasions, convinced him that he had found a spiritual leader in the apostolic and patristic mold, a model of leadership and service for monks and priests, abbots and bishops.

Known in Ireland as Maol Maedoc Ua Morgair, Malachy had been born into the reform begun at Cashel, for he was eleven years old and attending school in Armagh when Ceallach was appointed bishop there. Bernard notes the boy's excellent education and his spiritual wisdom imbibed from his devout mother. When he was eight years old, Malachy lost his father, who had been the Armagh school's chief lector. At an early age he "took to exercising himself in divine things by seeking solitude, keeping vigils, meditating on the law, eating sparingly and praying frequently."[21]

Bernard is at pains to show that, even when young, Malachy had the wisdom to place himself under an experienced master of the spiritual way. Imar O'Hagan, "a man of holy and austere life . . . who served God by fastings and prayers day and night," was founder and abbot of the monastery of Saints Peter and Paul at Armagh. Through him, Malachy advanced in wisdom, exercising humility, silence, and perseverance, the virtues which characterize monastic learning. "Schooled in asceticism" and given a rule of life by the old man, the youthful enthusiast soon "drew not a few imitators, encouraged by his example."[22]

---

[21] Bernard, *Life of Saint Malachy*, 1.1; CF 10:16.
[22] Bernard, *Life of Saint Malachy*, 2.5; CF 10:20.

Ordained priest, Malachy was chosen by Bishop Ceallach as his associate in the struggle for church renewal. The old bishop had seen him, when merely a deacon, "apply himself to every work of piety," including burying the dead, which "seemed to him not only a humble, but a humanitarian task." Under Ceallach, the young man went from place to place "sowing the holy seed" in a country that was moving away from God. Ordained priest, he gave the people "the law and life of discipline," working to uproot bad practices, "whatever he found disorderly, unsightly or deformed . . . establishing again the apostolic sanctions and the rulings of the holy fathers." He brought the neglectful back to the sacraments and, in the monasteries, confirmed the practice of psalm-singing at the canonical hours.[23]

By visiting the reforming Bishop Malchus in Munster, Malachy enhanced his understanding of the laws and teachings of the universal Church so that, when appointed bishop of Down and Connor three years later, in 1124, he was well prepared for the task. Like Malchus and Ceallach, the new bishop lived a semimonastic life. He carried out diocesan visitations on foot, with his brethren, in the manner of Saint Paul or Martin of Tours. In the process, he suffered the dangers and insults incidental to the work of renewal. In all these ways Malachy proved himself "an apostolic man."[24]

So impressed was Bernard by the sacrifices that the bishop's duties exacted of him, that he tells his readers, "Those who have tried to teach what they have not learned should read this." Celebrating him as a churchman untouched by avarice or ambition, the abbot exclaims, "Show me a man who is content with bare necessities, who despises superfluities!" In the preface to the *Life*, Malachy is eulogized as a saint, one of those who show the way, not by words, but example. "It is why we record their lives," says Bernard, for "they are mirrors who in our age are a rarity." As a "true heir of the apostles" Malachy is a light for others, while many of those who should be examples are "smoldering rather than blazing." He did not lord it over others but was servant of all. Everything he had was shared with the brethren.[25]

A similar impulse inspired Bernard, Athanasius, and Severus to write their lives of Malachy, Antony, and Martin. In this fellow-spirit

---

[23] Bernard, *Life of Saint Malachy*, 3.6–7; CF 10:21–23.
[24] Bernard, *Life of Saint Malachy*, 8.17; CF 10:34.
[25] Bernard, *Life of Saint Malachy*, 2.4; preface; CF 10:19; 11–12.

whom God had twice directed to his monastery Bernard found embodied the very qualities which he himself had promoted throughout his life. Indeed, this modest biography may represent the abbot's testament to his own life, dedicated, like Malachy's, to preaching the Gospel and furthering the cause of renewal. Here was a man from a country at the edge of the known world, who, as busy priest and bishop, had maintained his commitment to priesthood and asceticism. In him the abbot saw an apostolic man whose life harmonized with the spirit of the early Church. This celebration of a bishop humbly dedicated to service of God and neighbor casts a kindly light on the aspirations and motives of Bernard, who, at various times, could be so formidable or so benign, as he encountered the great difficulties and challenges of his time.

# 23

# FINDING JERUSALEM
## SPARKS FROM THE FIRE

B ernard was convinced that the ascetic way, with its absolute acceptance of the divine will, represented the ultimate expression of love for God, the high road to heaven. He never spared himself in his efforts to win individuals to that road. Geoffrey, his biographer and former secretary, claimed that when the abbot set out to bring people to God, the Holy Spirit gave his words such power that "hardly any love or affection for people or things was strong enough to withstand the force."[1] That the abbot had a unique capacity to move minds and hearts is seen in his successful appeal to the twenty students of Paris in the year 1140. His fervent belief in the efficacy of asceticism is evident in a letter to the bishop of Lincoln, in England, informing him that one of the canons of his cathedral, pausing at Clairvaux on a pilgrimage to Jerusalem, had "found a short cut to the holy city and arrived there very quickly." In the life of the monastery the man had found "a Jerusalem united to the one in heaven by whole-hearted devotion, conformity of life and by a certain spiritual affinity."[2]

Bernard consistently challenged students at the Paris schools to consider monasticism. Around 1125 he told Henry Murdac, another Englishman, who was "seeking the Word among written words," that if he wished to grasp the Word, he would "do so sooner by following him than by reading of him."[3] Henry became a Cistercian. Appointed abbot

---

[1] *Life of Saint Bernard*, 6; Webb and Walker, 32.
[2] Bernard, *Letters*, 67.1, *The Letters of Saint Bernard of Clairvaux*, trans. Bruno Scott James (London: Burns Oates, 1952) 91.
[3] Bernard, Ep 107.1; James, 155.

of the new foundation of Vauclair in 1134, he was elected third abbot of Fountains in England ten years later. Walter of Chaumont also heard from Bernard, who told him that his youth, intelligence, and knowledge were being wasted in pursuit of what was passing, when they could be of "so much greater use in the service of God." Yet another young man, Romanus, a subdeacon in Rome, was asked, "Why hesitate to give birth to the spirit of salvation which you have conceived already?"[4] When such men became monks, Bernard continued to be concerned for their welfare. To the parents of Geoffrey, who had just entered Clairvaux, he wrote, "Be comforted, do not worry, I shall look after him like a father and he will be to me a son until the father of mercies, the God of all consolation, shall receive him from my hands."[5]

The abbot of Clairvaux could use more forceful words when necessary. Writing to Fulke, a cleric who has renounced his vows as a canon regular of Saint Augustine for the more comfortable life of a secular priest, he employs language favored by both fathers and ascetics in their battle against temptation. Refusing to countenance Fulke's protestations that his uncle, the dean, has enticed him away from his commitment, he insists that the uncle's sin does not excuse Fulke's, for he has been drawn by flattery, "not dragged off with violence." Bernard concludes by invoking traditional Christian imagery of the battle for what is good:

> What business have you in towns, fancy soldier? Your brother soldiers, whom you have deserted by running away, are fighting and conquering, they are knocking on the gates of heaven and they are being opened unto them; they take the kingdom of heaven by force and are kings, while you trot round the streets and market places on your horse, clothed in scarlet and fine linen. . . . Where is your shield of faith, your helmet of salvation, your corselet of patience? Take up arms and act the man while the fight is still in progress.[6]

Even seasoned ascetics were the recipients of the abbot's counsel. Arnold, a Cistercian abbot who set off with a group of monks for the Holy Land, is begged to abandon a disastrous course of action and implored

[4] Bernard, Epp 105.1, 106; James, 152, 154.
[5] Bernard, Ep 112.2; James, 169.
[6] Bernard, Ep 2.2; 2.12; James, 11, 18.

"with tears, with all my might, in the name of Jesus Christ that you would spare his cross, the cross which redeemed those whom you are doing your utmost to destroy."[7] One of Bernard's own monks, Rainald, now abbot of Foigny and suffering agonies of doubt about his capacity to persist, complains that he finds many of those with him more of a burden than a comfort. He is gently reminded that, as abbot, he was given to them "not to be comforted, but to comfort," and, by God's grace, he will be able to comfort them all without needing to be comforted. He is told that he is abbot especially "of the sad, faint-hearted and discontented" and that, by consoling, encouraging, and admonishing them, "you do your duty and carry your burden and, by carrying your burden, heal those you carry."[8] Rainald became abbot of Foigny in 1122. Ten years later he returned to Clairvaux to serve as Bernard's secretary and accompany him on some of his most important journeys.

In 1133 Geoffrey, abbot of the lax Benedictine monastery of Saint Mary in York, England, asked for support against thirteen troublesome monks, one of whom was prior. The monks were demanding reform. Bernard's reply was notably unsympathetic. Subsequent repeated refusals by Geoffrey to listen to the ascetics' complaints led to the involvement of their archbishop. The conflict resulted in the foundation of Fountains Abbey by the reformers. Bernard was happy with the outcome but disclaimed responsibility, assuring Geoffrey that the monks had acted on their own initiative throughout. He nonetheless quoted "the blessed Gregory" to support his belief that the inspiration of God lay behind the new foundation: "The second best is unlawful for one who has chosen the best."[9] Geoffrey was told that, rather than attempting to impede the progress of his sons, he should take pride in them.

This exchange may suggest that Bernard was strict and unyielding, but a letter to Guy, abbot of Trois-Fontaine, demonstrates the humility underlying his exercise of authority. A rebellious monk has made Guy's life a misery. Every avenue has been tried, but the man remains convinced that he has been wronged. Concluding that the malcontent must leave the monastery, Guy seeks Bernard's advice. He is advised to listen to what the monk has to say about his grievance, "not only patiently, but willingly."

[7] Bernard, Ep 4.1; James, 21.
[8] Bernard, Ep 76.2; James, 107.
[9] Bernard, Ep 169.5; James, 239; Gregory the Great, *Pastoral Care*, 1.2–3; ACW 11:23–27.

Bernard goes further, disclosing to Guy his own experience of dealing with a similar case. Angered by a rebellious monk, he had commanded him, "with angry voice and threatening looks," to leave the immediate precincts of the monastery. On deciding to recall the man, he found that he had gone to a remote grange on monastic lands and was refusing to return until assured of reinstatement to his old position. The monk argued that, since he had been treated unjustly, he should not have to submit to judgment. Knowing that his own feelings could influence his decision, Bernard submitted the matter "to the consideration of the brethren." In his absence, they found in the monk's favor, because he had not been expelled in accordance with the Rule. The abbot accepted their decision.[10]

Yet another story helps to illustrate the variety of ways in which Bernard dealt with life's challenges. Recognizing the ability of Aelred, gifted master of novices and future abbot of Rievaulx in England, he asked him to write "some little thing" to help those who, wishing to abandon a life of sin, were "trying to follow the narrow way." Responding later to the diffident monk's reasons for delaying, Bernard assured him that neither his former rustic life among rocks and mountains, engagement in manual work, nor weakness in grammar released him from his obligation, for "knowledge that comes from the school of the Holy Spirit" is sweeter than that offered by the schools of rhetoric.

Judging that a little of his own robust rhetoric would dissipate the younger man's misgivings, Bernard suggested disobedience, lack of humility, or stubbornness as possible sources of the delay. Though conceding that the task would impose a heavy burden, which might appear to be "hard, even impossible," he insisted, "I persist in my opinion and repeat my command." Reminding the master of novices that rustic life among the mountains and the rocks leads to contemplation, the abbot of Clairvaux commanded him to "write down those thoughts that have occurred to you, in your long meditations, concerning the excellence of charity, its fruit, and its proper order." He even suggested a title for the book and proposed that his own letter be used as an introduction. Bernard's assessment of the modest abbot's talents was vindicated. Through the middle ages, Aelred's *Mirror of Charity* was celebrated as a spiritual classic. It is still in print in the third millennium.[11]

---

[10] Bernard, Ep 73.2; James, 102–3.

[11] Bernard, Ep 177; James, 246–47; Aelred of Rievaulx, *Mirror of Charity*, trans. Elizabeth Connor, CF 17 (Kalamazoo; Cistercian, 1990).

In 1125, almost two decades before the dispatch of the letter to Aelred, Bernard's convictions on the efficacy of Cistercian life in the service of God gave birth to his controversial *Apology*. The impetus for its composition came from his friend, William of Saint-Thierry, who was at that time a reforming Benedictine abbot. The book presents a picture of the monastic orders, with their differing charisms, all valid and contained within "Joseph's colorful robe," the Church. Diverse as they are, says Bernard, these orders "serve the same kingdom." Aware that all dedicated people regard themselves as sinners finding their way to God, he adapts John Cassian to suggest that just as different illnesses require different remedies, so each religious order has its own validity for those who enter. There are many orders, all with their origin in the early Christian community, which, holding everything in common, had distributed to each "as he had need."[12] The abbot confesses that he himself became a Cistercian because, as a sinner, "I knew that my soul was so weak as to require a stronger remedy."[13]

In the *Apology* Bernard regrets the decline in asceticism since the days of Antony and, while acknowledging the weaknesses of his own order, reserves his fiercest criticism for what he sees as the excesses of Cluny. Bernard's cousin Robert had deserted Clairvaux for that order in 1119, provoking a condemnation of the young man's seduction by Cluny's "sophistries," with Bernard exclaiming, "Arise, soldier of Christ! I say arise! Shake off the dust and return to the battle! You will fight more valiantly after your flight, and you will conquer more gloriously."[14] In the *Apology* he has Cluny in mind when, upbraiding abbots who enjoy "pomp and circumstance" and monks who have a preference for fine clothing, he denounces the "soaring heights, extravagant lengths and unnecessary widths" of certain monastic churches. He takes particular offense at expensive decorations and "novel images which catch the attention of those who go in to pray, and dry up their devotion." The result is that "one could spend the whole day gazing fascinated at these things, one by one, instead of meditating on the law of God."[15]

---

[12] Bernard, *Apologia*, 10.24, trans. Michael Casey, CF 1 (Shannon: Irish University Press, 1970) 59–60; see Acts 4:35.

[13] Bernard, *Apologia*, 3.5–7; CF 1: 38–42.

[14] Bernard, Ep 1.1, 1.13; James, 1, 8–9.

[15] Bernard, *Apologia*, 12.28–29; CF 1: 63–66.

With pungent satire and an armory of words as piercing as Jerome's, Bernard exaggerates the human foibles that cry out for correction. Belaboring monasteries whose monks fail to eat simply and sparingly, he depicts a world in which palates have become so "attracted to piquant flavors that ordinary things begin to pall." It is a far cry from the time of Antony and his contemporaries, he claims, when monks "often spent the whole day with fasting stomachs, but their minds were feasted." Professing astonishment at the lengths to which monastic cooks go to tempt the palate, Bernard satirically considers

> all the ways in which eggs are tampered with and tortured, or the care that goes into turning them one way and turning them back. They might be cooked soft, hard or scrambled. They might be fried or roasted, even occasionally stuffed. Sometimes they are served with other foods, and sometimes on their own. What reason can there be for all this variation except the gratification of a jaded appetite? [16]

The abbot's stinging humor, with its fluent and persuasive plea for austerity, was felt by popes, priests, and monks. Inevitably, publication of the *Apology*, with its austere vision of monasticism, affected relations between the Cistercians and the order of Cluny. Though the book moved Peter, abbot of Cluny, to initiate a reform, his concept of the ascetic life remained more all-embracing than that of Bernard, whom he asked, "What does it matter, if men of the same purpose and profession come by a different path to the same country, if by a variety of ways to the same life, if by manifold roads to the same Jerusalem which is above, the mother of us all?" [17] That Bernard's words and actions were in the prophetic mode is evident in a letter to Suger, abbot of the once notoriously decadent royal abbey of Saint Denis and former chief minister to the king, who had acted on his appeal for reform. Suger is warmly praised because, though his abbey had a history of serving the king rather than God, all has now changed and

> the labor of continence, the rigor of discipline, is relieved by the sweet tones of hymns and psalms. Shame for the past encourages

---

[16] Bernard, *Apologia*, 9.19–20; CF 1: 54–56.

[17] Peter the Venerable, Ep 1.10; A. Victor Murray, *Abelard and Saint Bernard: A Study in Twelfth-Century Modernism* (Manchester: Manchester University Press, 1967) 27–28.

the austerity of this new way of life. The men who pluck the fruit of a good conscience are inspired by a desire which shall not be frustrated, and a hope which shall not be confounded. Fear of future judgment gives place to the loving practice of brotherly charity. . . . Now the vaults of the great abbey, which once resounded to the hubbub of secular business, "echo only to spiritual canticles."[18]

Around the time that he was celebrating the transformation of Saint Denis, Bernard wrote to a group in no need of renewal, the Carthusians in the mountains of Dauphine. Expressing gratitude to their prior, Guy, for the inspiring letters which had "fired my heart like so many sparks from the fire which the Lord came to spread over the earth," Bernard says that he has not written till now, because he was loath to distract Guy from his contemplation of God: "I feared that in doing so I should be as one disturbing Moses on the mountain, Elias in the desert or Samuel watching in the temple."[19] The contents of this letter formed the substance of his theme in *On Loving God*.

Bernard expressed appreciation of another ascetic, Malachy, in noting his journey, in 1121, as a young reforming priest, from Armagh to Lismore, in Munster, where there was a famous monastery. There he "drank deeply" from the wisdom of the aged bishop and former monk Malchus. It was the same Malchus who had been the admirer of Anselm and an early enthusiast for religious renewal in Ireland. When the bishop was visited by Malachy, says Bernard, he "was an old man full of days and virtues, and the wisdom of God was in him."[20] Returning from Lismore, the young cleric went to Bangor "at father Imar's command," and rebuilt Comgall's monastery, which had been in ruins since the Viking attacks. It was "a work prepared and preserved by God for Malachy."[21]

Refusing the valuable landholdings which were attached to the monastic site, Malachy and his ten companions first built a chapel "of polished boards, firmly and tightly fastened together, an Irish work finely wrought." As he renewed this "holy place highly productive of saints . . . he felt that he was somehow replanting paradise." Aware that the

---

[18] Bernard, Ep 80.4; James, 112–13.
[19] Bernard, Ep 12.1–2; James, 41–42.
[20] Bernard, *Life of Saint Malachy*, 4.8; CF 10:24.
[21] Bernard, *Life of Saint Malachy*, 6.12; CF 10:30.

Bangor initiative was in harmony with the Cistercian ideal, Bernard must have been reminded of his own efforts to establish Clairvaux less than a decade before. The symbolism of Malachy's action is defined in Bernard's remark that, at Bangor, the Irishman "embraced the life because of the reputation of its former dignity and also because many bodies of the saints slept there." From that moment, says Bernard, God was served as in the old days, for "the devotion was the same, the numbers were fewer." He salutes Bangor, which had given birth to "many thousands of monks and many monasteries."[22]

To convey the degree of life, nourishment, hope, and happiness engendered by the earlier Irish monastic founders, Bernard turns to Scripture: "You visit the earth and bless it; you make it to be productive. The river of God is full of water. You prepare their grain, for you so prepare the earth, blessing the rivers, multiply its shoots. With drops of rain will it rejoice while causing growth." He presents the restoration of Bangor as an invocation of the spirit of Patrick and Columban, recalling that, in previous generations, it had produced "an army of saints which overflowed into foreign territory in the manner of a great flood."[23]

In the dramatic movement to mainland Europe of that earlier Irish monasticism, Bernard would have perceived a mirror image of the remarkable influence of Clairvaux, which, by the time of his death in 1153, was responsible for the foundation of sixty-eight daughter houses, from Ireland to Italy, from Germany to Spain. Bernard links Ireland and France by reminding his readers that Columban, "coming to our Gaulish parts, built a monastery at Luxeil and a great people was made here." His consciousness of Luxeil's contribution to the life of the French church must have been heightened by the fact that it is sited only eighty miles southeast of Clairvaux. Another French city well-known to the Irish, Saint Germanus's Auxerre, is a similar distance to the southwest.

The ascetic Malachy felt at home among the brethren at Clairvaux, where he paused in 1139 on his way to Rome to request pallia for the dioceses of Armagh and Cashel. Having briefly contemplated entering the monastery, he accepted the pope's advice that he should return to Ireland and serve as papal legate. Bernard would have concurred with the decision, for, knowing that the monastic way was not for all, he had

---

[22] Bernard, *Life of Saint Malachy*, 6.12, 6.14; CF 10:30, 31.
[23] Bernard, *Life of Saint Malachy*, 6.12; CF 10:30–31; see Ps 65:9–10.

discouraged several bishops from pursuing it. Among them was Thurstan of York, who was advised to "stay where you are and exhibit in a bishop the dress and holy life of a monk."[24] When Malachy asked Bernard to train four of his traveling companions to be "seed" for an Irish Cistercian foundation through which the people of Ireland "would be blessed," the abbot responded with characteristic enthusiasm and energy.[25]

After returning to Ireland, the bishop anticipated a swift response from Clairvaux, but the experienced Bernard counseled patience. He disclosed that, following discussion of the matter with his brethren, they were agreed that the little community would not be able to set out "until Christ is more fully formed" in them. They will be ready to "engage in the fight" when equipped with the spiritual strength by the Holy Spirit. Bernard asked Malachy to select a site "far removed from the turmoil of the world," to which he would soon send men "fashioned anew in Christ." In the opening sentences of this letter there are intimations of the abbot's difficulties at home: "Amongst all the many worries and troubles by which I am distracted, your brethren from a distant land, your letter and your gift of a staff are my comfort." Malachy is asked to pray for Bernard, "because we are betrayed, all of us, into many faults, and moving much amongst men of the world we collect much of the world's dust."[26]

Led by Christian O'Conachry, the monks arrived at Mellifont in 1142. They were twelve in all, four Irish and eight French. Bernard wrote positively to Malachy of the pioneers: "They are the seed which I am sending; now it is for you to water. God will give the increase." In another letter he expresses pleasure that the new foundation "flourishes exceedingly, both in temporal and in spiritual things." However, the enterprise faltered when the Irish, lacking the discipline of the French, "found it hard to accept observances that were strange to them," and the Clairvaux brethren, along with Christian, returned to Bernard. Submitting to Malachy's pleas, the abbot sent a second group, this time volunteers, as he did not oblige anyone to go against his will. There was one exception. Asked to return to Ireland, the indispensable Robert the builder "acceded to my request this time like an obedient son."[27]

---

[24] Bernard, Ep 173.2; James, 244.
[25] Bernard, *Life of Saint Malachy*, 16.39; CF 10:53.
[26] Bernard, Ep 383; James, 452–53.
[27] Bernard, Epp 383, 384, 385; James, 452–55, quotation at 455.

Bernard's evident concern for the monks who traveled to Ireland typified his pastoral attitude to the needs of his comrades. When confronting abuses, injustices, and error, he could employ language which was fiercely polemical, even hurtful. In the company of his brethren, he was full of "gentleness, understanding and concern, learning to consider the weak and feeble by sympathizing with their weaknesses."[28] As abbot and spiritual mentor, he shared Benedict's vision of a life founded on the principles of the spiritual fellowship exemplified in the Christian community in Acts, where "everything they owned was held in common."[29]

An instance of his care for the members of the community is seen in the case of Rualene. Bernard had appointed Rualene abbot of Saint Anastasius near Rome, at the request of the former abbot, Bernard Paganelli, now Pope Eugenius. Deeply unhappy, the young man wrote to Bernard, who in turn communicated with Eugenius, himself a former monk at Clairvaux: "A mother cannot forget the child she bore, and the grief I feel for him proclaims him to be my son." Asking that Rualene be permitted to return to Clairvaux, Bernard quoted Saint Ambrose: "No one does anything well if he does it unwillingly, even if what he does is good in itself, because the spirit of fear achieves nothing if it is not united to the spirit of love." The request was refused. After another fruitless attempt, Bernard asked Rualene to accept the pope's decision and "spare yourself and me, who for love of you has not spared myself."[30]

Anxious about the well-being of the new monastic community in Ireland, Bernard told Malachy of the differing aspirations and needs of the monks. With great subtlety, he sought to convey to his friend some of his own skills in guiding others. When sending Christian for the second time, he tells Malachy that if he can persuade recruits to identify with the order, it would be "very advantageous to the house, and you would be better obeyed." He addresses the bishop as a brother and a trusted friend in faith: "You command all the affection and all the devotion of which I am capable." He asks that he should never forget "the poor man who clings to you with such regard." So close are they, Bernard assures him, that he is able to send him his sons, "who are your sons too." Malachy is asked to open his heart to them and cherish them. "Never

[28] *Life of Saint Bernard*, 15; Webb and Walker, 62.
[29] Acts 4:32; see Acts 2:44–45.
[30] Bernard, Epp 331, 333; James, 413, 414.

on any pretext let your care and ardor for them flag or fade," he is told, "and never permit to perish what your hand has planted."[31]

During his time in France, Malachy visited the abbey of Arrouaise in Arras, where canons regular lived by the *Rule of Saint Augustine*. The order had been formally established in the mid-eleventh century by Peter Damian and Gregory VII. Malachy introduced it to Ireland.[32] In 1157, nine years after the death of the reforming bishop and four years after Bernard's, Irish kings and Church leaders assembled at Mellifont for the consecration of the just-completed chapel of the monastery. Among the seventeen bishops and abbots present was Christian, now bishop of Lismore and papal legate. One of those left behind at Clairvaux in 1140, he had returned to become abbot of the first group of brethren at Mellifont. The hopes of Bernard and Malachy for the Irish church were being realized.

---

[31] Bernard, Ep 385.1; James, 454–55.

[32] Aubrey Gwynn and R. Neville Hadcock, *Medieval Religious Houses in Ireland* (London: Longman, 1970) 148; Augustine, Ep 211; NPNF 1:563–68.

# 24

# FAITH AND REASON

Shortly after meeting Malachy for the first time, Bernard was embroiled in the historic encounter with Peter Abelard. It was a dispute which had its origin in a letter from Bernard's friend William of Saint Thierry, who feared that Abelard was imperiling the faith of Christians "in the Holy Trinity, the person of our mediator, Jesus Christ, the Holy Spirit, God's grace and the sacrament of our redemption."[1] A leading philosopher of the time, Peter Abelard was a product of the cathedral schools, soon to evolve into the universities, where masters licensed by the bishops taught students from across Europe. Rhetoric and logic were popular choices for those contemplating service in the Church or careers in education and public life.

Abelard had excelled in the study of dialectic from his youth. Besting his masters in logical debate and subjecting them to displays of withering wit, he attracted a large student following. When still in his early thirties, he established his own school of philosophy. Just over a decade later he turned to theology. Once again eminent teachers suffered the double insult of his intellectual brilliance and gift for ridicule. Anselm of Laon, who had studied under his saintly namesake at Bec, was dismissed by Abelard with the comment, "Anyone who came to him with a question for solution went away more puzzled than ever. . . . He had a wonderful command of words, but the sense was contemptible and devoid of reason. When he lit a fire, he filled the house with smoke instead of providing light."[2]

---

[1] *Life of Saint Bernard*, 24; Webb and Walker, 100.
[2] Watkin Williams, *Saint Bernard of Clairvaux* (Manchester: University Press, 1952) 293.

Augustine and Anselm had already subjected aspects of faith to rational scrutiny, as had Bernard's much-admired bishop and mentor in the early days at Clairvaux, William of Champeaux, who had been a renowned master at the cathedral schools of Paris. A noted product of Abelard's labors was *On the Divine Unity and Trinity.* He claimed that the book was written to satisfy his students' demand "for something intelligible rather than mere words on the subject," and in response to their assertion that "words were useless if the intelligence could not follow them." This theme was developed in the light of his own principle that "nothing could be believed unless it was first understood," and that "it was absurd for anyone to preach to others what neither he nor those he taught could grasp with understanding." The treatise was condemned at Soissons in 1121.[3]

It was not till almost twenty years later that William wrote to Bernard, who then read Abelard's work for the first time. To a monk steeped in the teachings of the fathers, its tenor represented a denial of the patristic tradition. The abbot was aware that Anselm, embarking on his study of the existence of God, had prayed, "Therefore, Lord, giver of understanding and faith, grant me to understand, to the degree you deem best, that you exist as we believe, and that you are what we believe you to be."[4] Augustine too had approached contemplation of the Trinity with a profession of belief, criticizing those who, putting reason first, "consider it beneath their dignity to begin with faith." Bernard concluded that, in Abelard's case, "mere human ingenuity is taking on itself to solve everything, and leaving nothing to faith."[5]

He arranged a private meeting with the philosopher, but the outcome was a challenge from a man confident of victory in public disputation. Asked by the bishops to meet the challenge at Sens, Bernard reluctantly assented. However, as he read headings from Abelard's works on the day appointed, his adversary refused to engage before a patently hostile audience of prelates and announced that he would appeal directly to Rome.[6] It was the action of one who contemplated the support of influential churchmen, some of whom were former pupils. It provoked

[3] Peter Abelard, *Historia Calamitatum,* trans. Betty Radice, *The Epistles of Abelard and Heloise* (London: Penguin Books, 1974) 78.

[4] Anselm, *Proslogion,* 2; Hopkins and Richardson, vol. 1, 93.

[5] Augustine, *On the Trinity,* 1.1; FCh 45:3.

[6] Bernard, Epp 238.1, 239.4; James, 316, 319.

a warning from Bernard to bishops and cardinals of the curia: "Read, if you please, that book of Peter Abelard which he calls a book of theology. You have it to hand, since, as he boasts, it is read eagerly by many in the curia." The recipients of the letter were asked to note what was written there about the Holy Trinity, the procession of the Holy Spirit, "and much else that is very strange indeed to Catholic ears and minds."[7]

Bernard's words and actions were reminiscent of Jerome's letter to Pope Damasus on the Arian crisis and Augustine's warnings to Sixtus during the Pelagian controversy. He alleged that Abelard was subjecting the articles of faith, the sacraments, and the Christian moral code to the full rigor of rational dialectic and was "holding up to scorn" the faith of ordinary Christians.[8] At the heart of his concern was the philosopher's teaching on the incarnation and death of Christ, which appeared to suggest that the primary objective was to give an example of love, not to ensure salvation for mankind. Bernard's trenchant language evokes memories of the doctrinal battles fought by Athanasius, Basil, Jerome, Augustine, and Leo: "Where he speaks of the Trinity, he savors of Arius; when of grace, he savors of Pelagius; when of the person of Christ, he savors of Nestorius. . . . He oversteps the landmarks placed by our fathers in writing about faith, the sacraments and the Holy Trinity." Bernard felt that Christians were being led astray because Abelard "approaches the dark cloud which surrounds God, not alone as Moses did, but with a whole crowd of his disciples."[9]

Abelard's handbook of sentences, *Sic et Non*, the most comprehensive teaching aid of the time, which embodied passages from both pagan philosophers and the fathers, included variant patristic comments on excerpts from Scripture. Bernard took issue with the author's instruction to students that they resolve contradictions on the principle that "by doubting we are led to inquire and by inquiry we perceive the truth."[10] In a long letter, Bernard contested this skeptical approach to articles of faith, asking, "What is more contrary to reason than to try by reason to transcend reason? And what is more contrary to faith than to refuse to believe anything that reason cannot reach?"[11] His ideal approach is

---

[7] Bernard, Ep 238.2; James, 316.
[8] Bernard, Ep 238.1; James, 316.
[9] Bernard, Epp 240, 244; James, 321, 325.
[10] Peter Abelard, *Sic et Non*, prologue, 16–17; Murray, 143.
[11] Bernard, Ep 190; James, 320 n.

found in Anselm's Augustinian declaration as he prepares to subject the mysteries of the incarnation and redemption to the light of reason:

> For no Christian ought to question the truth of what the Catholic Church believes in its heart and confesses with its mouth. Rather, by holding constantly and unhesitatingly to this faith, by loving it and living according to it he ought humbly, and as best he is able, to seek to discover the reason for its truth. If he is able to understand, let him give thanks to God. If he cannot, let him not toss his horns in strife but let him bow his head in reverence.[12]

It was just before the Council of Sens that Bernard first met Malachy, whom he was to celebrate as an exemplar of the qualities which he found lacking in Abelard. In recounting the Irishman's story, Bernard celebrates his humility, poverty, and dedication to prayer, noting their profound effect on the faithful, who "rushed to put themselves under his wise direction and his holiness, to be taught and corrected and to submit to his rule."[13] Here he sees the faith enhanced, not by a dazzling display of reasoning, but through Christian teaching and example.

The key to this perception of the gulf between Malachy and Abelard is found in Bernard's first work, *On Humility and Pride*, written just ten years after he became abbot of Clairvaux. Revealing how humility leads to truth, with Jesus the great exemplar, he invokes the spirit of Gregory the Great and "the blessed Benedict."[14] Tracing the steps of humility "which Benedict sets out in the seventh chapter of his Rule for monks," he reminds his readers that it was Jesus who had first shown the way, when saying, "Learn from me, for I am meek and humble of heart." Bernard confesses that, unlike Benedict, he himself is "more familiar with the downward path," the twelve steps of pride, which ultimately lead to the inability to distinguish good from evil. There are corresponding steps upward on Jacob's ladder of humility to love, truth, and a full relation between the believer and God.[15] Those desiring to return to the truth do not need to be told the road, for, as sinners, they can merely

---

[12] Anselm, *On the Incarnation of the Word*, 1; Hopkins and Richardson, vol. 3, 11.
[13] Bernard, *Life of Saint Malachy*, 14.32; CF 10:48.
[14] Bernard, *On Humility and Pride*, 1.1; *Selected Works*, 102.
[15] Bernard, *On Humility and Pride*, 2.3, 22.57; *Selected Works*, 103–4, 142–43; RB 7.10–66.

retrace their footsteps: "Go up by the same steps by which you came down in your pride."[16]

The parallels with the writings of Jerome, Augustine, John Cassian, Gregory, and Columban speak of Bernard's empathy with the fathers. His teaching on humility rests on the truth that God is the source of human beings' existence and of all their gifts. He characterizes Abelard as "a monk without rule, a prelate without responsibility," who "does not know his limitations, making void the virtue of the cross by the cleverness of his words."[17] The monk who wrote on pride and humility detects in Abelard a Luciferian strain, the same insatiable curiosity, the vanity, the efforts to "outdo others in performance," and the overwhelming arrogance. In the light of Bernard's criticisms, it is intriguing to find that Abelard himself was fully alive to the dangers of intellectual pride:

> It is not ignorance that makes a heretic, but pride. It is when, for example, someone wants, for novelty's sake, to make a name for himself and he boasts in putting forward something unusual, which he then tries to defend against all-comers in order to look superior to everyone, or at least not inferior. . . . Professors of dialectic very easily fall into this trap because they think they are so strongly armed with reasons that they are free to defend or attack whatever they like. Their arrogance is so great that nothing is thought beyond comprehension, or incapable of explanation, by their petty reasonings.[18]

In criticizing Abelard and praising Malachy, Bernard pointed out the contrast between the learning of the contemporary schools of the great cities and that of the monasteries. Fearing that the schools' current approach to faith was not deepening students' understanding of God, he found in monastic life Benedict's "school for the Lord's service," which, since its master is Christ, leads its members directly to truth.[19] It was a perception that inspired his commendation of the remoteness of the monastic setting to young Henry Murdac: "You will find much more heavenly dew amongst the woods than you will ever find among

---

[16] Bernard, *On Humility and Pride*, 9.27; *Selected Works*, 122–23.

[17] Bernard, Epp 238.1, 241; James, 316, 321.

[18] Peter Abelard, *Theologia Summiboni* 11.4-12, trans. M. T. Clanchy, *Abelard: A Medieval Life* (Oxford: Blackwell Publishers, 1997) 302.

[19] RB Prol. 45; Fry, 165.

books. Woods and stones will teach you what you can never hear from any master."[20]

Bernard felt that, while many students of the schools were destined for the Church, their scholastic curriculum and ethos encouraged ambition and worldliness, leading some to contemplate entering the priesthood without first envisaging a profound change in their lives. "Whence comes such zeal for preferment, such shameless ambition, such folly of human presumption?" he exclaimed.[21] In much current scholarly activity undertaken by clerics, he saw a restless wandering that lacked purpose.[22] This evoked his repetition of an observation of Paul's which had been echoed by Ambrose, Augustine, Leo, and Gregory. The disciples chosen by Jesus were neither orators nor philosophers, yet through them the work of redemption was brought to the world. "What did the apostles teach?" asked Bernard on one occasion, and answered, "Not to read Plato, not to spend time in the subtleties of Aristotle, not to be always discussing, while never coming to a knowledge of the truth. They taught us how to live."[23]

Despite these challenging words, the abbot of Clairvaux was not an enemy of reason. Since the Cistercians accepted only adults into their ranks, many of the monks entering the monastery were well educated. Among them were the twenty students addressed by Bernard at Paris in the year of his encounter with Peter Abelard. As a devotee of Augustine and Anselm, Bernard was keenly aware of the value of reason in illuminating the mysteries of faith. He himself had benefited from an excellent traditional schooling and was happy to see clerics engage in secular education when its ultimate purpose was the glory of God: "Perhaps you think that I have sullied too much the good name of knowledge, that I have cast aspersions on the learned and proscribed the study of letters. God forbid; I am not unmindful of the benefits its scholars conferred, and still confer, on the Church, by refuting her opponents and instructing the simple."[24]

---

[20] Bernard, Ep 107.2; James, 156.

[21] Bernard, *On Conversion*, 19.32; *Selected Works*, 92.

[22] Bernard, *On Humility and Pride*, 10.28; *Selected Works*, 123–24.

[23] Bernard, *Sermon on the Feast of SS Peter and Paul*; Murray, 9–10.

[24] Bernard, *On the Song of Songs*, 36.2, trans. Kilian Walsh, *On the Song of Songs 2*, CF 7 (Kalamazoo, MI: Cistercian Publications, 1976) 174.

To a monastic teacher like Bernard, the application of pure logic to the things of God threatened the older theological discourse, literal and allegorical. Augustine, who had not hesitated to apply reason to faith, had also learned from Ambrose the value of approaching passages in the Old Testament "by way of allegory," seeing in it a means of reading Scripture which "draws aside the veil of mystery and spiritually lays open things that, interpreted literally, seem misleading."[25] Bernard's contemplative discourse on God appealed, through words and example, to the heart, on which the divine word could be written indelibly. It also appealed to the will, source of moral action. As a monastic teacher who valued discernment or discretion, the spiritual wisdom favored by Cassian and Gregory the Great, he preferred the understanding of God gained through the faith and humility of a Martin or an Antony to the knowledge of a learned bishop, priest, or monk who was in thrall to the world.

In his biography of Malachy, Bernard surely presents the humble Irishman as a foil to the proud philosopher who "tries to explore with his reason what the devout mind grasps at once with vigorous faith," and "holding God suspect, will not believe anything until he has first examined it with his reason."[26] In a sermon on the first anniversary of his friend's death, he celebrates the manner in which Malachy's lips guarded sacred knowledge, his mouth meditated wisdom, and his tongue spoke judgment and mercy, "curing great wounds of souls."[27] As his earliest teacher, the bishop's mother had introduced him to the spiritual wisdom which is "more valuable than mere worldly knowledge."[28] These observations represent Bernard's implicit dismissal of any subjection of sacred beliefs to arid rational scrutiny alone. They account for his observation in the *Life of Malachy* that "you know of the just man that the law of his God is in his heart, not in a book."[29]

Abelard repeatedly professed acceptance of the authority of Scripture but could not resist the lure of displaying the intellectual virtuosity which brought him fame. That it was never his intention to reject Christian beliefs is seen in early professions of orthodoxy, and one in

[25] Augustine, *Conf*, 5.14.24, 6.5.8; Ryan, 131, 139–40.
[26] Bernard, Ep 249.1; James, 328.
[27] Bernard, *Sermon on the Passing of Saint Malachy*, 3; CF 10:99.
[28] Bernard, *Life of Saint Malachy*, 1.1; CF 10:15.
[29] Bernard, *Life of Saint Malachy*, preface; CF 10:12.

his final years, which were spent at Cluny: "I do not want to be a philosopher at the price of being rejected by Paul; nor yet an Aristotle at the price of being rejected by Christ, for there is no other name under heaven whereby I can be saved."[30] A similar claim in the prologue to his early work on theology is clearly sincere, yet contains the characteristic tincture of pride which invariably colored his writing and led to his condemnation:

> If in this work I have by my fault ranged outside the orbit of Catholic meaning or language, let it be pardoned in consideration of my intention; I am always ready to make satisfaction for wrong statements, either by correcting them or deleting them, whenever any of the faithful has established my error on rational or on scriptural grounds.[31]

There is an element of irony in the development of theological studies in the years following the clash between these two talented men. Though Bernard succeeded in having the philosopher's work condemned by Rome, Abelard's application of dialectic was to become an accepted tool of theological discourse. Just two years before the episode at Sens, Bernard, at the request of the bishop of Lucca, wrote to Gilduin, abbot of Saint Victor, asking him to support Peter Lombard, a student who would be spending "a brief time" in Paris.[32] The student remained in Paris, becoming a famed master of the schools and, shortly before his death, the city's archbishop.

Later in the twelfth century Peter Lombard's *Book of Sentences* was published. Like Abelard's *Sic et Non* the collection contained copious scriptural readings and excerpts from authorities on theological topics, to which reference was made when aspects of faith were subjected to intellectual scrutiny. The authorities included Augustine, Jerome, John Damascene, and individuals from Lombard's own day. There were even selections from *Sic et Non*. The compendium was arranged in four books: on the mystery of the Trinity, the creation and the fall of man, the redemption through the incarnation, and the continuation of that

---

[30] Quoted in James, "Note on the Controversy," 314.
[31] Watkin Williams, *Saint Bernard of Clairvaux*, 301.
[32] Bernard, Ep 442; James, 508.

redemption through the sacraments.[33] Inevitably, there was debate, even criticism, surrounding the *Sentences*, but Lombard always guided his students toward conclusions consonant with orthodox belief. His work provided a basis for theological study through the later middle ages.

The application of reason to faith remains a valued means of exploring the Gospel teachings and presenting them to the world. Its foremost exponent, Thomas Aquinas, recognized the limitations of reason in relation to the mysteries of religion but demonstrated that there were many truths of faith which can be illuminated by philosophical scrutiny.[34] Abelard's methods, applied with a bravura which was daring and, to some, dangerously challenging, had become the norm in more cautious hands. Bernard's way, faithful to the contemplative traditions of the fathers and the ascetics in rejecting the subjection of Christian belief to an arid logic that threatened its unity, continued to be an essential complement to the philosophical scrutiny of the divine mysteries.

[33] Copleston, *Medieval Philosophy*, 168.
[34] Copleston, *Medieval Philosophy*, 306–7.

# 25

# A LIGHT NOT QUENCHED
## BERNARD AND THE BISHOPS

Bernard shared the fathers' view that the Christian body's spiritual health rests on the quality of its leaders. A devotee of Gregory the Great, he reminded bishops that, as successors of the apostles and primary teachers of the faith, they must be servants of God and not slaves of worldly values. There should be no place in priests' lives for ambition, the "mother of hypocrisy," which seeks advancement, honors, and the ability to lord over others. True pastors must have "the compassion of Moses, the patience of Job, the mercy of Samuel and the holiness of David."[1] Bernard had an especial admiration for William of Champeaux, who had ordained him and invested him as abbot of Clairvaux. Both men were said to be so devoted to things of the spirit that, "from the moment of their first private talk together, they became one heart and one mind in the Lord."[2]

The abbot's firmly held views inevitably led him to intervene when he felt that certain episcopal appointments would either sustain or inhibit the faith of Christians. In 1126 he asked the pope to confirm the appointment of Alberic, selected to fill the vacant see of Chalons. He gave an assurance that the priest was a credit to the church in France, as he was "irreproachable in faith and doctrine, prudent alike in divine and human affairs."[3] Bernard feared that Alberic's consecration would be frustrated by a secular authority which cared nothing for spiritual matters. It was a fear which proved to be well-founded.

[1] Bernard, Ep 129.5; James, 193.
[2] *Life of Saint Bernard*, 12; Webb and Walker, 54.
[3] Bernard, Ep 14; James, 49.

The abbot had a particular distaste for status seekers. To Philip, who had intruded himself into the archbishopric of Tours, he expressed his sorrow: "Oh, if you did but know, even you! If you set yourself to learn, you will soon know grounds for grief; and then in your grief, my grief will bear fruit."[4] Bernard invariably supported Church leaders whose work for renewal was being resisted or belittled. When there was dissension in the Diocese of Treves, he defended the bishop against lying allegations which were being given credence by Rome, bluntly telling the pope that his treatment of the matter was "not, to my mind, a good thing for the diocese."[5] Intervening when the bishop of Troyes was attacked while attempting to reform his clergy, he alleged that, while the man was being ill-used for doing what was right, there was failure to criticize bishops who had ignored the misconduct of clergy living in such a way that "malice distills from their pampered lives." These prelates were doubly blameworthy because they "throw what is holy to the dogs and cast pearls before swine, who turn upon them and tread them down."[6]

The magnitude of the risks taken by Bernard in the cause of reform is evident in a conflict which occurred in 1127. Stephen, bishop of Paris, attempted to renew the practices of his cathedral canons, who resisted the reform, then gained the approval of the king. The aristocracy joined in. There was violence, intimidation, even murder. Seeking protection, Stephen fled to the archbishop of Sens. He turned to Bernard, who stood by him fearlessly. A letter of protest was sent to King Louis in the name of the entire Cistercian order. When Louis won the pope's support, Bernard immediately wrote to Rome, expressing astonishment that it had acted after hearing the testimony of only one side, and that a lie.[7] The king's party then attacked Henry, archbishop of Sens, who had embraced reform under Bernard's tutelage. Old accusations of simony against the archbishop were resurrected by his opponents. Again Bernard wrote to the pope. Describing the king as "another Herod," he claimed that, not only were the bishops being threatened, but "zeal for righteousness, piety of life and religion itself" were also being overthrown.[8]

---

4 Bernard, Ep 157; James, 227.
5 Bernard, Epp 218–22; James, 297–304.
6 Bernard, Ep 158; James, 228.
7 Bernard, Ep 49; James, 77.
8 Bernard, Ep 52; James, 82.

Experiences like these enhanced Bernard's regard for Malachy and added perspective to his portrayal of the Irishman, which skillfully depicts the obstacles confronting a bishop who was administering a see in which religious practice had waned. An acute lack of clergy in Ireland had left a generation of Christians of Down and Connor Diocese starved of religious instruction and contact with the sacraments. Appointed their bishop when barely thirty, Malachy was presented with a stark choice, to "withdraw in disgrace or fight in danger." He could act as a hireling, or as a shepherd who would "stand his ground rather than flee, being prepared to give up his life for his sheep if need be."

Presenting his friend's ministry as an example to others, Bernard extols his quiet perseverance and tact. Accompanied by his brethren, Malachy made all visitations on foot, in the apostolic manner. He rebuilt churches and ordained clergy. Those who had fallen by the wayside he admonished, in a body or privately, sometimes roughly, sometimes gently, in a manner that was most helpful to each. Yet while large numbers embraced the sacraments, there was resistance from those who saw renewal as a threat to comfortable attitudes and practices. "Good Jesus!" exclaims the bishop's biographer, "what your soldier suffered in your name at the hands of wicked men."[9]

Over a decade before he first met Malachy, Bernard had experienced similar resistance in his own reforming ministry. A critical communication from Haimeric, papal chancellor, suggests how numerous his enemies were. Forced to defend himself vigorously against accusations that he was meddling in matters for which he had no authority, he claimed that he had been "summoned and dragged" to defend the rights of the Church, even against "a violent tyrant armed against the Church by the apostolic authority." With characteristic directness, Bernard insisted that his silence would not end the Church's troubles "so long as the Roman Curia continues to pass judgments to the prejudice of the absent in order to please those that are at hand." Indeed, were Haimeric to confine him to dealing only with his monastic responsibilities, he would be perfectly happy:

> May it please you to bid the noisy and importunate frogs to keep to their holes and remain content with their ponds. See

[9] Bernard, *Life of Saint Malachy*, 8.17; CF 10:34.

that they are heard no more in the councils of the mighty or seen in the palaces of the great, that no necessity and no authority may have the power to drag them into public affairs and embroil them in disputes.[10]

The "importunate frog" was not to be confined to his pool. Immediately after the reproof from Rome, albeit from a man whom he admired and respected, Bernard had to travel even more widely. In 1130, two candidates for the see of Rome were nominated by opposing groups of cardinals. The impasse derived from continued interference of the great Roman families in church affairs. Approached for guidance and help, Bernard supported Innocent II, whom he judged the worthier man and a genuine supporter of religious renewal. When Cardinal Peter Leonis persisted in the schism as Anacletus II, Innocent was unable to enter Rome. Much of his time in exile was spent in France. During seven turbulent years Bernard made his way to various parts of Europe and persuaded many churchmen to support Innocent. The schism ended in 1137. Innocent was installed in Rome two years later, after a final attempt at usurpation of the see on the death of Anacletus. One of the first foreign bishops received by him was Malachy, whom he named papal legate to Ireland.

Bernard's memories of these challenges to episcopal authority surely colored his description of Malachy's appointment to Armagh, which took place in the year before the Roman schism began. Bishop Ceallach was determined that, on his death, the see of Armagh would not revert to a lay coarb and, invoking "the authority of Saint Patrick," named Malachy in his "last testament." As a token, he sent his pastoral staff, the ancient bachal Isu, to the younger man, who was consecrated for Armagh. However, there was a challenge. Claiming succession as coarb, or abbot, in accordance with the O'Sinach family tradition, Muirchertach gained administrative control of the lands and property of the see. Malachy's fellow bishops, including Gille and Malchus, urged him to enter Armagh, but he refused, fearing that it would be "impossible for him to enter the office peaceably." As the years passed, he was repeatedly pressed to assume full responsibility, and finally agreed. It was on the understanding that "when the whole affair is settled and the Church is

---

[10] Bernard, Ep 51.2–3; James, 80–81.

enjoying peace, you will permit me to return to my former spouse, my lady poverty, from whom I am being snatched away." He was speaking of his attachment to the see of Down and Connor.[11]

In the biography, Bernard clearly exploits another parallel between Innocent's troubles and those of Malachy, who, like the pope, experienced a second challenge to his appointment. When he entered Armagh on Muirchertach's death, a new coarb, Niall, made off with the see's insignia, which included the *Book of Armagh* and the bachal Isu. Now thirty-eight years old, Malachy persisted with typical fortitude. Disregarding the warnings of friends, he accepted an invitation by supporters of Niall to discuss peace with the words, "Who would grant me to leave behind this example sealed with my own blood?" On meeting the bishop, the bloody-minded plotters were so disarmed by his calm demeanor that they "honored rather than assaulted him." Thereafter, Niall's resistance began to waver.[12]

Malachy received the insignia of Armagh in 1137, the year in which the Roman schism was resolved. Bernard notes that, throughout his ordeal, the bishop's prudence and fortitude had been worthy of the ascetics. These virtues fortified him again when dealing with a king who had broken his word after coming to terms with an enemy through episcopal mediation. Seizing his opponent, the ruler put him in chains. Widespread bloodshed threatened. Malachy vainly demanded the captive's release. Vowing that they would eat nothing till the man was freed, he and his brethren fasted and prayed for two days. "Unable to withstand the power of prayer," the leader fled. Pursued by the bishop, he submitted to him in the end.[13] The high and mighty were not the only beneficiaries of Malachy's sense of justice and truth. On the first anniversary of his death, Bernard spoke of his compassion for orphans, widows, and the poor. He celebrated his protection of the oppressed, on whose behalf he had "resisted the proud and lashed out at tyrants."[14]

Bernard too showed courage when dealing with injustice. In the name of his fellow Cistercians, he wrote to King Louis in 1142 about atrocities committed against innocent villagers during a military campaign. The devastated villages, fired by the royal forces, were sited on the

[11] Bernard, *Life of Saint Malachy*, 10.19–21; CFS 10:37–40.
[12] Gwynn, 214; Bernard, *Life of Saint Malachy*, 12.25–26; CF 10:43.
[13] Bernard, *Life of Saint Malachy*, 27.60; CF 10:75–76.
[14] Bernard, *Homily on the Anniversary*, 2; CF 10:108.

lands of Count Theobald of Champagne, who was in dispute with the king. Many lost their lives. Bernard vowed that should Louis take similar action in future, "the sons of the Church" would stand and fight "with the weapons that are permitted to us, that is, with prayers and lamentations to God, not with shields and swords."[15] Some time earlier, he had written to Theobald about *his* unjust treatment of an opponent. The count, who was refusing to show mercy to a defeated enemy, was reminded that he who "judges strictly" will not be able to overlook his unjust judgments. "Do you not fear that, 'as you have judged, so you will be judged?'" he was asked. "Do you not realize that God can disinherit Count Theobald quite as easily as Count Theobald has disinherited Humbert?"[16]

Throughout his *Life of Malachy*, Bernard presents Malachy as one who has no interest in authority for its own sake, and whose humility is a reproach to those who enter the clerical state for the wrong reasons. When the death of Niall, pretender to Armagh, in 1139, brought no further conflict to the see, Malachy, as promised, made way for another devotee of renewal. It was Gelasius, abbot of Derry, known in his own language as Gilla mac Liag mac Ruaidri, who had himself been traditional coarb of Saint Columba. Malachy returned to his "Lady Poverty," this time to administer Down alone. Another bishop was appointed to Connor, the more prestigious portion of the see, while the saint was happily restored to Bangor. There, says Bernard, "he lived in the religious community which he himself had founded, without ecclesiastical or worldly benefices."[17] Bernard points out the moral for worldly bishops "who dispute about boundaries, stirring up endless enmity among themselves for a mere village." To such "a tribe of men," but not to Malachy, he says, the ancient prophecy applies: "They have ripped up the fertile lands of Gilead to enlarge their borders."[18]

Bernard struggled to have bishops of Malachy's stature appointed in France. Never slow to reprove a churchman who behaved in a nonapostolic manner, he could be as scathing as Jerome in berating those who were a scandal to the faithful. Though praising Suger, abbot of Saint Denis in Paris, for joining the reform movement, he told him that the "detestable impropriety" of his former way of life was now being followed

[15] Bernard, Ep 297.3; James, 365.
[16] Bernard, Ep 39.2; James, 71–72.
[17] Bernard, *Sermon on the Passing of Saint Malachy*, 6; CF 10:102.
[18] Bernard, *Life of Saint Malachy*, 14.31; CF 10:47; see Amos 1:13.

by his friend Stephen Garlande, archdeacon of Notre Dame and dean of Orleans. As royal seneschal, Garlande also had charge of the king's forces. In holding this position, said Bernard, he "puts the army before his clerical state and secular business before the Church." He also prefers "human things to divine and earthly to heavenly things." Bernard urged Suger to "prove yourself a true friend to him by doing what you can to make him a friend of the truth."[19]

Bishops and cardinals who were among the pope's advisers did not escape the censure of the abbot, who observed that "the monasteries welcome all sorts of men in the hope of doing them good, but the curia has more readily welcomed good men than it has made men good."[20] Nor did Bernard hesitate to reprove the pope himself when, in 1139, at the Second Lateran Council, Innocent deposed those bishops who had sided with the usurper Anacletus. They included Peter of Pisa, whose vital support Bernard had won to end the schism. The disappointed abbot informed the pope that his display of revenge had undermined the spirit of the settlement. Having spared no effort on Innocent's behalf, Bernard asked him to judge his own actions in the light of the promises given:

> Were you not pleased to appoint me as your representative for the reconciliation of Peter of Pisa, should God call him from the foul condition of schism? If you deny this, I can prove it by as many witnesses as there were men in the curia at the time. And after this was not the man received back to his position according to your plighted word? Who then has advised you, or rather beguiled you into revoking what you had once granted, and going back on your word which your lips had uttered?[21]

Bernard's interest in episcopal appointments was accompanied by a determined personal rejection of offers of several sees. Langres, Chalons, Reims, and Genoa, even Ambrose's Milan, all hoped to secure him at one time or another, but he refused each in turn. "His soul had no desire for such preferments, no desire for miter or ring," wrote his first biographer.[22]

---

[19] Bernard, Ep 80.10–13; James, 116–18.

[20] Bernard, *On Consideration*, 4.11, trans. George Lewis (Oxford: Clarendon Press, 1908) 109.

[21] Bernard, Ep 283; James, 354.

[22] *Life of Saint Bernard*, 21; Webb and Walker, 85.

Many of the abbot's own monks became bishops, and a namesake from his monastery at Clairvaux was elected pope as Eugenius III in 1145.

Bernard never failed to fight hard for the pastoral leadership which would advance and support the faith and practice of Christians. However, there were times when his espousal of episcopal candidates had a less than happy outcome. On returning from Rome in 1138 he assisted in the selection of a bishop for Langres, his own diocese, and two candidates were selected as potential appointees. In his absence, a third person was quickly chosen and consecrated. When Bernard appealed, there was further negotiation and a monk from Clairvaux was finally installed.[23] This caused a setback in his relations with Peter the Venerable, for the disappointed candidate was a monk of Cluny.

Three years later, intervention in the contested succession to the see of York, in England, led to lengthy complications. Archbishop Thurstan had died and William Fitzherbert, nephew of the king, was chosen to succeed. The abbots of several Cistercian monasteries, including Fountains and Rievaulx, challenged the decision. Bernard accepted their judgment and wrote to Rome, alleging simony, "on the authority of truthful men."[24] It was six years before the disagreement was resolved by the suspension of Fitzherbert and the election of Henry Murdac, abbot of Fountains and an old disciple of Bernard's. However, the continuing hostility of the king meant that Henry was unable to occupy the see till 1151. When Henry died in 1153, the year of Bernard's own death, William at last entered York. The dispute had extended into four pontificates.

Though sometimes misguided, Bernard always sought what was good and true. His ideal was a worthy episcopate leading a faithful Christian body, at whose heart were monasteries inspired by the example of the fathers and the early ascetics. From bishops he asked the highest standard, that of the apostolic age, and, in his *Conduct and Duties of Bishops*, warns against ambitious prelates subjecting religious affairs to the interests of secular powers. The evils surrounding such behavior are identified as pride, avarice, love of luxury, and the trappings of power.[25] Recognizing that Malachy was free of such vices, he challenges

---

[23] Bernard, Epp 179–86; James, 249–59.

[24] Bernard, Epp 187.1, 188–208; James, 261, 262–84.

[25] Bernard, Ep 42; James, 7; Bernard of Clairvaux, *On Baptism and the Office of Bishops*, trans. Pauline Matarasso, CF 67 (Kalamazoo, MI: Cistercian Publications, 2004) 37–81.

worldly bishops to look at this embodiment of an ideal, a bishop whose actions were beyond reproach, a man whose life from boyhood had been a preparation for the episcopal responsibility he was to undertake. Malachy was "a man truly holy, a man of our own time, of outstanding wisdom and virtue, a burning and shining light still not quenched, but only withdrawn."[26]

The *Life of Malachy* records the saint's travels, as papal legate, through the length and breadth of Ireland, from Coleraine to Lismore, from Antrim to Cork. Extending his spiritual care to all, without distinction of "sex, age, condition or profession," he held councils "far and wide," and led by example.[27] Bernard's rhetoric, heightened in the manner of Jerome, presents an unflattering picture of an Irish Church sorely in need of renewal. He is unsparing in his depiction of those who, in earlier days, had resisted or spurned Malachy's efforts. They were "superstitious, lacking in faith, undisciplined, Christians in name, but pagans in heart." Yet, responding to the bishop's patient persistence, "their hardness of heart yielded, their barbarity was quelled; the disobedient house began to be relaxed little by little."[28] Bernard celebrates the outcome for the people: "Religion is planted everywhere, it takes root and is nursed along. His eyes are on them, his care is for their needs."[29]

In 1148 Malachy convened a reform synod on Inis Padraig, near Dublin. The island had been Patrick's point of departure for the journey to Saul which signaled the commencement of his ministry. It was agreed that the legate should go once more to Rome to request pallia for the dioceses of Armagh and Cashel. On the way, he again called at Clairvaux, where he died, surrounded by his ascetic friends. Preaching the funeral sermon, Bernard assured the brethren that the deceased had been a man of faith, prayer, and wisdom, who, in preaching the good news, "cured the great wounds of souls."[30] Having risked his life for truth, he returned to his original see, "where he lived in the religious community which he himself founded, without ecclesiastical or worldly benefices." Enduring with good cheer everything that was hard and contrary, Malachy was "not ensnared by enticements" and now enjoys his reward, for he is at

---

[26] Bernard, *Life of Saint Malachy*, preface; CF 10:12.

[27] Bernard, *Life of Saint Malachy*, 18.42; CF 10:56.

[28] Bernard, *Life of Saint Malachy*, 8.16–17; CF 10:33–35; see Ezek 2:5–6.

[29] Bernard, *Life of Saint Malachy*, 18.42; CF 10:56–57.

[30] Bernard, *Sermon on the Passing of Saint Malachy*, 3; CF 10:99.

peace, a fellow citizen of the saints and a member of the household of God. Surely, exclaimed Bernard, "he was gold," tried in the fire of tribulation.[31] His listeners were asked to imitate the holiness of a man who, through faith and humility, had overcome the world.

Bernard's remarkable esteem for the imperturbable faith and purpose shown by the Irishman in the course of a demanding life may reflect awareness of the intense pressures in his own. From around 1130, when he was forty years old, he had been repeatedly summoned from the monastery to support the Church through various crises. In more than one respect he was another Gregory the Great, wrenched from monastic peace and pitched into the turmoil of the world. Repeatedly called upon to give leadership, he was tugged in every direction. His situation also resembled that of Augustine, who, shortly before his death, commented, "Even from early manhood, so much authority was attributed to me that, whenever it was necessary for someone to speak to the people and I was present, I was seldom allowed to be silent and listen to others and be 'swift to hear and slow to speak.'"[32]

The abbot's first biographer speaks of the conflict in Bernard's heart between a great desire for souls and the desire "to remain hidden from the attention of the world."[33] Words to his monks, written during one of his absences from Clairvaux, reinforce this perception: "I am forced to move in affairs that trouble the peace of my soul, and are not perhaps quite compatible with my vocation." He assures the brethren of his continuing affection with the reminder that, while they suffer the loss of a single person, he is suffering "from the absence of each and all of you, and this is something quite different and harder to bear." On another occasion, they learn that they are their abbot's only consolation "in this evil hour, this land of exile."[34]

Reflecting on the numerous letters he had to write, he told a friend, "Let us give our heads respite from dictating, our tongues from chattering, our hands from writing, our messengers from running to and fro, and apply ourselves to meditating day and night on the Law of God, which is the law of charity."[35] Unease at the renown attached to his name

---

[31] Bernard, *Sermon on the Passing of Saint Malachy*, 5–6; CF 10:101–2.
[32] Augustine, *Retractions*, prologue; FCh 60:4; see Jas 1:19.
[33] *Life of Saint Bernard*, 9; Webb and Walker, 45.
[34] Bernard, Epp 144.1, 146.1; James, 212, 214.
[35] Bernard, Ep 93.1; James, 139.

is evident in a letter to Cardinal Deacon Peter. Praised by the cardinal, Bernard candidly analyzes the situation in which he finds himself. All the regard for him, he insists, is based not on merit, but on reputation, a sort of empty fame. Peter is told that, in honoring Bernard, he is acknowledging "not what I am, but what I am believed to be. It is not me you love when you love me in the way you do, but something, I know not what, which is in me but not of me. To be honest, I do know what it is you love in me; it is nothing at all. For what does not exist, even if you think it does, is without any doubt nothing at all."[36]

In the adulation which accompanies fame Bernard perceives the emptiness that lies at the heart of any life lived solely in the context of the world. He tells Peter that it is a void which can be only approached through faith and filled by love of God. When Christians learn to cling to the God who always is and is always happy, they too live forever and are always happy. Drawn away from that love to embrace what is worthless, human beings can be reduced to nothingness. However, they can be cured by faith. Drawing even closer to God through understanding and love, they can delight in the truth, which is Christ. Without this support, says Bernard, people in their ignorance can commend what does not exist and be silent about what does. He concludes by adapting Augustine's words: "If you do not believe, you shall not understand, so it can be equally well said, "If you do not desire God ardently, you will not love him perfectly."[37]

Bernard's last years were overshadowed by the failure of the second crusade, called in response to the capture of Edessa. Despite his initial reluctance to promote the venture, he applied himself vigorously to the task, persuading the emperor and many members of the German nobility and their French counterparts to become associated with the enterprise, which ended in failure. The crusaders' return in 1149 was accompanied by recrimination and criticism, much of it directed at Bernard. Meanwhile his old enemies in church and state persisted in their assaults. What the abbot endured through the tensions created by his engagement with the world is manifest in one letter, written in a moment of supreme frustration following untrue allegations about his interference in a monastic appointment:

---

[36] Bernard, Ep 19.1; James, 52.
[37] Bernard, Ep 19.2; James, 53.

May my monstrous life, my bitter conscience, move you to pity;
I am a sort of modern chimera, neither cleric nor layman. I
have kept the habit of a monk, but I have long ago abandoned
the life. I do not wish to tell you what I dare say you have heard
from others: what am I doing, what are my purposes, through
what dangers I pass in the world, or rather down what preci-
pices I am hurled. If you have not heard, enquire and then,
according to what you hear, give your advice and the support
of your prayers.[38]

Despite his often painful experience of society, Bernard did not
retreat permanently to the monastery. Like Gregory at the court of Constantinople, he maintained the spirit of contemplation in the context of
working in the world. That he struggled to reconcile the paradox of his
double life is evident in *On Consideration*, written for the guidance of
Pope Eugenius, a former monk of Clairvaux. Both title and theme come
from Gregory's *Pastoral Rule*, in which consideration is presented as the
wisdom which enables the dedicated individual to reach wise decisions,
particularly in reconciling activity and contemplation. Invoking Pope
Gregory's image of Jacob's wives, Leah and Rachel, the abbot reminds
Eugenius that, having left the latter, he has lost the pleasure of cloistral
solitude and will bear burdens which could absorb all his being, wearing
away his spiritual life.[39]

The danger is that, little by little, the heart could be hardened, for
mortal men will always struggle to relate their earthly concerns to the
realm of wisdom, virtue, eternity, and the highest good. There is hope,
however, for "if your consideration deals with these things so that
through them it seeks what is above, it does not go into exile."[40] True
piety finds time for consideration, for its true object, "be still and know
that I am God," engenders truth, peace, and justice. Through the virtues
of prudence, justice, fortitude, and temperance it imparts knowledge of
divine and human affairs.[41] Consideration brings strength, says Bernard,
for when Rome faced an imminent threat of destruction, it enabled Pope

---

[38] Bernard, Ep 326.4; James, 402.
[39] Bernard, *On Consideration*, 1.1–2, 1.4; trans. John D. Anderson and Elizabeth
T. Kernan, CF 37 (Kalamazoo, MI: Cistercian Publications, 1976) 25–26, 29–30.
[40] Bernard, *On Consideration*, 1.2; 5.1; CF 37:27; 139.
[41] Bernard, *On Consideration*, 1.6–8; CF 37:33–38.

Gregory to write his commentary on "the very obscure final section of Ezekiel."[42]

In all his efforts to renew the faith of monks, clergy, and laity, Bernard sought to carry what he called the "burden of truth," which, he insisted, is in fact light, for not only is it no burden for the man who carries it, but it even carries him. "And what can be lighter than a burden which not only does not burden, but even carries him on whom it is laid? It is the burden which the Virgin bore and by which she was borne and not burdened."[43] This delightful play on words and their deeper meaning typified the abbot's perpetual contemplation of the inner reality, which he communicated to others with such ease. Bernard believed that the ascetic Malachy, carrying the burdens of responsibility lightly, had shown fortitude in face of criticism and "laid down laws filled with justice, moderation and honesty."[44] Malachy's life on earth had been of infinite worth, for "he conquered foreign peoples to the light yoke of Christ, restoring his inheritance to him even to the ends of the earth."[45]

Bernard wrote to the bishop's brethren in Ireland, regretting the loss of "such a valuable leader." It is an act of filial piety to grieve, he says, but one of even greater filial piety to rejoice "with him in the life he has found." They have gained an advocate "in the court of heaven" who, before dying, had commended them to the care of Bernard, who assures them that he will fulfill that commitment, spiritual and material. They are not to take it ill, he says, that their spiritual leader "should have his tomb with us."[46] During the funeral service, Malachy was eulogized by the abbot as a man who "came from the ends of the earth to be buried here in our earth." Now he is at peace, "a fellow citizen of the saints and a member of the household of God."[47] The bishop died on 2 November 1148. Bernard died five years later, on the thirteenth calends of September. Two days later, in accordance with his wishes, he was buried beside his friend, "before the altar of our Lady, to whom he had been the most devoted of priests."[48]

---

[42] Bernard, *On Consideration*, 1.12; CF 37:43.
[43] Bernard, Ep 75.2; James, 104.
[44] Bernard, *Life of Saint Malachy*, 3.7; CF 10:22.
[45] Bernard, *Homily on the Anniversary*, 1; CF 10:107.
[46] Bernard, Ep 386.1–3; James, 455–56.
[47] Bernard, *Sermon on the Passing of Saint Malachy*, 1; 5; CF 10:97; 101.
[48] *Life of Saint Bernard*, 32; Webb and Walker, 126; Adriaan H. Bredero, *Bernard of Clairvaux* (Edinburgh: T & T Clark, 1996) 68, 72.

This final gesture of the abbot of Clairvaux was in keeping with the spirit of the fathers and ascetics, who recognized that the bonds of faith forged by Christians transcend those which are solely a product of the earthly city. Malachy had attained that absolute fulfillment sought by all Christians. "Shall I weep for him who is beyond all weeping?" asks Bernard. "He is dancing, he is triumphing, he has been led into the joy of the Lord; and I should mourn for him? I desire these things for myself."[49] He had hailed his friend as "an apostolic man, the apostolic model, true heir of the apostles," celebrated by comrades who have shared the same tent with him in the battle for what is good and true.[50] Augustine too had spoken of what awaited those faithful pilgrims to the heavenly city, who, having served God and neighbor by helping to establish an earthly peace, can enjoy the "only peace deserving of the name . . . the perfectly ordered and completely harmonious fellowship in the enjoyment of God, and of each other in God."[51]

---

[49] Bernard, *Life of Saint Malachy*, 75; CF 10:92.
[50] Bernard, *Life of Saint Malachy*, 19.44; CF 10:58.
[51] Augustine, *City of God*, 19.17; Bettenson, 878.

# Epilogue
## The Legacy of the Fathers

Two millennia after the birth of Christ, in an age which celebrates its material knowledge and success, many still pursue the quest for truth, while individual Christians continue to seek a more secure foundation for their faith. During the patristic age, dedicated men and women ensured that the way of faith became a living reality for believers. Martin's mentor, Hilary of Poitiers, contrasted the fleeting "earthly satisfactions" offered by the world with God's gift to human beings of "the safe and peaceful harbor of the impregnable faith."[1] In AD 107 Ignatius of Antioch portrayed believers as "the strings of a lyre," who, in harmony with their bishops, take the keynote of God to sing, as a single choir, "in unison, through Jesus Christ to the father."[2]

Christians will appreciate the richness of these images, which rests on the New Testament revelation that salvation has come through the incarnation, death, and resurrection of the Word of God. In that testament there is another narrative, the gradual dawning of the apostles' awareness that the kingdom proclaimed by Jesus is not of this world. The fathers were alive to the problem of making the life of faith a living reality in a world that is endlessly fascinating, challenging, and rewarding. Led by Augustine and Basil, they presented a theology of salvation which enabled peoples of various races, degrees, and times to be faithful members of the spiritual kingdom, while engaging fully in the lives of their communities.

The apostolic and patristic teaching, which embraces the innate goodness of creation, the fall, and the redemption, calls inhabitants of

[1] Hilary of Poitiers, *The Trinity*, 1.1–2, 12.1; FCh 25:3–4, 501.
[2] Ignatius, *Letter to the Ephesians*, 4; FCh 1:89.

the two cities to serve God and the common good. Basil, Ambrose, and Leo asked Christians to seek God in service of their neighbors. Jerome's gift for languages brought them closer contact with his Word. Augustine deepened their appreciation of the mysteries by relating reason and faith. Introducing the Gospel message to their times, followers of the fathers like Bede, Anselm, and Bernard invoked the wisdom of those "brilliant lights" of the early Church. Firmly grounded in Scripture and the apostolic age, transcending cultures and generations, the patristic writings still offer rich sources of pastoral care, instruction, guidance, and consolation.

By encountering these gifted mentors, today's Christians, living in a world that is largely indifferent to the faith, return to the deepest source of their commitment, the mercy and generosity of God. They can benefit from Augustine's advice to Proba on prayer, appreciate Basil's letter on the delights of ascetic life, or be moved by Jerome's tribute to Paula and Marcella. Pope Gregory's exchanges with Augustine of Canterbury in the course of that anxious monk's mission to the English offer support to clergy perplexed by pastoral challenges. Augustine of Hippo's characteristic openness, resolve, courage, and concern for the spiritual well-being of his people strike a chord in modern societies. Readers of Jerome's letters recognize that his natural pugnacity does not diminish the rich legacy of his learning or the generosity of his contribution to God's service.

Contemporary Christians find that the lives of those early spiritual leaders chime with their own, since they encapsulate human weakness, conversion, and renewed commitment to the Gospel message. The need for perennial reform, felt by individual Christians and the entire body of believers, can be more readily addressed by looking to the experience and example of the fathers. Augustine's desire that his works be "carefully preserved for posterity" signaled a determination that his account of God's transformative intervention in his life and the life of the Church should be widely known.[3] The same hope inspired Athanasius's *Antony*, Jerome's *Malchus*, Severus's *Martin*, and Gregory's portrait of Benedict. The contribution of the humble Patrick testifies to his profound faith and offers solace to Christians experiencing opposition and discouragement.

Ambrose, Basil, and their peers have inspired generations of Christians to celebrate the divine benevolence, source of the earth's natural

---

[3] Possidius, *Life of Saint Augustine*, 31.6; Augustinian Press, 130.

gifts and beauties. The hexamera and related commentaries on the first six books of Scripture inspire gratitude for God's munificence. John Chrysostom delivered sixty-seven homilies on Genesis. Contemplating the words, "In the beginning, God created the heavens and the earth," Basil exclaims, "What ear is worthy of the sublimity of this narrative? How well prepared should that soul be for the hearing of such stupendous wonders?"[4] At the end of the *Confessions*, Augustine rejoices that the divine generosity is being recognized and reciprocated: "Your creation sings praise to you so that we may love you, and we love you so that praise may be offered to you by your creation."[5]

Followers of the fathers and ascetics have mediated their wisdom on the love and mercy of God to new generations. Prominent among them was Bernard, who, rivaling those illustrious predecessors in his ability to express appreciation of the extent of God's care for humanity, described the "law of the Lord" as the love of one who does not seek his own. All things were made in accord with this law, which unites the Trinity in the bond of peace. It is the divine essence, which is found in John's phrase "God is love."[6] In his letter to the monks of Chartreuse, the abbot insisted that even the Lord of all is not outside this law, for God lives by it, and observed it in creating and governing the universe.[7] That Anselm, who died just three years before Bernard entered Cîteaux, shared the abbot's patristic vision of the human soul's bond with God is manifest in his *Meditation on Human Redemption*:

> What then is the strength and power of your salvation and where is it found? Christ has brought you back to life. He is the Good Samaritan who healed you. He is the good friend who redeemed you and set you free by laying down his life for you. Christ did all this. So the strength of your salvation is the strength of Christ.[8]

[4] Basil, *Homily*, 1.3, *On the Hexameron*, trans. Agnes Clare Way, *The Exegetic Homilies*, vol. 46 (Washington, DC: CUAP, 1981) 3.

[5] Augustine, *Conf*, 13.33.48; Boulding, 377.

[6] Bernard, *On Loving God*, 13.36; *Selected Works*, 201–2; 1 John 4:8.

[7] Bernard, Ep 12.4; James, 44.

[8] Bernard, Ep 12; James, 41–42; Anselm, *Prayers and Meditations*, trans. Benedicta Ward (Middlesex: Penguin Books, 1973) 239.

Christians continue to be challenged by these spiritual forebears. Augustine's ideas on human destiny, responsibility and justice, peace and war are as relevant today as they were in the early fifth century. Basil's exhilaration on discovering the joys of contemplation in the wilderness may strike a chord in the modern urban consciousness. Antony's retreat to the remoteness of the desert to pursue a life of simplicity and prayer resonates in increasingly complex societies. The work of John Chrysostom, Basil, and Gregory the Great for the sick, the hungry, and the dispossessed continues. A world marked by extremes of want and plenty, poverty and wealth can learn from the Gospel-based ascetic and patristic emphasis on frugality and sharing, expressed so well by Leo and seen by believers as a reflection of the generosity of God.

These and other insights of the ascetics, the fathers, and their successors continue to illuminate the profound worth of the pristine Christian message in an often divided, jaded, and unequal world. Born of the wisdom that inspired the apostles' and fathers' mission to renew the face of the earth, they confirm the truth of Irenaeus's felicitous image of the Gospel teaching received from Jesus which, passed on in the Church, "by the Spirit of God renews its youth and, as if it were some precious deposit in an excellent vessel, causes the vessel itself containing it to renew its youth also."[9]

---

[9] Irenaeus, *Against Heresies*, 3.24.1; ANF 1:458.

# Bibliography

## Primary Sources

Adomnán. *Life of Saint Columba.* Translated by Richard Sharpe. London: Penguin Books, 1995.

———. *De Locis Sanctis.* Edited by Denis Meehan. Dublin: Dublin Institute for Advanced Studies, 1958.

Aelred of Rieuvalx. *The Mirror of Charity.* Translated by Geoffrey Webb and Adrian Walker. London: A. R. Mowbray, 1962.

*Aldhelm: The Prose Works.* Translated by Michael Lapidge and Michael Herren. Cambridge: D. S. Brewer, Rowman and Littlefield, 1979.

Saint Ambrose. *Select Works and Letters: On the Duties of the Clergy; On the Mysteries; Concerning Widows; Concerning Virgins.* Translated by Rev. H. De Romestin, MA, DD. Edited by Philip Schaff and Henry Wace. A Select Library of the Nicene and Post-Nicene Fathers of the Christian Church, Second Series, Vol. 10. Grand Rapids, MI: Eerdmans, 1997.

———. *Letters.* Translated by Sister Mary Melchior Benenka, OP. Edited by Roy Joseph Deferrari. The Fathers of the Church, Vol. 26. Washington, DC: Catholic University of America Press, 1967.

———. *The Theological and Dogmatic Works: On the Mysteries; The Sacraments; The Holy Spirit; The Incarnation.* Translated by Roy Joseph Deferrari. Edited by Hermigild Dressler, OFM. The Fathers of the Church, Vol. 44. Washington, DC: CUAP in association with Consortium Books, 1977.

———. *The Hexameron.* Translated by John J. Savage. Edited by Hermigild Dressler, OFM. The Fathers of the Church, Vol. 42. Washington, DC: CUAP in association with Consortium Books, 1977.

———. *On Virginity.* Translated by Daniel Callam, CSB. Toronto: Peregrina, 1996.

*Annals of Ulster to AD 1131.* Edited by Seán Mac Airt and Geróid Mac Niocaill. Dublin: Institute for Advanced Studies, 1983.

*Anselm of Canterbury: The Major Works*. Edited by B. Davies and G. R. Evans. Oxford: University Press, 1988.

*The Works of Saint Anselm of Canterbury Vol. 1: Monologion and Proslogion*. Edited and translated by J. Hopkins and H. Richardson. London: SCM Press, 1974.

*The Works of Saint Anselm of Canterbury, Vol. 3: Incarnation of the Word and Cur Deus Homo*. Edited and translated by J. Hopkins and H. Richardson. New York: Edwin Mellen Press, 1976.

*The Letters of Saint Anselm of Canterbury, Vol. 1*. Translated by Walter Frohlich. Cistercian Studies Series 96. Kalamazoo, MI: Cistercian Publications, 1990.

*The Letters of Saint Anselm of Canterbury, Vol. 2*. Translated by Walter Frohlich. Cistercian Studies Series 97. Kalamazoo, MI: Cistercian Publications, 1993.

*The Letters of Saint Anselm of Canterbury, Vol. 3*. Translated by Walter Frohlich. Cistercian Studies Series 142. Kalamazoo, MI: Cistercian Publications, 1994.

*The Prayers and Meditations of Saint Anselm*. Translated by Sister Benedicta Ward. Middlesex: Penguin Books, 1973.

*Antiphonary of Bangor Vol. 2*. Edited by F. E. Warren, BD. Henry Bradshaw Society. London: Harrison and Sons, 1895.

*The Apostolic Fathers*. Translated by Joseph M.-F. Marique, SJ; Gerald G. Walsh, SJ; and Francis X. Glimm. Edited by Hermigild Dressler, OFM. The Fathers of the Church, Vol. 1. Washington, DC: CUAP, 1981.

*The Apostolic Fathers: The First Epistle of Clement to the Corinthians. The Epistles of Ignatius; The Epistle of Polycarp of Smyrna; The Martyrdom of Polycarp; Didache*. Translated by Maxwell Staniforth. Early Christian Writings. New York: Dorset Press, 1993.

*The Apostolic Fathers with Justin Martyr and Irenaeus*. Revised by A. Cleveland Coxe, DD. Edited by Rev. Alexander Roberts, DD; and James Donaldson, LLD. The Ante-Nicene Fathers of the Christian Church, Vol. 1. Grand Rapids, MI: Eerdmans, 1996.

*The Book of Armagh*. Edited by John Gwynn, DD, DCL. Dublin: Hodges Figgis, 1913.

Saint Augustine. *Expositions on the Book of the Psalms*. Translated by Cleveland Coxe, DD. Edited by Philip Schaff, DD, LLD. A Select Library of the Nicene and Post-Nicene Fathers of the Christian Church, First Series, Vol. 8. Grand Rapids, MI: Eerdmans, 1996.

———. *Discourses on the Psalms 1*. Translated by Dame Scholastica Hegbin and Dame Felicitas Corrigan. Edited by Johannes Quasten and Walter J. Burkhardt, SJ. Ancient Christian Writers, No. 29. London: Longmans Green, 1960.

———. *Discourses on the Psalms 2*. Translated by Dame Scholastica Hegbin and Dame Felicitas Corrigan. Edited by Johannes Quasten. Ancient Christian Writers, No. 30. London: Longmans Green, 1961.

————. *Sermons on the Liturgical Seasons.* Translated by Sister Mary Sarah Muldowney. Edited by Hermigild Dressler, OFM. The Fathers of the Church, Vol. 38. Washington, DC: CUAP in association with Consortium Books, 1958.

————. *On the Trinity.* Translated by Stephen McKenna, CSSR. Edited by Hermigild Dressler, OFM. The Fathers of the Church, Vol. 45. Washington, DC: CUAP, 1981.

————. *The Retractions.* Translated by Sister Mary Inez Bogan, RSM, PhD. Edited by Roy Joseph Deferrari. The Fathers of the Church, Vol. 60. Washington, DC: CUAP, 1968.

————. *Letters.* Translated by J. G. Cunningham. Edited by M. A. Philip Schaff, DD, LLD. A Select Library of the Nicene and Post-Nicene Fathers of the Christian Church, First Series, Vol. 1. Peabody, MA: Hendrickson, 1999.

————. *Letters 83–130.* Translated by Sister Wilfrid Parsons, SND. Edited by Roy Joseph Deferrari. The Fathers of the Church, Vol. 18. Washington, DC: CUAP, 1966.

————. *Letters 131–164.* Translated by Sister Wilfrid Parsons, SND. Edited by Roy Joseph Deferrari. The Fathers of the Church, Vol. 20. Washington, DC: CUAP, 1965.

————. *Letters 165–203.* Translated by Sister Wilfrid Parsons, SND. Edited by Hermigild Dressler, OFM. The Fathers of the Church, Vol. 32. Washington, DC: CUAP in association with Consortium Books, 1977.

————. *Letters 204–270.* Translated by Sister Wilfrid Parsons, SND. Edited by Hermigild Dressler, OFM. The Fathers of the Church, Vol. 32. Washington, DC: CUAP in association with Consortium Books, 1977.

————. *Letters 1–29.* Translated by Robert B. Eno, SS. Edited by Thomas P. Halton. The Fathers of the Church, Vol. 81. Washington, DC: CUAP, 1989.

————. *On Genesis.* Translated by Roland J. Teske, SJ. Edited by Thomas P. Halton. The Fathers of the Church, Vol. 84. Washington, DC: CUAP, 1991.

————. *On the Work of Monks; On the Christian Life; The Usefulness of Fasting.* Translated by Mary Sarah Muldowney, RSM, PhD. Edited by Roy Joseph Deferrari. The Fathers of the Church, Vol. 14. Washington, DC: CUAP, 1981.

————. *Treatises on Marriage and Other Subjects: The Good of Marriage.* Translated by Charles T. Wilcox, MM. Edited by Roy Joseph Deferrari. The Fathers of the Church, Vol. 27. Washington, DC: CUAP, 1969.

————. *The Care to be Taken for the Dead.* Translated by John A. Lacy, MA. Edited by Roy Joseph Deferrari. The Fathers of the Church, Vol. 27. Washington, DC: CUAP, 1969.

————. *Christian Instruction.* Translated by John J. Gavigan, OSA. Edited by Roy Joseph Deferrari. The Fathers of the Church, Vol. 2. Washington, DC: CUAP, 1966.

―――. *The City of God*. Translated by Henry Bettenson. London: Penguin Books, 2003.

―――. *The Confessions*. Translated by John K. Ryan. New York: Image Books, 1960.

―――. *The Confessions*. Translated by Maria Boulding. Edited by John E. Rotelle, OSA. The Works of Saint Augustine. Hyde Park, NY: New City Press, 2008.

―――. *Against Julian*. Translated by Matthew A. Schumaker, CSC. Edited by Hermigild Dressler, OFM. The Fathers of the Church, Vol. 35. Washington, DC: CUAP, 1981.

―――. *Free Choice of the Will: Grace and Free Will*. Translated by Robert Russell, OAS. Edited by Roy Joseph Deferrari. The Fathers of the Church, Vol. 59. Washington, DC: CUAP, 1968.

―――. *The Anti-Pelagian Writings: On Nature and Grace; On the Predestination of the Saints; On the Gift of Perseverance*. Translated by Peter Holmes, DD, LLD; and Robert Ernest Wallis, PhD. Revised by Benjamin B. Warfield, DD. Edited by Philip Schaff. NPNF, First Series, Vol. 5. Grand Rapids, MI: Eerdmans, 1997.

―――. *Political Writings*. Edited by E. M. Atkins and R. J. Dodaro. Cambridge: University Press, 2001.

Saint Basil. *Letters 1–185*. Translated by Sister Agnes Clare Way, CDP. Edited by Hermigild Dressler, OFM. The Fathers of the Church, Vol. 13. Washington, DC: CUAP, 1951.

―――. *Letters 186–368*. Translated by Sister Agnes Clare Way, CDP. Edited by Hermigild Dressler, OFM. The Fathers of the Church, Vol. 28. Washington, DC: CUAP, 1969.

―――. *On the Hexameron*. Exegetic Writings. Translated by Sister Agnes Clare Way, CDP. Edited by Hermigild Dressler, OFM. The Fathers of the Church, Vol. 46. Washington, DC: CUAP, 1981.

Bede. *Ecclesiastical History of the English People*. Translated by Leo Sherley-Price. Revised by R. E. Latham. London: Penguin Books, 1990.

*RB 1980: The Rule of St. Benedict*. Edited by Timothy Fry et al. Collegeville, MN: Liturgical Press, 1981.

*The Letters of Saint Bernard of Clairvaux*. Translated by Bruno Scott James. London: Burns Oates, 1952.

Saint Bernard of Clairvaux. *Opera: Vols. 1 & 2*. Edited by J. Leclercq, OSB; C. H. Talbot; and H. M. Rochais. Rome: Editiones Cistercienses, 1958.

―――. *Treatises 1: An Apologia to Abbot William*. Translated by Michael Casey, OCSO. Cistercian Fathers Series 1. Shannon: Irish University Press, 1970.

―――. *The Life and Death of Saint Malachy the Irishman*. Translated by Robert T. Meyer. Kalamazoo, MI: Cistercian Publications, 1978.

————. *Song of Songs 1, 2.* The Works of Bernard of Clairvaux. Translated by Kilian Walsh, OCSO. CF 4, 7. Kalamazoo, MI: Cistercian Publications, 1979.

————. *Selected Works.* Translated by G. R. Evans. New York: Paulist Press, 1987.

————.*On Consideration.* Translated by John D. Anderson and Elizabeth T. Kernan. Kalamazoo, MI: Cistercian Publications, 1976.

*The Life of Saint Bernard of Clairvaux by his Contemporaries.* Translated by Geoffrey Webb and Adrian Walker. London: A. R. Mowbray, 1960.

Saint Boniface. *Letters.* Translated by Ephriam Emerton. New York: Columbia University Press, 1940.

*The Reign of Charlemagne.* Edited by H. R. Loyn and John Percival. Documents of Medieval History 2. London: Edward Arnold, 1975.

*Sancti Columbani Opera: Letters, Sermons, Rule, Penitential and Songs.* Translated by G. S. M. Walker. Dublin: Dublin Institute for Advanced Studies, 1957.

Saint Cyprian. *Treatises: The Unity of the Church; The Lord's Prayer; Works and Almsgiving.* Translated and edited by Roy Joseph Deferrari. The Fathers of the Church, Vol. 36. Washington, DC: CUAP in association with Consortium Books, 1977.

————. *The Lapsed and the Unity of the Catholic Church.* Translated by Maurice Bévenot, SJ. Edited by Johannes Quasten, STD; and Joseph C. Plumpe, PhD. Ancient Christian Writers, No. 25. Westminster, MD: Newman Press, 1957.

*The Didache or Teaching of the Apostles.* Translated by Francis X. Glimm, STL. Edited by Hermigild Dressler, OFM. The Fathers of the Church, Vol. I. Washington, DC: CUAP, 1981.

*Early Christian Lives: Life of Antony by Athanasius, Life of Paul of Thebes by Jerome, Life of Hilarion by Jerome, Life of Malchus by Jerome, Life of Martin of Tours by Sulpicius Severus, Life of Benedict by Gregory the Great.* Translated by Carolinne White. London: Penguin Books, 1998.

*Egeria's Travels.* Translated by John Wilkinson. Oxford: Oxbow Books, 2006.

Eusebius. *Ecclesiastical History.* Translated by Kirsopp Lake, DD, DLitt. Loeb Classical Library, Vol. 1. London: Wm. Heinemann, 1926.

Gildas. *The Ruin of Britain and Other Works.* Translated and edited by M. Winterbottom. London: Phillimore, 1978.

Saint Gregory the Great. *Selected Epistles: Books 1–8; Pastoral Rule.* Translated by Rev. James Barmby, DD. Edited by Philip Schaff and Henry Wace. NPNF, Second Series, Vol. 12. Grand Rapids, MI: Eerdmans, 1997.

————. *Selected Epistles: Books 9–14.* Translated by Rev. James Barmby, DD. Edited by Philip Schaff and Henry Wace. NPNF, Vol. 13, Second Series. Grand Rapids, MI: Eerdmans, 1997.

———. *Pastoral Care*. Translated by Henry Davis, SJ. Edited by Johannes Quasten, STD; and Joseph C. Plumpe, PhD. Ancient Christian Writers. Westminster, MD: Newman Press, 1950.

———. *Dialogues*. Translated by Odo John Zimmerman, OSB. Edited by Hermigild Dressler, OFM. The Fathers of the Church, Vol. 39. Washington, DC: CUAP, 1983.

Saint Gregory of Nazianzen. *Select Orations and Letters: Panegyric on Basil*. Translated by Charles Gordon Browne, MA; and James Edward Swallow, MA. Edited by Philip Schaff and Henry Wace. NPNF, Second Series, Vol. 7. Grand Rapids, MI: Eerdmans, 1996.

———. *Sermons*. Translated by Jane Patricia Freeland, CSJB; and Agnes Josephine Conway, SSJ. Edited by Thomas P. Halton. The Fathers of the Church, Vol. 93. Washington, DC: CUAP, 1995.

———. *Three Poems*. Translated by Denis Molaise Meehan, OSB. Edited by Thomas P. Halton. The Fathers of the Church, Vol. 75. Washington, DC: CUAP, 1987.

———. *Funeral Orations*. Translated by Leo P. McCauley. Edited by Roy Joseph Deferrari. The Fathers of the Church, Vol. 22. Washington, DC: CUAP, 1968.

———. *Select Orations*. Translated by Martha Vinson. Edited by Thomas P. Halton. The Fathers of the Church, Vol. 107. Washington, DC: CUAP, 2003.

Saint Gregory of Nyssa. *Ascetical Works: The Life of Saint Macrina*. Translated by Virginia Woods Callahan. Edited by Roy Joseph Deferrari. The Fathers of the Church, Vol. 58. Washington, DC: CUAP, 1967.

*The Epistolae Vagantes of Pope Gregory VII*. Edited and translated by H. E. J. Cowdrey. Oxford: Clarendon Press, 1972.

*The Register of Pope Gregory VII 1073–1085*. Translated by H. E. J. Cowdrey. Oxford: University Press, 2002.

*The Correspondence of Pope Gregory VII*. Translated by Ephriam Emerton. Records of Civilization 14. New York: Octagon Books, 1966.

Gregory of Tours. *The History of the Franks*. Translated by Lewis Thorpe. London: Penguin Books, 1983.

Hermas. *The Shepherd*. Translated by M.-F. Marique, SJ, PhD. Edited by Hermigild Dressler, OFM. The Fathers of the Church, Vol. 1. Washington, DC: CUAP, 1981.

Saint Hilary of Poitier. *The Trinity*. Translated by Stephen McKenna, CSSR. Edited by Roy Joseph Deferrari. The Fathers of the Church, Vol. 25. Washington, DC: CUAP, 1968.

Saint Irenaeus. *Against Heresies*. Revised by A. Cleveland Coxe, DD. Edited by Rev. Alexander Roberts, DD; and James Donaldson, LLD. The Ante-Nicene Fathers of the Christian Church, Vol. 1. Grand Rapids, MI: Eerdmans, 1996.

Saint Jerome. *Letters and Select Works.* Translated by Hon. W. H. Fremantle, MA. Edited by Philip Schaff and Henry Wace. NPNF, Vol. 6. Grand Rapids, MI: Eerdmans, 1996.

————. *Selected Works: Against the Luciferians, Against Jovinian, Against Vigilantius, Preface to Commentary on Ezekiel.* Translated by Hon. W. H. Fremantle, MA. Edited by Philip Schaff and Henry Wace. NPNF 6. Grand Rapids, MI: Eerdmans, 1996.

————. *On Illustrious Men.* Translated and edited by Thomas P. Halton. The Fathers of the Church, Vol. 100. Washington, DC: CUAP, 1999.

————. *On the Priesthood.* Translated by W. R. W. Stephens, MA. Edited by Philip Schaff and Henry Wace. NPNF, Vol. 9. Grand Rapids, MI: Eerdmans, 1996.

John Cassian. *Institutes, Conferences and On the Incarnation.* Translated by Rev. Edgar C. S. Gibson, MA. Edited by Philip Schaff and Henry Wace. NPNF, Second Series, Vol. 11. Grand Rapids, MI: Eerdmans, 1998.

————. *The Conferences,* trans. Boniface Ramsey. ACW 57. New York: Paulist, 1992.

————. *Institutes,* trans. Boniface Ramsey. ACW 58. New York: Newman Press, 2000.

————. *On the Incarnation; Against Nestorius.* Translated by Edgar C. S. Gibson, MA. Edited by Philip Schaff and Henry Wace. NPNF, Second Series, Vol. 11. Grand Rapids, MI: Eerdmans, 1998.

Saint John Chrysostom. Homily 6, *On Prayer.* http://www.vatican.va/ documents/ spirit_20010302_giovanni-crisostomo_it.html.

Saint John of Damascus. *Writings: The Fount of Knowledge.* Translated by Frederic H. Chase Jr. Edited by Bernard M. Peebles. The Fathers of the Church, Vol. 37. Washington, DC: CUAP, 1970.

John of Salerno. *Saint Odo of Cluny.* Edited by Dom Gerard Sitwell. London: Sheed and Ward, 1958.

Jonas. *Life of Saint Columban.* Translated and edited by Dana Carlton Munro. Felinfach: Llanerch Publishers, 1993.

*The Letters of Lanfranc Archbishop of Canterbury.* Edited and translated by Helen Clover and Margaret Gibson. Oxford: Clarendon Press, 1979.

Pope Saint Leo the Great. *Letters.* Translated by Brother Edmund Hunt. Edited by Roy Joseph Deferrari. The Fathers of the Church, Vol. 34. Washington, DC: CUAP, 1963.

Saint Leo. *Sermons.* Translated by Jane Patricia Freedland, CSJB; and Agnes J. Conway, SSJ. Edited by Thomas P. Halton. The Fathers of the Church, Vol. 93. Washington, DC: CUAP, 1995.

————. *The Letters and Sermons.* Translated by Rev. Charles Lett Feltoe, MA. Edited by Philip Schaff and Henry Wace. NPNF, Second Series, Vol. 12. Grand Rapids, MI: Eerdmans, 1997.

*The Acts of the Christian Martyrs*. H. Musurillo. Oxford: Clarendon Press, 1972.

Óengus. *Martyrology*. Translated by Whitley Stokes, DCL. London: Henry Bradshaw Society, 1905.

Origen. *Against Celsus*. Translated by Rev. Frederick Crombie, DD. Edinburgh: T & T Clark, 1872.

*The Letters of Saint Patrick*. Translated by Daniel Conneely. Maynooth: An Sagart, 1993.

*The Works of Saint Patrick: Confession and Letter to the Soldiers of Coroticus*. Translated by Ludwig Bieler. Edited by Johannes Quasten, STL; and Joseph C. Plumpe, PhD. Ancient Christian Writers, No. 17. Westminster, MD: Newman, 1953.

*The Patrician Texts in the Book of Armagh*. Translated and edited by Ludwig Bieler. Dublin: Dublin Institute for Advanced Studies, 1979.

*The Writings of Bishop Patrick*. Translated by Aubrey Gwynn. Dublin: Dublin Institute for Advanced Studies, 1955.

Paulinus of Nola. *Letters*. Translated by P. G. Walsh. Edited by Johannes Quasten, Walter J. Burkhardt, and Thomas C. Lawler. Ancient Christian Writers, Vols. 35 and 36. London: Longmans, Green, 1967.

*The Irish Penitentials*. Edited by Ludwig Bieler. Dublin: Dublin Institute for Advanced Studies, 1963.

*The Letters of Abelard and Heloise: Historia Calamitatum*. Translated by Betty Radice. London: Penguin Books, 1974.

*The Book of Pontiffs*. Translated by Raymond Davis. Liverpool: Liverpool University Press, 1989.

Possidius. *The Life of Saint Augustine*. Translated by Matthew O'Connell. Edited by John E. Rotelle, OSA. The Augustinian Series, Vol. 1. Villanova, PA: Augustinian Press, 1988.

Prosper of Aquitaine. *In Defense of Saint Augustine*. Translated by P. De Letter, SJ, PhD. Edited by Johannes Quasten, STD; and Joseph C. Plumpe, PhD. Ancient Christian Writers, No. 32. London: Longmans, Green, 1963.

———. *The Call of All Nations*. Translated by P. De Letter, SJ, PhD. Edited by Johannes Quasten, STD; and Joseph C. Plumpe, PhD. Ancient Christian Writers, No. 14. London: Longmans, Green, 1952.

———. *Against Cassian*. Translated by Peter De Letter, SJ, PhD. Ancient Christian Writers, No. 32. London: Longmans, Green, 1963.

*The Stowe Missal, Vol. 2*. Translated by Sir George F. Warner. London: Henry Bradshaw Society, 1915.

*Walahfrid Strabo's Life of Saint Gaul*. Edited by Maud Joynt. London: Society for Promoting Christian Knowledge, 1927.

Tertullian. *Apology*. Translated by Sister Emily Joseph Daly, CSJ, PhD. Edited by Hermigild Dressler, OFM. The Fathers of the Church, Vol. 10. Washington, DC: CUAP, 1977.

Tertullian, Cyprian, and Origen. *On the Lord's Prayer*. Translated by Alistair Stewart-Sykes. Crestwood, NY: Saint Vladimir's Seminary Press, 2004.

*The Western Fathers: Being the Lives of SS. Martin of Tours by Sulpicius Severus, Ambrose by Paulinus, Augustine of Hippo by Possidius, Honoratus of Arles and Germanus of Auxerre*. Translated by F. R. Hoare. London: Sheed and Ward, 1954.

## Secondary Sources

Allott, Stephen. *Alcuin of York: His Life and Letters*. York: William Sessions, 1974.

Attwater, Donald. *The Penguin Dictionary of Saints*. Harmondsworth: Penguin Books, 1975.

Bieler, Ludwig. *Ireland, Harbinger of the Middle Ages*. London: 1963.

Bonner, Gerald. *Saint Augustine of Hippo: Life and Controversies*. London: SCM Press, 1963.

Bredero, Adriaan H. *Bernard of Clairvaux: Between Cult and History*. Edinburgh: T & T Clark, 1996.

Brown, Peter. *Augustine of Hippo*. London: Faber and Faber, 1967.

Byrne, Francis John. *Irish Kings and High-Kings*. Dublin: Four Courts Press, 1973.

Cachia, Nicholas. *Image of the Good Shepherd as a Source of the Ministerial Priesthood*. Rome: Gregorian University Press, 1997.

Calkins, Robert G. *Illuminated Books of the Middle Ages*. London: Thames and Hudson, 1983.

Carey, John. *King of Mysteries: Early Irish Religious Writings*. Dublin: Four Courts Press, 1998.

Charles-Edwards, T. M. *Early Christian Ireland*. Cambridge: University Press, 2000.

Clanchy, M. T. *Abelard: A Medieval Life*. Oxford: Blackwell, 1997.

Clark, Mary T., RSCJ. *Augustine*. Outstanding Christian Thinkers Series. Edited by Brian Davies, OP. London: Geoffrey Chapman, 1996.

Copleston, Frederick. *Medieval Philosophy*. A History of Philosophy, Vol. 2. London: Continuum, 2003.

Cowdrey, H. E. J. *Pope Gregory VII: 1073–1085*. Oxford: Clarendon Press, 1998.

Dix, Dom Gregory. *The Shape of the Liturgy*. London: Adam and Charles Black, 1975.

Dudden, F. Homes. *The Life and Times of Saint Ambrose, 2 Vols*. Oxford: Clarendon Press, 1935.

———. *Gregory the Great: His Place in History and Thought, 2 Vols*. London: Longmans, Green, 1905.

Dumville, David, ed. *Saint Patrick, A.D. 493–1993*. Woodbridge, Suffolk: Boydell Press, 1993.

Eadmer. *The Life of Saint Anselm*. Edited and translated by R. W. Southern. London: Thomas Nelson and Sons, 1962.

Einhard. *Life of Charlemagne*. Translated by Evelyn Scherabon and Edwin H. Zeydel. Coral Gables, FL: University of Miami Press, 1972.

Etchingham, Colmán. *Church Organisation in Ireland AD 650 to 1000*. Kildare, Ireland: Laigin Publications, 1999.

Evans, G. R. *Bernard of Clairvaux*. Oxford: University Press, 2000.

———. *The Mind of Saint Bernard of Clairvaux*. Oxford: Clarendon Press, 1983.

———. *Anselm and Talking about God*. Oxford: Clarendon Press, 1978.

———. *Anselm and a New Generation*. Oxford: Clarendon Press, 1980.

Fleming, John. *Gille of Limerick c. 1070–1145*. Dublin: Four Courts Press, 2001.

Godman, Peter. *Poetry of the Carolingian Renaissance*. London: Duckworth, 1985.

Gougaud, Louis. *Christianity in Celtic Lands*. Dublin: Four Courts Press, 1992.

Gwynn, Aubrey. Edited by Gerard O'Brien. *The Irish Church in the Eleventh and Twelfth Centuries*. Dublin: Four Courts Press, 1992.

Gwynn, Aubrey, and R. Neville Hadcock. *Medieval Religious Houses in Ireland*. London: Longman, 1970.

Halphen, Louis. *Charlemagne and the Course of the Carolingian Empire*. Translated by Giselle de Nie. New York: North Holland, 1977.

Hanson, R. P. C. *Saint Patrick, His Origins and Career*. Oxford: Clarendon Press, 1968.

———. *The Life and Writings of the Historical Saint Patrick*. New York: Seabury Press, 1983.

Harbison, Peter. *The High Crosses of Ireland, Vols. 1 and 2*. Bonn: Dr. Rudolf Habelt Grubh, 1992.

Hartmann, Grisar. *History of Rome and the Popes in the Middle Ages, Vol. 2*. London: Kegan Paul, Trench, Trubner, 1912.

Henderson, George. *From Durrow to Kells*. London: Thames and Hudson, 1987.

Henry, Francoise. *Irish Art in the Early Christian Period*. London: Methuen, 1940.

———. *Irish Art in the Romanesque Period*. London: Methuen, 1973.

———. *Irish High Crosses*. Dublin: Published for the Cultural Relations Committee of Ireland at the Three Candles, 1964.

———. *Irish Art during the Viking Invasions*. London: Methuen, 1973.

Hillgarth, J. N., ed. *Christianity and Paganism, 350–750*. Philadelphia: University of Pennsylvania Press, 1986.

Jackson, K. H. *Language and History in Early Britain*. Edinburgh: University Press, 1971.

James, Bruno S. *Saint Bernard of Clairvaux*. London: Hodden and Stoughton, 1957.

Jedin, Hubert, and John Nolan, eds. *History of the Church, Vols. 1 and 2*. London: Burns Oates, 1980.

Jungmann, Josef A. *The Early Liturgy.* London: Darton, Longman & Todd, 1959.

Kelly, J. N. D., DD. *Early Christian Creeds.* London: Longman, 1976.

———. *Golden Mouth: The Story of John Chrysostom, Ascetic, Preacher, Bishop.* London: Duckworth, 1995.

———. *Jerome: His Life, Writings and Controversies.* London: Duckworth, 1975.

———. *The Oxford Dictionary of the Popes.* Oxford: Oxford University Press, 1986.

———. *Early Christian Doctrines.* London: Adam and Charles Black, 1973.

Kenney, James F. *Sources for the Early History of Ireland, Vol. 1: Ecclesiastical.* New York: Columbia University Press, 1929.

Lancel, Serge. *Saint Augustine.* Translated by Antonia Nevill. London: SCM Press, 2002.

Lapidge, Michael, and Richard Sharpe. *A Bibliography of Celtic/Latin Literature 400–1200.* Dublin: Royal Irish Academy, 1985.

Lawrence, C. E. *Medieval Monasticism.* London: Longman, 1990.

Lebreton, Jules, and Jacques Zeiller. *The Emergence of the Church in the Roman World.* A History of the Early Church, Book 2. New York: Collier Books, 1962.

Llewellyn, Peter. *Rome in the Dark Ages.* London: Faber and Faber, 1971.

Markus, R. A. *Christianity in the Roman World.* London: Thames and Hudson, 1974.

———. *Saeculum: History and Society in the Theology of Saint Augustine.* Cambridge: University Press, 1988.

———. *Gregory the Great and His World.* Cambridge: University Press, 1997.

McCracken, George E., and Allen Cabaniss. *Early Medieval Theology.* The Library of Christian Classics, Vol. 9. London: SCM Press, 1957.

McKitterick, Rosamond. *Carolingian Culture: Emulation and Innovation.* Cambridge: University Press, 1994.

———. *The Frankish Kingdoms under the Carolingians 751–987.* London: Longman, 1983.

Murphy, Gerard, trans. and ed. *Early Irish Lyrics.* Dublin: Four Courts Press, 1998.

Murray, A. Victor. *Abelard and Saint Bernard: A Study in Twelfth-Century "Modernism."* Manchester: Manchester University Press, 1967.

Ní Chatháin, P., and M. Richter., eds. *Ireland and Europe in the Early Middle Ages: Texts and Transmission.* Dublin: Four Courts Press, 2002.

Ó Corráin, Donnacha. *Ireland before the Normans.* Dublin: Gill and Macmillan, 1972.

O Cróinín, Dáibhí. *Early Medieval Ireland.* London: 1995.

O'Dwyer, Peter. *Céli Dé: Spiritual Reform in Ireland 750–900.* Dublin: Editions Tailliura, 1981.

O'Keefe, Tadhg. *Romanesque Ireland: Ideology and Architecture in Twelfth-Century Ireland*. Dublin: Four Courts Press, 2003.

O'Laverty, Rev. James. *A Historical Account of the Diocese of Down and Connor*, Vol. 2. Dublin: M. H. Gill and Son, 1880.

O'Loughlin, Thomas, ed. *Adamnan at Birr*. Dublin: Four Courts Press, 2001.

———. *Celtic Theology: Humanity, World and God in Early Irish Writings*. London: Continuum, 2001.

De Paor, Liam. *Saint Patrick's World: The Christian Culture of Ireland's Apostolic Age*. Dublin: Four Courts Press, 1993.

Quasten, Johannes. *Patrology, Vol. 2*. The Ante-Nicene Literature after Irenaeus. Antwerp: Spectrum Publishers, 1953.

Quasten, Johannes. *Patrology, 3 Vols*. The Golden Age of Patristic Literature. Westminster, MD: Newman Press, 1960.

Reeves, William, DD. *Culdees of the British Islands*. Felinfach: Llanerch Publications, 1994. Reprint of Dublin: M. H. Gill, 1864.

Richards, Jeffrey. *Consul of God*. London: Routledge and Kegan Paul, 1980.

Ryan, John. *Irish Monasticism: Origins and Early Development*. Dublin: Irish Academic Press, 1992.

Smyth, A.P., ed. *Seanchas*. Dublin: Four Courts Press, 2001.

Southern, R. W. *Saint Anselm: A Portrait in a Landscape*. Cambridge: University Press, 1991.

———. *Saint Anselm and His Biographer*. Cambridge: University Press, 1963.

Stevenson, J. *Creeds, Councils and Controversies*. London: SPCK, 1989.

———. *A New Eusebius*. London: SPCK, 1980.

Stokes, Margaret. *Six Months in the Apennines*. London: George Bell and Sons, 1892.

Straw, Carole. *Gregory the Great: Perfection in Imperfection*. London: University of California Press, 1988.

Tacitus. *Agricola*. Translated by Sir W. Peterson. Loeb Classical Library. London: William Heinemann, 1980.

Van der Meer, F. *Augustine the Bishop: The Life and Work of a Father of the Church*. Translated by B. Battershaw and G. R. Lamb. London: Sheed and Ward, 1983.

Virgil. *The Eclogues*. Translated by Guy Lee. London: Penguin Books, 1988.

———. *The Aeneid*. Translated by J. W. Mackail. London: MacMillan, 1908.

Wallace-Hadrill, J. M. *The Frankish Church*. Oxford: Clarendon Press, 1983.

Wallach, Liutpold. *Alcuin and Charlemagne*. Ithaca, NY: Cornell University Press, 1995.

Williams, Watkin. *Saint Bernard of Clairvaux*. Manchester: University Press, 1952.

# INDEX